GOVERNMENT, RELIGION AND SOCIETY IN NORTHERN ENGLAND 1000–1700

Government, Religion and Society in Northern England 1000–1700

EDITED BY
JOHN C. APPLEBY AND PAUL DALTON

SUTTON PUBLISHING

First published in 1997 by
Sutton Publishing Limited · Phoenix Mill
Thrupp · Stroud · Gloucestershire · GL5 2BU

Reprinted 1998

British Library Cataloguing in Publication Data
A catalogue record for this book is available from the British Library.

ISBN 0 7509 1057 7

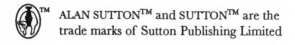

^{TM} ALAN SUTTON™ and SUTTON™ are the
trade marks of Sutton Publishing Limited

Typeset in 10/15 Baskerville.
Typesetting and origination by
Sutton Publishing Limited.
Printed in Great Britain by
MPG Books Ltd, Bodmin, Cornwall

CONTENTS

EDITORS' INTRODUCTION

This volume represents the proceedings of a conference held between the 10th and the 12th of April 1995 at Liverpool Institute of Higher Education, which has subsequently become Liverpool Hope University College. The idea for the conference grew out of discussions between the editors, and was encouraged and supported by the then Rector of college, Dr James Burke, the Pro-Rector, Dr John Elford, and our colleagues in the department of history who were all concerned to further promote the research profile of the college. Without this support it would not have been possible either to hold the conference or publish the proceedings in the present format.

The editors' aims were to provide a suitable forum for the discussion of several central themes in the history of northern England over a period which cuts across conventional chronological categories. This was felt to be particularly appropriate given the strength of deep-rooted and often hostile images of the region which can be traced in the historical record back at least to the Middle Ages, and which survive in certain forms to the present, as Dr Helen Jewell's recent study has shown.[1] The north–south divide has become a commonplace of modern political, social, economic and cultural discourse, though it is more often asserted than analysed. To take but one very recent example, an article in *The Guardian*, which has its roots in the north, referred to Ampleforth (North Yorkshire) as 'a Catholic enclave in one of the most feudal corners of England'.[2] Despite the journalistic rhetoric, this description raises fundamental questions concerning the perceived image of the north within a national context, and the extent to which this image approaches reality. Above all, these questions are related to the creation of a specific stereotype in which the north is often portrayed as distinct, remote, separate, feudal, backward, lawless,

[1] Helen M. Jewell, *The North–South Divide: The Origins of Northern Consciousness in England* (Manchester, 1994).

[2] 'Smells, Bells and Scandals', *The Guardian*, 9 March 1996, p. 23.

undeveloped, and only loosely attached to the metropolitan centre of English power and administration. This stereotype has always had major implications for the way in which the north and its people have been and are still regarded.

The papers in this volume seek to explore and illuminate the reality of life in northern England from a variety of perspectives, over a broad historical period. One of the central themes is the operation and problems of government in the north, related to which are the issues of lordship and local power and administrative structures, state-building within the British Isles, the development of – and importance of the border in – Anglo-Scottish relations, the impact of warfare and political instability, the nature of cross-border connections, and the extent of northern political and administrative assimilation and integration. The second major theme of the volume is religion. The diverse papers on this subject address the spiritual, political and social functions of the church, and the potential contradiction between them, as well as the role of the occupants of religious houses both before and after the Reformation. Religious change and continuity raise issues concerning the nature of religious life and the degree of religious conservatism in the north. Several papers demonstrate the wide-ranging social implications of these governmental and religious themes. Some contributors address the question of the distinct identity and perception of the north, and challenge long-standing popular and preconceived notions about the region which have implications for the construction of regional identities within the British Isles and demonstrate the problems of defining the north and northernness.

We would like to thank Liverpool Hope University College for the excellent facilities provided to host the conference and for financial assistance towards the costs of publishing the proceedings. Our thanks are also due to the many individuals who supported and helped to organise the conference. In addition to Dr Burke and Dr Elford, we are grateful to our current Rector and Chief Executive, Professor Simon Lee, and our other Pro-Rector, Dr Susan O'Brien, for the support they have shown for this project since joining our college in September 1995. We would also like to thank our speakers for presenting their papers, the quality of their contributions, the promptness and efficiency with which they submitted their manuscripts for publication, and the courtesy and understanding with which they dealt with editors working to tight word limits and strict deadlines. We are also grateful to our colleagues in the history department who supported the conference and helped it to run smoothly. Our then head of department, Dr John McGurk, our new head of department, Dr Janet Hollinshead, and Dr Fiona Pogson kindly agreed to sit on the conference steering committee, attended the conference throughout, chaired papers, and helped us in many other ways. Additionally, we thank Mrs Anne Kermode, Miss Dorothy O'Hanlon, Dr Neil Jamieson, Dr Jenny Kermode, Dr Chris Lewis and Mrs Doreen Heaney for their help and support. The formal conference dinner was held at The Athenaeum in Liverpool, and we are grateful to Mr Alan Andrews for his memorable and amusing after-dinner speech about the history of the club, Mrs Teal and her staff for the splendid meal, and Mr E.H. Seagroatt, the club librarian, for organising the excellent book display. The publication of the volume has been greatly assisted by the efficiency of Roger Thorp and his staff at Sutton Publishers. We would like to thank them for the care they have taken at every step in the publishing process and for helping us to publish the volume so soon after the conference.

When originally planning the conference the editors envisaged that it might be the first in a series devoted to the history of northern England. Our commitment to this has been reaffirmed by the positive reaction we have received to our conference both within and outside our college.

John Appleby
Paul Dalton

Liverpool, April 1996

LIST OF CONTRIBUTORS

Dr John C. Appleby is Senior Lecturer in History at Liverpool Hope University College

Dr N.J. Higham is Reader in History at the University of Manchester

Dr Paul Dalton is Lecturer in Medieval History at Liverpool Hope University College

Dr W.M. Aird is Lecturer in Medieval History at the University of Wales, Cardiff

Dr Keith J. Stringer is Reader in Medieval British History at the University of Lancaster

Dr Graeme White is Principal Lecturer in Medieval History at University College Chester

Dr Alan Young is Principal Lecturer in Medieval History at the University College of Ripon and York, St John

Professor Barbara English is Professor of History at the University of Hull

Dr Janet Burton is Lecturer in Medieval History at the University of Wales, Lampeter

Dr A.D.M. Barrell is Lecturer in Later Medieval History at The Queen's University, Belfast

Professor A.J. Pollard is Professor of History at the University of Teesside

Dr Jenny Kermode is Senior Lecturer in Local History at the University of Liverpool

Professor Claire Cross is Professor of History at the University of York

Dr Maureen M. Meikle is Senior Lecturer in History at the University of Sunderland

Dr Fiona Pogson is Lecturer in Early Modern History at Liverpool Hope University College

Dr Michael Mullett is Senior Lecturer in History at the University of Lancaster

LIST OF ABBREVIATIONS

BI	Borthwick Institute of Historical Research, York
BIHR	*Bulletin of the Institute of Historical Research*
BL	The British Library, London
EHR	*English Historical Review*
LP	*Letters and Papers, Foreign and Domestic, of the Reign of Henry VIII* (London, 1862–1932)
PRO	Public Record Office, London
SHR	*Scottish Historical Review*
Summerson, *Carlisle*	Henry Summerson, *Medieval Carlisle: The City and the Borders from the Late Eleventh to the Mid-Sixteenth Century*, Cumb. and Westm. Antiq. and Arch. Soc., Extra Series, 25 (1993)
TCWAAS	*Transactions of the Cumberland and Westmorland Antiquarian and Archaeological Society*
TRHS	*Transactions of the Royal Historical Society*
VCH	*Victoria County History*

1

PATTERNS OF PATRONAGE AND POWER: THE GOVERNANCE OF LATE ANGLO-SAXON CHESHIRE

N.J.Higham

This paper explores interaction between different status groups within Cheshire's free, landholding community *TRE (Tempus Regis Edwardi)* on the basis of Domesday Book. It must be emphasized that the results are tentative.[1] There is some, admittedly less than conclusive, evidence that the rulers of Mercia had held significant estates in Cheshire in the tenth century,[2] but by 1066 the seignorial situation looks very different. At that date Cheshire was one of only three shires in all Domesday England to be entirely devoid of royal lands.[3] Direct royal interest was then limited to two-thirds of the revenues from that part of Chester which lay outside the bishop's holding, the profits of the shire court, a similar proportion of the tolls on salt leaving the several wiches and the land geld. In contrast, Earl Edwin of Mercia, and to a lesser extent his brother, Morcar, earl of Northumbria, dominated the ranks of landholders, with the bishop of Lichfield a poor third. The last Anglo-Saxon bishop was Leofwine, formerly abbot of Coventry, a religious house which was peculiarly favoured by Edwin's grandfather, the great Earl Leofric, and his wife, Countess Godiva. We should assume that both the abbacy itself and, at that stage, the diocese of Lichfield were appointments to which the powerful earl could expect to advance his own candidates. Leofwine had held both

---

[1] See *VCH Cheshire*, i, pp. 316–25; N.J. Higham, *The Origins of Cheshire* (Manchester, 1993), pp. 182–202.

[2] N.J. Higham, 'The Cheshire Burhs and the Mercian Frontier to 924', *Trans. of the Lancs. and Cheshire Antiq. Soc.*, 85 (1988), 214–19.

[3] D.H. Hill, *An Atlas of Anglo-Saxon England* (Oxford, 1981), p. 101.

successively, which implies that he was an intimate political associate of Leofric's dynasty and so a key member of the affinity of the latter's young and inexperienced grandson in 1066 when, indeed, he was probably its elder statesman. It is unlikely to have been coincidental that his name was identical with that of Earl Leofric's own father, Ealdorman Leofwine. He may well have been a distant member of their kin or of a family connected with it for at least a generation previously.

It would be wrong, therefore, to imagine that the bishop was in any important sense independent of the earl.[4] The probability of close collaboration between these two is borne out in Domesday Book.[5] Here the shire court is recorded as supporting the bishop's claims to three and a half hides in Bettisfield and Iscoyd, although not to a further hide in Tilston. All these lands were in 1066 recorded as being in the hands of the earl and it seems that earl and bishop were effectively managing their landed resources in close co-operation, with the earl perhaps a tenant of these diocesan estates. Certainly Earl Edwin's substantial estates at Malpas, Bettisfield, Iscoyd and Worthenbury would have made it comparatively easy for his stewards to manage small and scattered holdings of the bishop in Maelor Saesneg, in their joint interest. Indeed, this very intermingling suggests that the bishop's interest may well have derived from the larger holdings of the earls at some stage, perhaps even in the recent past. The peculiar pattern of estates in this southern corner of *Dudestan* hundred may imply that English control was in some doubt and that the region was already in some sense thought of as Welsh territory, in which case there may have been good political reasons for the earl to hold these estates.[6] Both bishop and earl were arguably patrons of the same group of local thegns, particularly in the Dee valley, where, for example, another Edwin seems to have been a prominent associate of the earl in Malpas parish and may also have overseen the bishop's lands nearby.[7] A

[4] Higham, *Origins*, pp. 193–4.

[5] P. Morgan (ed.), *Domesday Book: Cheshire* (Chichester, 1978), f. 264b. Hereafter referred to as *DB*.

[6] Higham, *Origins*, pp. 75–7.

[7] *DB*, f. 266c.

somewhat enigmatic reference in Domesday Book to 'the bishop's men' suggests that his tenants had significant holdings in the Welsh marches of Cheshire, west of the Dee.[8]

Nor was St Werburgh's truly independent of the earl. This minster and the bishop's church of St John's were the only institutions in the region to appear in 'Florence of Worcester's' list of those religious houses which had been enriched by Earl Leofric.[9] There can be little doubt that this minster was considered by Earl Edwin to be his own family monastery, much as it was later to be that of the Norman earl, Hugh Lupus. Once again Domesday Book provides supporting evidence.[10] At Burwardsley in the south-west of the county, the reeves of Earls Edwin and Morcar had sold one hide taken away from the church of St Werburgh to a certain *Ravenchel*. The minster was obviously a participant in this transaction, and may well have likewise formally purchased this small estate from its patrons, the house of Leofric, only to have it requisitioned and resold some time between 1062 and 1066.

Earl Edwin and his associates had a controlling and strategic interest in Chester and its locality as well as in the supervision of local assets. These included the courts of the hundreds, from two of which, Frodsham and Macclesfield, the third penny went to the local court of the earl.[11] To other comital manors were attached further exceptional assets, such as the urban burgages (presumably in Chester) which paid their dues at Weaverham.[12] What is more difficult to identify is the pattern of interdependence and interaction between the leaders of local society and other ranks *TRE*. This is partly because some of the men named as holding land *TRE* may have died before or during 1066. Earl Edwin and his brother fought, and lost, a bloody battle against the Norwegians in September 1066, only a few weeks before the battle of Hastings. The core of their army was presumably made up of their affinity in north-west

[8] Ibid., f. 263a.

[9] See Higham, *Origins*, p. 186.

[10] *DB*, f. 264c.

[11] Ibid., f. 263d.

[12] Ibid., f. 263c. *In civitas* is most unlikely to refer to any city other than Chester.

Mercia and neighbouring parts of Wales and it seems likely that the Cheshire thegnage suffered significant losses on the very eve of the Norman takeover.

Another problem is the lack of defining detail attached to the names of Cheshire's landholders *TRE*. The earls appear to have been always designated by title and the bishop's estates are grouped, but few other landholders are identified by anything other than their names. To illustrate the problem, let us take two examples of different kinds. First the name *Edric* which occurs as the middle one of the three holders *TRE* of Prenton, the sole holder of Tittenley and the name of both holders of the two manors of Broomhall.[13] Use of the plural in the latter confirms that the Domesday scribe believed these to be two quite separate individuals who held adjacent manors within the same township, despite having the same name and despite their respective holdings being consolidated to form a single demesne manor in the lordship of William Malbank two decades later. In 1066, although there are only four references to the name in association with three place-names, we can be fairly confident that there were at least two individuals concerned. Secondly, the names *Dot* and *Dodo*, which occur eighteen times.[14] It may be that it is legitimate to assume that *Dodo*, the holder of two manors at Hartford, was a distinguishable individual. But what of the rest of these instances? In theory each could specify a different person; alternatively, all could refer to the same individual. It is equally possible, of course, that some medial point on this scale is more appropriate.

To what extent, therefore, is it possible to reconstruct the vertical ties which held this late pre-Conquest community together? Ultimately it is not possible to produce anything like a complete picture but it is possible to make some useful headway. Let us take, by way of illustration, the 1086 barony of Dunham, a small lordship of a mere eight manors which had been granted by Earl Hugh to Hamo de Mascy. The manors were as indicated in Table 1.

---

[13] Ibid., ff. 265b, 265d.

[14] *Dot: DB*, ff. 263d (Coddington), 264b (Cholmondeley), 264c (Shocklach, Bickerton), 265a (*Calvintone*), 265c (Aston, Shavington), 265d (Wilkesley, Stapeley), 266a (Millington), 266d (Mobberley), 267a (High) Legh, Wincham, Peover), 267b (Witton), 267c (Appleton); *Dodo*, 267a (Hartford, both manors held by one individual).

Table 1

THE BARONY OF DUNHAM, 1086

Manor	*TRE* holder
In Bucklow Hundred	
Dunham	*Elward*
Bowdon	*Elward*
Hale	*Elward*
Sunderland and Baguley	*Elward, Suga, Vdeman* and *Pat* as 4 manors
Ashley	*Elward*
Alretune	*Aelward*
In Hamestan Hundred	
Bramhall	*Brun, Hacun* (elsewhere *Hacon*) as 2 manors
In Warmundestrou [Wilaveston] Hundred	
Puddington	*Vlvric*

The consistency with which the name *Elward* (including *Aelward* as a variant) occurs as a precursor to that of Hamo de Mascy is impressive and this grouping of manors and their collective passage to a single Norman lord surely implies that these instances all refer to a single individual.[15] The name also occurs elsewhere. We can be reasonably confident that the core group of manors at and around Dunham was held by a single individual. But what of the identity of these further instances where estates which were isolated from that core failed to pass to Hamo de Mascy?

It may be possible to make some progress even here. One way of distinguishing important landholders from others is to identify the tenure of those manors to which exceptional assets were attached, such as cornmills, churches and priests, fisheries and salthouses.[16] The appropriateness of these criteria can of course be checked by reference to the estates of the earls. Both Earls Edwin and Morcar feature prominently in each category and Edwin has the distinction of holding the only two manors, Frodsham and Weaverham, to

[15] *VCH Cheshire*, i, p. 320.
[16] Ibid., p. 300; Higham, *Origins*, pp. 194–8.

exhibit all four characteristics. These attributes do, therefore, seem relevant to the status of individual landholders *TRE*. It is comforting to find *Elward* a prominent member of this group of approximately twenty-nine landholders, holding both a mill and a priest with a church at Bowdon. This was, of course, a church of some considerable status, with half a hide of land in 1086 and parochial responsibilities throughout the whole of the northern half of Bucklow hundred. The association of *Elward*, presumably as patron and rector, with this important minster indicates that he was a man of considerable status. The presence of a fishery at Shurlach is consistent with this distant manor also being held by the same individual. Shurlach was held, *TRE*, by two men, *Elward* and *Bers*, both of whom were 'free', so like most Cheshire landholders free at law and with the right to choose their own lords. There were no royal thegns in the area at that date so all presumably chose someone else as lord. For *Elward*, the obvious option was either Earl Edwin or his brother, Morcar, lord of Acton and the dominant figure in *Warmundestrou* hundred, where an *Elward* was named as holding Worleston. The name *Bers* does not occur elsewhere in Cheshire's Domesday folios, so his association with *Elward* at Shurlach is most likely to have been an unequal one. *Elward* is named first and this arguably indicates superiority in many instances, although this is not an invariable rule. The presence of a fishery suggests that one at least of these landholders was of high status and the association of this *Elward* with the lord of Bowdon seems the most plausible solution, in which case *Bers* looks very much like his *minister* or reeve, holding a part of this manor as tenant in return for managing the whole for his superior lord. It is possible, therefore, that all, or certainly the majority, of references to *Elward* in Domesday Cheshire refer to the same individual who was a major landholder and who had his capital manor at Bowdon at the core of a conglomerate of manors within that parish, all of which then passed to Hamo de Mascy. What of the other constituent manors of the barony of Dunham which do not have *Elward* as the named holder *TRE*?

The name *Brun* (Brown) occurs against four other manors *TRE* (Chelford, Alderley, Norbury and Siddington), in each instance as the sole landholder. All five manors lie in *Hamestan* hundred, they total five hides, including all Bramhall, but twenty-three ploughlands with the same proviso. This latter figure is very impressive by the standards of Cheshire landholdings, where most manors had only a handful of ploughlands and rarely more than twice as many as they had hides. The grouped pattern of all these holdings suggests that all had in 1066 been held by an individual. The concentration of these manors along the western edge of *Hamestan* hundred may also be significant, since they lie very close to Bowdon parish. There can be no serious doubt that *Brun* was well acquainted with *Elward, TRE*, and it is quite possible that close relations then existed between them.

Brun was perhaps the superior of *Hacon* at Bramhall. A *Hacon* was otherwise mentioned as sole holder only of Poole, a small manor in *Warmundestrou* hundred, but the name also occurs at Worleston in the same hundred, being named first of three holders, namely *Hacon, Elward* and *Elric*, of another small manor.[17] The recurrence of *Elward* herein is unlikely to be a coincidence, rather the names *Elward, Hacon* and *Brun* seem to be interlocked as members of a particular and hierarchically organized group of landholders whose local leaders were *Elward* and perhaps *Brun*, but who had links to the outside world via the unequal relationship pertaining between that local leadership and the house of Leofric. They may, of course, also have been linked dynastically or through kinship.

The name *Elric* recurs in a context which implies that he also had ties with the earls. Burwardsley was said to have been held *TRE* as three manors by *Elric, Colbert* and *Ravenchel*.[18] These were presumably, therefore, three individual farms, all within the same township. The artificiality of this sub-division between the tenants of three free landholders implies recent sub-division of a pre-existing manor. These holdings had presumably, therefore, been created, probably for the purpose of rewarding service, and it is probable that it was the earls who had taken this step, since it was the holding of *Ravenchel* here to which St Werburgh's asserted their title in 1086, claiming that the reeves of the earls had taken it from them and sold it to him. This can only have occurred between c. 1062, when Edwin became titular earl of Mercia, and 1066. If *Ravenchel* had obtained his holding here from the earls' estate managers, it seems likely that

---

[17] *DB*, ff. 266d (Bramhall), 265d (Poole, Worleston).
[18] Ibid., f. 264c.

what look like equal thirds in other parts of the township had derived from the same source, albeit without reference to St Werburgh's. Elsewhere *Elric* held Stapeley in partnership with *Dot* and may have been his reeve or ministerial tenant for the administration of this half-hide manor and was named also as the holder of Chorley and Baddiley, both of which were tiny holdings.[19] In each case *Elric* is likely to have been the same individual. He may have been in each instance either a ministerial tenant or the landholder by inheritance, purchase or marriage, but it seems quite clear that this collection of tiny manorial holdings and fragments thereof places *Elric* in a very different category to an *Elward* or *Dot*.

Going back to the situation at Sunderland and Baguley, neither *Suga* nor *Pat* occurs elsewhere in Cheshire's Domesday folios so each was probably a tenant or dependant of *Elward*. The name *Vdeman* (Woodman) does occur again but only in a single instance at Bickley in south-west Cheshire, a small manor.[20] It is difficult to judge whether or not the Bickley *Vdeman* should be identified with the associate of *Elward*. In 1066 the south-west was dominated by a substantial group of manors held by Earl Edwin at and around Malpas (then *Depenbach*), which seem to have been managed on his behalf by another prominent thegn named Edwin. The Bickley *Vdeman* was perhaps a member of his circle of associates. In favour of a separate identity is the fact that this name is one which we might expect anywhere associated with woodland and its management, as is the case in both these localities. Yet the occurrence of both *Ravenchel* and *Vdeman* in the context of the earls' patronage in Malpas parish may imply that the latter should be identified with the only other occurrence of the name elsewhere. Certainly, there can be no more than two individuals called *Vdeman* in the ranks of *TRE* landholders and there may have been only one. Whichever, this individual (or pair of individuals) was (or were) of low status. It is possible that *Vdeman* was a well-disguised survivor of the Norman Conquest. Bickley was held of Robert Fitz Hugh by one Fulk, whose sole tenement this was and who was

[19] Ibid., ff. 265d (Stapeley, Chorley, Baddiley, but note the variant name, *Aluric* herein, which might imply a different individual).

[20] Ibid., f. 264c.

probably a man-at-arms serving at Malpas Castle, but he had one plough here in demesne as well as two *bordarii* with their own plough. A reeve presided over the entirety on behalf of its new tenant. Such a manor hardly warranted the employment of a reeve unless such was already *in situ* and it would certainly not be surprising if that were to be the same man who had held it, arguably in a ministerial capacity, in 1066.

Thus, the barony of Dunham had at least a degree of coherence even before the Norman Conquest. A single individual named *Elward* had held five of Hamo's eight manors as sole landholder and was associated with others, probably as the superior lord, in a further two instances. His holdings were relatively compact geographically and although the total hidage appears small this block of estates was sufficient to make him the most powerful landholder in north-east Cheshire. It seems reasonably certain that he was also the principal holder of Shurlach, where his ministerial tenant, *Bers*, managed his principal fishery, and also held land at Worleston, where *Hacon* and *Elric* were also landholders, probably in association with him and possibly as his tenants. Worleston was clearly in the orbit of Earl Morcar, whose only substantial Cheshire estate lay at Acton in *Warmundestrou* hundred, and *Elric* was similarly rubbing shoulders with the reeves of the earls at Burwardsley, much as was *Vdeman* at Bickley.

Elward therefore emerges as a significant local figure, patron of a minster church and the holder of almost every manor in its parish. His affinity was not, however, isolated, but integrated into the greater whole of the Mercian earldom, beneath which arguably existed an entire mêlée of interlocking and interactive systems of local patronage. Nor was this system impermeable. Men like *Elric* were arguably associates not just of *Elward* but also of other leading figures, such as the thegn Edwin, and of the reeves of the earls themselves. Integration was therefore not solely horizontal but also occurred vertically.

In the later Middle Ages ambitious men sought career paths in the service of the state, the leadership of local society and of the Church, and often in complex combinations of all three, and they married in the hope of augmenting their patrimony. It seems likely that men of a range of status which compares closely with that of the later gentry were pursuing similar objectives by comparable means in the decades prior to the Norman Conquest.

To round off our treatment of the barony of Dunham, it is worth examining occurrences of the name *Vlvric* who was recorded as the precursor of Hamo de Mascy at Puddington in *Wilaveston* hundred. *Vlvric* occurs *TRE* against the impressive total of nine manors, but this is a group which differs fundamentally from that of *Elward* being entirely without manorial assets indicative of exceptional status.[21] In contrast, these manors are characterized by their small size, peripheral status and dispersed distribution. Additionally, none was held in combination with any other individual, in direct contrast with *Elward*, for example. In total these manors were assessed for tax on 10.66 hides and were credited with twenty-six ploughlands. If they were all held by one individual, then this was clearly sufficient to sustain the status of a late Anglo-Saxon thegn, yet there are obvious problems concerned with the exploitation of these estates. They were scattered across six of Cheshire's twelve hundreds, with never more than three in one hundred (Ollerton, Butley and Bredbury were all in *Hamestan* hundred). There is obviously a strong temptation to attribute these various estates to a whole series of different minor holders, even as many as nine, until it is noted that *Vlvric* survived to 1086 as the holder of the three manors in *Hamestan* hundred. Admittedly, these are the least scattered of his holdings but this fact is at least sufficient to make one stop and reconsider the evidence. *Vlvric* held the core of his manors in *Hamestan* hundred, a sub-division of the shire which was dominated by two great estates, both of which were the property of Earl Edwin. These were the manors of Macclesfield and Adlington. Despite the fact that their tenurial status and internal organization were very different, the descriptions of these two estates exhibit strong similarities. Both were credited with twenty ploughlands; each was worth £8 in 1066 and 20s. in 1086. These similarities are so marked as to suggest that both were being managed by a single reeve, whose response to a series of set questions posed by the Domesday inquisitors took, for his own convenience, the form of a division of his totals in each respect into two equal parts. If there was a reeve

[21] Ibid., ff. 264a, 264d (Alsager, Spurstow, Peckforton), 265a, 265c (Bredbury, Wistaston), 266c (Pulford, Puddington), 267d (Butley, Ollerton). Unusually all these manors were listed as in his sole tenure.

responsible for the important court of Macclesfield in 1086, to which the third penny of the hundred was attached and where there was a comital residence, it may well have been *Vlvric*, who still held Butley, the sole manor to be named between the townships of Adlington and Macclesfield. A few yards from the boundary of that township lies the minster church of Prestbury, unnamed in Domesday Book and entirely unrecorded pre-Conquest yet productive of late Anglo-Saxon stone carving, so almost certainly already in existence in 1066. The close proximity of Macclesfield, Adlington, Prestbury and Butley suggests that *Vlvric* may well have been a survivor of the numerous ministerial classes who had run Cheshire on behalf of Earl Edwin before 1066, in which case his tenure of a thin scattering of small estates elsewhere may have derived either from further official duties, from grants of small manors in return for services already performed or from inheritance. Whichever, it seems quite possible that the long-lived *Vlvric* who survived at Butley, Cheadle and Ollerton may well have been the holder of many, even all, of the nine manors which were assigned to that name in 1066.

These arguments are far from conclusive but imply that the number of landholders *TRE* was in practice rather smaller than suggested by a brief glance at Domesday Book. The earls had reeves looking after their interests in Cheshire, and these ministerial figures may be identifiable by close attention to the landholding community. We can distinguish between different groups of those landholders, in part by the number and value of their holdings. A clear contrast exists between the five to ten hide estate of figures such as *Elward* and *Vlvric* and the single holding of a *Bers* or *Pat*. Another distinction would seem to be between well-established holdings congregating around assets which are indicative of high status and involving sub-tenancies and ministerial tenancies of their own, and bundles of widely dispersed, small estates with neither exceptional assets nor minor landholdings. In the former category, *Elward* is the figure who has been highlighted here but we could as easily have examined, for example, the holdings of Edward, focused on his hall and church at Great Budworth, or Thored, a close associate of the bishop who possessed mills at Allington and Barrow and a fishery at Allington. As an exemplar of the latter category we have focused on *Vlvric* but, again, there were several other candidates available. It seems very likely that *Elward* and *Vlvric* had come to their landholdings by very different routes. The route of *Elward* has all the hallmarks of a long-established patrimony, while that of *Vlvric* was arguably very largely the fruit of his own labours. Whether such guesswork is accepted or not, it seems clear that the bland record of land tenure offered us by Domesday Book conceals a complex pattern of estate formation, of social hierarchies and of interactions between an agglomeration of affinities of different sizes and levels, all within the overall fabric of a dynastically focused, regional affinity which had coalesced over a period of half a century or so.

In conclusion, Cheshire had a system of government which consisted of the shire itself, the court to which that shire was answerable, and a sub-set of hundredal courts, which the local community was obliged to attend regularly. These lesser divisions display signs of rather greater antiquity than does the structure of the shire itself. Alongside the civil system of royal government was a pattern of parishes, both large and small, with an unusual predominance in this underpopulated and poor shire of extensive, multi-township parishes attached still to minster churches. Only a small number, primarily St Werburgh's and St John's, had substantial communities of clergy, or canons, or significant assets. Church patronage was shared between the bishop of Lichfield and well-established secular lords and patrons, of whom by far the most authoritative were undoubtedly the earls; but the role of men of the rank of *Elward* in their own localities should not be ignored. The number of single township parishes may have increased in the recent past, with some erosion of the great *parochiae* of several minsters, particularly in the west of the shire.

There were no royal estates present and the king's assets amounted to little more than the tolls on the salt wiches, the profits of justice and a share of other urban and shire revenues and obligations. These were arguably collected primarily by, or on behalf of, the earl. There were no royal thegns present and the king must have seemed a very distant figure to many in this regional community in the mid-eleventh century. By contrast, Chester was by this stage the capital of one of the greatest earldoms in England. The power of the earls was least contested in Cheshire where they apparently ruled supreme, yet their territorial assets outside were far more valuable. The earldom of Earl Edwin which focused on Chester dominated much of Shropshire and Staffordshire. So, in the last generation before the Conquest does the spectre of the *Wr(e)ocensæte* rise up to trap us and persuade us that that community retained a relevance to the political geography of England under Edward the Confessor?[22]

Cheshire itself lay at the hub of Edwin's earldom where there existed a hierarchy of lordships cemented by commendation which was headed by the bishop and the earls, but this system probably encompassed the entire landholding community of the shire. There were no other credible patrons with any influence locally who might have deflected a proportion of Cheshire's manorial landholders from commending themselves to the house of Leofric or its closest ecclesiastical ally. It was this community in arms, the *Cestrenses*, who were later to spearhead Mercian resistance to King William. Beneath this unifying fabric was a mêlée of holdings of different types, some more ministerial than others and some of a type closer to later gentry estates, all tied together in some sense by the complex of overlapping commendations which bound individuals together in unequal relationships. Our vision of all this is understandably murky but it is worth recalling that this was a political establishment which was capable, at need, of deploying militarily to the extent of fighting a battle of international importance, even against an enemy as fearsome as Harald Hardrada and his Norwegians, whom it took on at Gate Fulford on 20 September 1066. It seems certain that many of Cheshire's landholders were there present, yet the threat of intervention remained. Only when William had effectively cut communications between London and Chester by his slow progress around the Home Counties did the *witan* in the capital finally concede the crown to him. Once Hastings had been fought and lost, their sole remaining weapon of any military consequence was the following of the house of Leofric, centred on Chester and Cheshire. The arrival of the Norman army at Berkhamstead signalled the fact that Watling Street was effectively closed to William's enemies and the leaders of the English, at London, no longer capable of effective resistance to his claims to the throne.

[22] Higham, *Origins*, pp. 114–25, 182–91.

2

THE GOVERNMENTAL INTEGRATION OF THE FAR NORTH, 1066–1199[*]

Paul Dalton

In 1086 it is likely that the regions we know today as Northumberland, Cumbria and County Durham did not form part of the kingdom of England.[1] East of the Pennines the country between the Humber and the Forth had anciently formed the kingdom of Northumbria. In the ninth century Northumbria contracted as the Scots pressed southwards, as most of the land between the Tyne and the Tees was granted to the religious community of Lindisfarne which by 995 had moved to Durham, and as Vikings captured York in 867. Although the West Saxon kings claimed dominion over Northumbria, they only ended Scandinavian control of York in 954 and were powerless to prevent the Scots conquering Lothian between 954 and c. 973. Their dominion was more nominal than real. West of the Pennines, the region between the Solway and the River Duddon came during the course of the tenth century to be dominated by the Britonic kingdom of Strathclyde, which became subject to Scottish 'overlordship' and after c. 1018 was under direct Scottish rule. In 1086, '[t]he fact that the Domesday Commissioners did not concern themselves with, broadly speaking, the territory north of the River Tees, the Howgill Fells, and lower Lonsdale must surely signify that the lands to the north of this approximate line were not seen . . . as forming part of the English realm'.[2]

[*] I would like to thank Liverpool Hope University College for financial assistance toward the research costs for this paper.

[1] For the following details, see G.W.S. Barrow, 'The Scots and the North of England', in E. King (ed.), *The Anarchy of King Stephen's Reign* (Oxford, 1994), pp. 231–3, 236; idem, 'The Anglo-Scottish Border', *Northern History*, 1 (1966), 21–42; Alfred P. Smyth, *Warlords and Holy Men: Scotland AD 80–1000* (London, 1984), pp. 215–38; D.P. Kirby, 'Strathclyde and Cumbria: A Survey of Historical Development to 1092', *TCWAAS*, n. s., 62 (1962), 77–94; P.A. Wilson, 'On the Use of the Terms "Strathclyde" and "Cumbria"', *TCWAAS*, n. s., 66 (1966), 57–92.

[2] Barrow, 'Scots and the North', p. 233.

It was under the Anglo-Norman kings that the border between England and Scotland was established at the Solway in 1092 and at the Tweed by 1121. But the extent to which the far north was integrated within England is open to question.[3] Building on the work of Sir James Holt and Geoffrey Barrow this paper will assess the extent and limitations of English government in Durham, Northumberland and Cumbria between 1066 and 1199.[4] Although it is based partly on the records of central administration that may give a distorted image of purposeful, centralized government it shows that considerable progress had been made toward the governmental integration of the far north by 1199.

Between 1066 and 1135 the Anglo-Norman kings considerably developed English administration in the far north. The process owed much to military might and the establishment of castles at important administrative and population centres. Fortresses were built at Durham in 1072, Newcastle in 1080, Carlisle in 1092, and Bamburgh by 1130, and with the possible exception of Durham all were royal.[5] But there was much more to the establishment of English government than military power. The towns in which the castles were situated or which grew up around them, and large tracts of the countryside beyond, were brought for the first time within the royal demesne or forest.[6] At Carlisle William Rufus re-established the town and brought in peasants to settle the region. Thirty years later Henry I probably constructed walls around Carlisle and set the town on a firm footing. In 1133 it became the focus of a new bishopric which was subject to the archbishopric of York and in Anglo-Norman eyes effectively detached English Cumbria from the diocese of Glasgow; and by 1135 it had a mint which issued royal coins made of silver

[3] Compare J.C. Holt, *The Northerners: A Study in the Reign of King John* (2nd edn, Oxford, 1992), pp. 197–216; and Helen M. Jewell, *The North–South Divide: The Origins of Northern Consciousness in England* (Manchester, 1994), pp. 37–40, 57–66.

[4] Holt, *Northerners*, pp. xv–xxxii, 194–216; G.W.S. Barrow, 'Northern English Society in the Twelfth and Thirteenth Centuries', *Northern History*, 4 (1969), 1–28; idem, *Kingdom of the Scots* (London, 1973), pp. 7–68; idem, 'Frontier and Settlement: Which Influenced Which? England and Scotland, 1100–1300', in Robert Bartlett and Angus MacKay (eds), *Medieval Frontier Societies* (Oxford, 1989), pp. 3–21.

[5] William E. Kapelle, *The Norman Conquest of the North: The Region and Its Transformation, 1000–1135* (London, 1979), pp. 120–57.

[6] Summerson, *Carlisle*, i, pp. 28–9, 91.

from royal mines at Alston. In the early years of Stephen's reign this mint was supplemented by others at Durham and Newcastle which by then were also well-established towns.[7]

English government was also extended by the settlement of Norman (or French) nobles who replaced or subjected the Northumbrian aristocracy. At the highest level, the bishopric of Durham was held by churchmen with continental origins from 1071, and the earldom of Northumberland was finally removed from native hands in 1075.[8] By 1135 Norman settlement was well advanced, although many native far northern aristocrats retained their lands. Large parts of the region had been divided up into compact baronies focused on castles; and several new religious houses, which played a crucial part in opening up the region to English royal authority, had been founded to supplement the communities of Hexham and Durham which were brought within the fold of the Anglo-Norman Church.[9]

By 1135 the Anglo-Norman kings had also taken steps to bring the far north within the shire system. They divided Cumbria into two administrative regions, Westmorland and Carlisle. Westmorland comprised the lordships of Appleby and Kendal, and was not quite a shire in the accepted sense, having no sheriff, but was accounting at the exchequer in 1129–30 because Appleby was then in the king's hands.[10] Some progress toward the shiring of Carlisle had also taken place. The 1129–30 pipe roll records debts of Odard the sheriff 'for the old farm of the pleas of Carlisle which belong to the shrievalty'.[11] However, the man

[7] Ibid., pp. 1–40; *Pipe Roll 31 Henry I*, p. 142; Mark Blackburn, 'Coinage and Currency', in *Anarchy*, pp. 152–5.

[8] T. Arnold (ed.), *Symeonis Monachi Opera Omnia*, Rolls Series (London, 1882–5), i, pp. 105–6; ii, pp. 195, 205–7, 225–6.

[9] Kapelle, *Norman Conquest*, pp. 146–57, 191–230; G.W.S. Barrow, 'The Pattern of Lordship and Feudal Settlement in Cumbria', *Journal of Medieval History*, 1 (1975), 117–38; Judith A. Green, 'Aristocratic Loyalties on the Northern Frontier of England, *c.* 1100–1174', in Daniel Williams (ed.), *England in the Twelfth Century* (Woodbridge, 1990), pp. 84–94; Janet Burton, *Monastic and Religious Orders in Britain, 1000–1300* (Cambridge, 1994), pp. 11–15, 31–3, 40–1, 51–3, 58–9, 67–9, 78–9.

[10] Judith A. Green, *The Government of England Under Henry I* (Cambridge, 1986), p. 132.

[11] *Pipe Roll 31 Henry I*, p. 142; Judith A. Green, *English Sheriffs to 1154* (London, 1990), pp. 23, 31; idem, *Government*, p. 264; W.P. Hedley, *Northumberland Families* (Newcastle upon Tyne, 1968–70), i, pp. 142–3.

who accounted for Carlisle in 1129–30, Hildret, is not described as sheriff, the pipe roll entries for Carlisle are limited in detail, and the shrievalty does not appear to have incorporated Copeland or Gilsland.[12] East of the Pennines, the land of St Cuthbert's, Durham, remained throughout the period under consideration as a great liberty governed by the bishop of Durham.[13] Further north, sheriffs of Northumberland appear from c. 1103, and in 1129–30 Northumberland was accounted for at the exchequer.[14]

The Anglo-Norman kings also brought the far north within the royal judicial system by 1135. This was achieved by the use of writs, the establishment of shire courts and the employment of three new types of royal justices. There were justices who held *ad hoc* courts which were special sessions of the county or hundred courts; local 'justiciars' who heard pleas of the crown; and itinerant justices who visited several counties in turn to hear common pleas.[15] The pipe roll of 1129–30 reveals that Eustace Fitz John, lord of Alnwick, and Walter Espec, lord of Wark, had heard pleas in Northumberland, Carlisle and Westmorland; that Eustace had heard them in Durham; and that Espec had also heard forest pleas.[16]

Although English royal control of the far north lapsed during Stephen's reign, when the Scots attached Cumbria and Northumberland to their kingdom, under Henry II this control was restored and intensified.[17] In 1157 Henry compelled Malcolm IV to surrender Cumbria and Northumberland. In 1158 Henry visited Carlisle and probably granted it a charter, and the sheriffs of Carlisle and Northumberland accounted at the exchequer.[18] At about the same

---

[12] *VCH Cumberland*, i, p. 310.

[13] J. Scammell, 'The Origin and Limitations of the Liberty of Durham', *EHR*, 81 (1966), 449–73.

[14] *Pipe Roll 31 Henry I*, p. 35; Green, *English Sheriffs*, p. 65.

[15] P. Brand, *The Origins of the English Legal Profession* (Oxford, 1992), pp. 7–8; H.A. Cronne, 'The Office of Local Justiciar in England Under the Norman Kings', *University of Birmingham Historical Journal*, 6 (1957–8), 19–38, esp. 30, 33, 35.

[16] Paul Dalton, *Conquest, Anarchy and Lordship: Yorkshire 1066–1154* (Cambridge, 1994), pp. 96–100, 306–7; idem, 'Eustace Fitz John and the Politics of Anglo-Norman England: The Rise and Survival of a Twelfth-Century Royal Servant', *Speculum*, 71 (1996), 358–83.

[17] For Stephen's reign, see Barrow, 'Scots and the North'; Dalton, *Conquest*, chapter 5; Keith J. Stringer, *infra*, pp. 40–62.

[18] Summerson, *Carlisle*, i, pp. 58–60; *Pipe Roll 4 Henry II*, pp. 119, 177.

time Henry created the barony of Gilsland for Hubert de Vaux, a long-time servant of the king, and included it in the shrievalty of Carlisle. Henry also established other new men in northern baronies and castles, reinforced the allegiance of local families, and strengthened his northern fortresses.[19] After the disruption of the Scottish invasion of 1173–4, he reorganized the administration of the far north. Until then he had allowed Robert son of Troite and then his son Adam, local lords with cross-border connections, to hold the shrievalty of Carlisle, but in 1174 they were replaced by Robert de Vaux, lord of Gilsland.[20] Shortly afterwards the county of Cumberland emerged in more fully developed form.[21] In 1176–7 the shrievalty of Carlisle was designated as the shrievalty of Cumberland. In 1178 the sheriff of Cumberland's accounts included the barony of Copeland for the first time. Henry also placed the escheated lordship of Appleby in the hands of the justiciar, Ranulf de Glanville, who despite substantial independence from exchequer supervision was styled sheriff of Westmorland. Administrative control was tightened further in 1185 when the far northern shrievalties, which until then had been controlled by a close-knit group of northern families, were granted to men more firmly linked to the royal government. Henry replaced the sheriffs of Northumberland and Cumberland, Roger de Stuteville and Robert de Vaux respectively, with Roger de Glanville and one of the royal stewards, Hugh de Morewick, and charged the outgoing sheriffs with various offences, and summoned them to account for pledges. Hugh was replaced by his brother, Nicholas, in 1187, and in 1188 Nicholas was replaced in turn by William Fitz Aldelin, who was a royal steward, marshal and justice, a frequent witness of royal charters, and retained office until 1197. Under King Richard such appointments continued.[22]

[19] *VCH Cumberland*, i, p. 306 and note 1; Judith A. Green, 'Anglo-Scottish Relations, 1066–1174', in Michael Jones and Malcolm Vale (eds), *England and Her Neighbours, 1066–1453: Essays in Honour of Pierre Chaplais* (London, 1989), pp. 70–1; Dalton, *Conquest*, pp. 229–30.

[20] *Public Record Office, London: Lists and Indexes No. IX. List of Sheriffs* . . . (New York, 1963), p. 26.

[21] *Pipe Roll 23 Henry II*, pp. 120, 123; *Pipe Roll 24 Henry II*, p. 126; *VCH Cumberland*, i, pp. 310–11.

[22] Holt, *Northerners*, pp. 202–3; Julia Boorman, 'The Sheriffs of Henry II and Their Role in Civil Litigation 1154–89' (unpublished Ph.D thesis, University of Reading, 1989), pp. 20, 104, 131, 147–8, 467–9.

Henry II also developed the administration of justice. In 1162–3 the itinerant justice Richard de Lucy visited Carlisle and possibly presided in Northumberland.[23] In 1166 the king instituted a regular series of judicial eyres intended to include the far north.[24] The itinerant justices visited several shires in turn to deal with civil and criminal cases, supervise local government and gather information. They gave judgements in assemblies that were 'individual local sessions of a national court', the king's court, and 'helped make possible the emergence of a national law and custom of England'.[25] In Cumberland and Northumberland regular eyres began in 1168–9. Thereafter, Cumberland received fourteen or fifteen visitations before 1199, an average of one every 2.1 to 2.2 years; Northumberland received thirteen eyre visitations, an average of one every 2.4 years; and Westmorland, where eyres did not begin until 1177–8, received only six visitations, an average of one every 3.7 years.[26] With the exception of Durham, which received only one visitation (because it was a liberty), the far northern counties were visited more frequently by royal justices than some shires in southern England, and only marginally less frequently visited than many other counties south of the Trent. Moreover, the far north also experienced frequent visitations of forest justices. Although eyres became much more infrequent in the region after 1216, they ensured that by 1199 royal justices were familiar figures in its administration.

The judicial visitations raise questions about the scope and effectiveness of the justices' authority. The tightening of judicial control is indicated by the 'frequent impositions for criminals escaped or cases not presented; heavy payments for offences against the forest law; amercements for default or failure to appear before the justices in the shire court . . . [and] for interference in the new royal judicial processes'.[27] It is also evident in the fact that the authority of

---

[23] Doris Mary Stenton (ed.), *Pleas Before the King or His Justices 1198–1202*, Selden Soc., 67, 68, 83, 84 (1953–67), iii, pp. li–liii.

[24] J.C. Holt, 'The Assizes of Henry II: The Texts', in D.A. Bullough and R.L. Storey (eds), *The Study of Medieval Records: Essays in Honour of Kathleen Major* (Oxford, 1971), pp. 101–5.

[25] Brand, *Legal Profession*, pp. 14–18.

[26] These figures are based on information in *Pleas Before the King*, iii, pp. liii–cxlvii.

[27] Holt, *Northerners*, pp. 201–2.

the justices could reach into the remote countryside. In 1170 the justices William Basset and Alan de Neville the younger visited Tynedale and imposed fines, including one of three marks on Richard of Emmethaugh for failing to produce someone for whom he had gone bail. 'After another six years, Richard had paid all but 10s. of this fine, for which he was being pursued by the great justiciar Ranulf Glanvill.'[28] Some far northerners served as, or sat with, royal justices and provided jurors. They also had agreements recorded, and legal disputes settled, before royal justices. At York in 1204 a Cumberland tenant, John Cole, came before the itinerant justices and accused Adam nephew of Hugh of killing Jordan nephew of John. Adam came to deny the accusation. In the same court appeared William Dragespere and Robert de Claville who accused fourteen men of being accessories to the killing, twelve of whom were also charged with robbing their accusers and two other men of 100 marks which the accusers were taking to the exchequer to pay for a fine which their lord, William Briwerre, had made with the king for the land and heir of Hugh de Morville. The dispute shows the effectiveness of royal management of far northern wardships. It also reveals that one of the lords involved was so eager to submit it to the judgement of royal justices that he did not wait for them to come to Cumberland.[29]

Some northern litigants travelled to the royal court for justice. Early in Henry II's reign the abbot of Furness and William de Lancaster, lord of Kendal, and thirty freemen of Furness and Westmorland came before the king at Woodstock to settle a dispute over land in the remote Furness Fells.[30] In 1197 a dispute between the royal justice Henry of Whiston and the priory of Carlisle over the advowson of the church of Lodore in Cumberland was settled before the justiciar at Westminster. In 1204 Richard de Lucy, lord of Copeland, demanded an inquest on the customs and services due to him, and brought his tenants into the king's court to test their claims.[31] But the enforcement of royal justice was

---

[28] Barrow, 'Northern English Society', 27.

[29] *Pleas Before the King*, iii, pp. 138–9, no. 930.

[30] R.C. Van Caenegem (ed.), *English Lawsuits from William I to Richard I*, Selden Soc., 106, 107 (1990–1), ii, no. 364; Barrow, 'Northern English Society', 27–8.

[31] *Pleas Before the King*, iii, p. cxix; *VCH Cumberland*, i, p. 300, n. 1.

far from completely effective, and could sometimes take time. Cases were often settled by compromise agreements rather than final decisions of courts. Some were only heard before the justices after the intervention of influential magnates and payment.[32] However, by 1199 there was clearly a demand from many far northerners for English royal justice.

Despite these developments the governmental organization of the far north remained to some extent anomalous. By *c.* 1250, and possibly from before 1066, there existed a distinct law of the March.[33] The hundreds and wapentakes into which the shires of most of England were divided were virtually absent from the far north. The region was divided into administrative units known as wards and 'shires',[34] which should not be confused with county shires. The Anglo-Norman and Angevin kings laid a new form of seignorial lordship over these units, but the covering was often no more than a thin veneer. Their new baronies encompassed rights and authority normally inherent within hundreds, and often incorporated thanage and drengage tenure and judicial officials known as sergeants of the peace who seem to have been the successors of thanes and drengs. Some of them also rendered ancient tributes to the king such as cornage, a render of cattle.

Some of the new baronies were liberties embodying jurisdictional privileges which set them apart from county administration. The greatest of them was that of the bishop and community of Durham which covered most of modern County Durham and Islandshire, Norhamshire and Bedlingtonshire in Northumberland. Its liberties included freedom from encroachment by a county court, exemption from the king's geld and (by *c.* 1150 and perhaps before) enjoyment of pleas of the crown in the bishop's own lands, the right to issue writs of right, and (usually) the exclusion of royal writs and officers.[35] In

---

[32] *Pleas Before the King*, i, p. 111.

[33] William W. Scott, 'The March Laws Reconsidered', in Alexander Grant and Keith J. Stringer (eds), *Medieval Scotland . . .* (Edinburgh, 1993), pp. 114–30.

[34] See Richard Lomas, *North-East England in the Middle Ages* (Edinburgh, 1992), pp. 22–3, 30 n. 6; Summerson, *Carlisle*, i, pp. 6–8 and notes; *VCH Cumberland*, i, pp. 313–21, 330–5; R.R. Reid, 'Barony and Thanage', *EHR*, 35 (1920), 185–91.

[35] Scammell, 'Liberty of Durham', 449–73; G.V. Scammell, *Hugh du Puiset, Bishop of Durham* (Cambridge, 1956), pp. 155, 185, 189–90.

Northumberland the major liberties included the estates of Tynemouth Priory, Hexhamshire, Redesdale and Tynedale, the latter being outside English control from 1157 to 1286. In Cumbria, the lords of Copeland and possibly Allerdale appear to have enjoyed the right to hear pleas of the crown, and their lordships retained elements of independence from county administration in the late twelfth century and beyond.[36]

The governmental incorporation of the far north was a slow, piecemeal process which in certain periods suffered serious reverses, and which remained limited and insecure in 1199. The process was subject to the ebb and flow of complicated cross-currents which hindered as well as promoted it. One such current was the ambition of Scottish kings to add the region to their dominions, which was kept at bay for much of the period 1066–1199 but which was largely realized in Stephen's reign, and disrupted English government several times in the late eleventh century and again during 1173–4. Another fluctuating current was the attitude of the English kings, whose far-flung interests prevented them from consistently devoting themselves to the incorporation of the far north, and who rarely visited the region. Although William Rufus, Henry I and Henry II showed some determination to govern the region, Stephen and Richard were prepared or forced to delegate control there to the Scots or their own magnates.

The most complicated and changeable current of all was that of magnate obedience and cooperation, which was essential to government. How far it flowed in the favour of English kings, and to what extent the relationship between them and the far northern magnates was strengthened between 1066 and 1199, are difficult questions to answer. Although the crown could strengthen its relationship with local magnates by promoting their attachments to court, and could hope to reinforce its control over them by placing *curiales* in positions of power within the localities and by manipulating patronage, such policies were not consistently implemented and their effects might be short-lived. The attitude of local magnates to the invasion of royal government could be ambivalent, changing and sometimes hostile, as King John found in 1214–15. As in the case of Gilbert Fitz Reinfrey, who served as a royal sheriff in

---

[36] Reid, 'Barony and Thanage', 194, 197; *VCH Cumberland*, i, pp. 310, 329.

Yorkshire and Lancashire in the early thirteenth century, but who purchased the freedom of his lordship of Kendal from suit of the shire court of Westmorland in the 1190s and went on to join the rebellion of 1214–15, magnates might welcome and participate in the invasion when it served their interests but seek to evade or oppose it when it did not.[37] They might exploit their local offices and positions for their own profit and advantage, sometimes with little regard for royal authority. And although they might occasionally be called to account, punished for their failings and dismissed from office, for much of the period 1066–1199 the crown seems to have been reluctant to interfere with them. The curial families of one generation often became the local families of the next as they were absorbed into local society by the acquisition of land and marriage. As the thirteenth century began the curial Glanvilles had become an established northern family, and a member of an established northern family, William de Stuteville, rather than a *curialis* held the shrievalties of Cumberland and Yorkshire and had only recently relinquished the shrievalty of Northumberland.[38]

The task of controlling the far northern barons was made even harder by their close links with Scotland.[39] These links show that 'communities on both sides of [the border] had an affinity that no amount of emphasis on their emerging national differences as Englishmen or Scots was ever entirely to obscure'.[40] By the last quarter of the twelfth century most of the far northern Anglo-Norman or Anglo-French barons seem, if their conduct during the Scottish invasions of 1173–4 is anything to go by, to have been more firmly attached to England than to Scotland. However, the actions of many of these

---

[37] W. Farrer, *Records Relating to the Barony of Kendale*, ed. John F. Curwen, Cumb. and Westm. Antiq. and Arch. Soc. Record Series, 4, 5 (1923–4), i, pp. xiii–xv, 3–6, 378; Holt, *Northerners*, pp. xxv, 1 n., 2, 31, 50, 57, 61, 65, 86, 104, 130, 137, 142, 153–4, 156, 224, 228–9, 235–6, 238.

[38] Richard Mortimer, 'The Family of Rannulf de Glanville', *BIHR*, 54 (1981), 1–16; *List of Sheriffs*, pp. 26, 97, 161.

[39] Holt, *Northerners*, pp. 208–10; G.W.S. Barrow, *The Anglo-Norman Era in Scottish History* (Oxford, 1980), pp. 1–117.

[40] Keith J. Stringer, 'Identities in Thirteenth-Century England: Frontier Society in the Far North', in Claus Bjorn *et al.* (eds), *Social and Political Identities in Western History* (Copenhagen, 1994), pp. 31–2.

barons in the period 1214–16 show how the balance could change if English government was pressed too hard. Moreover, the attachment to England of the native far northern aristocrats who had survived the Norman Conquest may never have been strong. Many fought for the Scots in 1138, and some supported William the Lion in 1173–4. In more peaceful times some tried to divide or balance their allegiance to the Scottish and English kings by using the concept of liege lordship. In a document possibly issued *c.* 1131, but which may be later, Prior Algar of Durham conceded to Dolfin son of Uchtred the territory of Staindrop and Staindropshire, in return for which Dolfin was to become the liegeman of St Cuthbert and the prior and monks, saving his fealty to the king of England, the king of Scotland, the bishop of Durham 'and his liege lord'.[41]

Paradoxically, the functioning and application of English government in the far north helped to create conditions which in certain circumstances encouraged the detachment of the region, or at least parts of it, from English control. This can be seen in the aspirations of towns like Newcastle and Carlisle which despite owing their emergence partly to royal and baronial authority, and despite being bastions of this authority, were seeking self government.[42] It can also be seen in the 1130s and 1140s when the Scots used the existing system of local government and lordship in the far north to exercise their authority there. It can be seen again in King John's reign when associations of local aristocrats manipulated local administrative institutions to help structure and express their resistance, bring down royal government and place the far north under the control of the king of Scots.[43]

In conclusion, despite the cross-currents affecting governmental integration, by 1199 the overall progress had, from an English perspective, been undoubtedly forward. In many respects the government applied since 1066 by English kings in the far north was the same as in other areas of England. These kings and their magnates had extended their power to the Tweed and the

---

[41] Paul Dalton, 'Scottish Influence on Durham 1066–1214', in David Rollason *et al.* (eds), *Anglo-Norman Durham 1093–1193* (Woodbridge, 1994), p. 349.

[42] Summerson, *Carlisle*, i, pp. 59–2, 94, 97, 100–3; T. Thomson and C. Innes (eds), *The Acts of the Parliaments of Scotland* (Edinburgh, 1814–75), i, p. 33.

[43] Holt, *Northerners*, pp. xxiv–xxvii, xxix–xxxii.

Solway and had gone some way to converting and modifying old forms of tenure and obligations. In the bishopric of Durham by 1210 ministerial services performed by thanes and drengs had largely given way to rent payments. In Cumberland, Westmorland and Northumberland the process was much slower, but was clearly underway by the same time.[44] In parts of the far north cornage renders had been commuted to money payments or replaced by new forms of military and socage tenure. Even in Cumbria, where cornage tenure was still thick on the ground in the 1190s, the baronies of Copeland, Gilsland and Kendal were by then all held by knight service.

It was Henry II more than any other English king in the period 1066–1199, perhaps, who did most to extend English government in the far north. In his reign there seems to have been a hardening of the English attitude towards the Scots.[45] Henry advanced the shiring of the north, tightened central control of its shrievalties, systematized the judicial visitations of its shire courts, and promoted the development of its towns and defences. The potency of royal administration in the far north is clear even within the northern liberties, the autonomy of which should not be overestimated. The liberty of Durham was subject to royal laws and the king's peace, and sometimes experienced direct royal intervention. The bishops who controlled it were appointed by the king and never possessed the full range of civil pleas in their courts. By 1208 the knights and free tenants of Durham had obtained a royal writ commanding the sheriff of Northumberland to intervene if the bishop distrained their stock contrary to security and pledge, that they were not to be impleaded concerning their free holdings except according to the assizes of the kingdom and by the king's writ, and that they could use these assizes in the bishop's court.[46] By 1199 the itinerant justices who enforced these assizes were regular visitors to the far north and were opening up the region to the common law which was gradually superseding local and peculiar customs, so helping to bind the parts of England together. The binding was most marked when English kings and their officials

[44] Ibid., pp. xix–xx.

[45] Green, 'Anglo-Scottish Relations', pp. 68–70.

[46] Scammell, 'Liberty of Durham', 449–73.

took direct action to impose their authority in the far north. When this happened English government could weigh heavily on the region. This is evident in the general eyre and the forest eyre which were sent out in 1198 when King Richard needed money to defend Normandy, and in the reaction which these eyres provoked in some northerners. The justices of 1198 spent several months north of the Humber, and in addition to their ordinary duties tallaged towns and the royal demesne. Their activities were supplemented by those of exchequer officials who imposed additional taxes. According to the northern chronicler, Roger of Howden, admittedly a hostile witness, by the general eyre and 'other vexations . . . the whole of England from sea to sea was reduced to poverty', and no sooner had the justices departed than the kingdom had to suffer a forest eyre which was 'another kind of torment'.[47] Although Howden's response to the eyre foreshadows the resentment which was provoked by King John's aggressive governmental intervention in the north, there can be no clearer statement than this of the advance and effectiveness of English royal government in the region by the end of the twelfth century.

[47] William Stubbs (ed.), *Chronica Magistri Rogeri de Houedene*, Rolls Series (London, 1868–71), iv, pp. 62–3.

3

NORTHERN ENGLAND OR SOUTHERN SCOTLAND? THE ANGLO-SCOTTISH BORDER IN THE ELEVENTH AND TWELFTH CENTURIES AND THE PROBLEM OF PERSPECTIVE*

W.M. Aird

For the year 1092 the E version of the *Anglo-Saxon Chronicle* recorded that, 'King William went . . . to Carlisle and restored the city and erected the castle; and drove out Dolfin who had ruled the country, and garrisoned the castle with his men and then came south and sent many peasant people back there with their wives and cattle to live there and cultivate the land.' William Rufus's annexation of Carlisle and its region in 1092 imposed a new frontier between those subject to the king of the English and those subject to the king of the Scots, dividing, in the process, the community of the ancient British kingdom of Strathclyde/Cumbria at the River Solway.[1] This may have been a response to Malcolm III of Scotland's invasion of Northumbria in the previous year. Control of southern Cumbria was the key to the defence of the Norman settlement in northern England for, hitherto, the Scots had been able to attack Yorkshire and Northumbria from the west through the Vale of Eden and the

*I am grateful to Professor Peter Coss at the University of Wales, College of Cardiff, who read a draft of this paper, and to the Department of History, University of Sheffield for its assistance in enabling me to attend the conference.

[1] D.C. Douglas and G.W. Greenaway (eds), *English Historical Documents II 1042–1189* (2nd edn, London, 1981), pp. 176–7; P.A. Wilson, 'On the Use of the Terms "Strathclyde" and "Cumbria"', in *TCWAAS*, n. s., 66 (1966), 57–92; D.P. Kirby, 'Strathclyde and Cumbria: A Survey of Historical Development to 1092', *TCWAAS*, n. s., 62 (1962), 77–94.

Tyne Gap as well as from the north across the River Tweed. The refortification and settlement of Carlisle was a clear statement by Rufus that he would no longer tolerate a Scots-controlled salient pushing deep into the north of his realm.[2] For Malcolm III the loss of Carlisle represented the English annexation of the southern portion of a region whose people had previously acknowledged a Scots overlord.[3] Malcolm attempted to negotiate with Rufus in the autumn of 1093 at Gloucester, but the Norman king refused to see Malcolm unless he agreed to submit his grievances to the judgement of Rufus's *curia*, as if the Scots king were an ordinary baron. Malcolm refused, stating that he would only treat with the Norman king 'upon the borders of their realms, where the kings of the Scots were accustomed to do right by the kings of the English, and according to the judgment of the chief men of both kingdoms'.[4] This statement suggests that Malcolm did not consider himself to be the English king's inferior.[5] On his return to Scotland Malcolm gathered an army and then attacked Northumbria but was killed by Earl Robert de Mowbray and his men on 13 November 1093.[6] Thereafter Rufus was able to exploit the struggles for the throne of Scotland by sponsoring his own candidates, Malcolm's sons, Duncan and Edgar, against their uncle, Donald. With Edgar's accession in 1097 Anglo-Scottish relations achieved a stability which was to last until the death of Henry I in 1135.[7] The succession struggle within the Anglo-Norman realm during Stephen's reign enabled Malcolm's son, David I, to reoccupy Carlisle and once more to extend

---

[2] F. Barlow, *William Rufus*, (London, 1983), pp. 288–98.

[3] Ibid., p. 297; Judith A. Green, 'Anglo-Scottish Relations, 1066–1174', in Michael Jones and Malcolm Vale (eds), *England and Her Neighbours, 1066–1453: Essays in Honour of Pierre Chaplais* (London, 1989), pp. 53–72. Earl Siward of Northumbria may have exercised jurisdiction in southern Cumbria: Kirby, 'Strathclyde and Cumbria', 93; William E. Kapelle, *The Norman Conquest of the North: The Region and its Transformation, 1000–1135* (London, 1979), pp. 43–7.

[4] B. Thorpe (ed.), Florence of Worcester, *Chronicon ex Chronicis* (London, 1848–9), ii, p. 31, translated in A.O. Anderson, *Scottish Annals from English Chroniclers, A.D. 500–1286*, (London, 1908; reprinted Stamford, 1991), p. 110.

[5] Malcolm's stipulation that the two kings should meet on the border bears comparison with the *hommage de paix* occasionally rendered by the Norman dukes to the French kings. See C.W. Hollister, 'Normandy, France and the Anglo-Norman *Regnum*', *Speculum*, 51 (1976), 202–42.

[6] Anderson, *Scottish Annals*, p. 113.

[7] A.A.M. Duncan, 'Earliest Scottish Charters', *SHR*, 37 (1958), 132–5.

Scottish lordship into southern Cumbria and Northumbria. The Scots maintained control of these areas until 1157 when Henry II forced the young Malcolm IV to surrender Carlisle and its region together with his younger brother William's earldom of Northumberland.

The history of the development of the Anglo-Scottish border has focused on the nature of the relationship between the kings of England and Scotland.[8] This is not surprising since the question of the border dominated Anglo-Scottish relations throughout the Middle Ages. However, this has tended, until relatively recently, to obscure the distinctiveness of the border region in the eleventh and twelfth centuries. It is necessary to remember that in this period the border was merely a notional political construct dividing communities which had more in common with each other than with their nominal political overlords, whose influence was remote. It is the purpose here, therefore, to examine a crucial period in the establishment of this border and to do so neither from the perspective of the Norman kings, nor from that of their Scots rivals, but rather from that of those who gradually came to realize they were living on a frontier. Attention will be focused on the French settlement on both sides of the frontier, its effect on the native aristocracy and the composition of border society, and on the ecclesiastical configuration of the region.

At the Norman Conquest the power of the Anglo-Saxon monarchy in the north was, at best, precarious. Although the Norman settlement of Yorkshire proceeded steadily in the years after the notorious 'harrying of the north' it was by no means complete by 1086, and it is likely that the omission of the modern counties of Durham, Northumberland, Cumberland and Westmorland as well as parts of Lancashire from the Domesday survey is indicative not only of the extent of effective French settlement but also perhaps of the Conqueror's realm.[9] In 1086 Cumberland and Westmorland still constituted the southernmost part of the kingdom of Strathclyde/Cumbria whose rulers looked north to Dunfermline for overlordship rather than south to London and

[8] See G.W.S. Barrow, 'The Scots and the North of England', in E. King (ed.), *The Anarchy of King Stephen's Reign* (Oxford, 1994), pp. 231–7.

[9] For Yorkshire, see Paul Dalton, *Conquest, Anarchy and Lordship: Yorkshire, 1066–1154* (Cambridge, 1994), pp. 19–78.

Winchester. On the other side of the Pennines, to the north of the River Tees, lay Anglian Northumbria, a region composed of the rump of the ancient kingdom of Bernicia which had once stretched to the Forth.[10] The Scandinavian invasions and settlement of the late ninth and tenth centuries had divided Northumbria at the Tees, which marked the approximate northern extent of Danish occupation. By the beginning of the eleventh century and probably much earlier, the region from the Forth to the Tweed had been annexed by the expansionist Scottish monarchy.[11] The Northumbrian earls, based at Bamburgh, and the bishop and community of the church of St Cuthbert maintained relations with both the expanding Scottish and English kingdoms, and it is uncertain which of the two kings they considered to be their natural ally.[12] West Saxon royal authority was acknowledged in the tenth century by the earls of Bamburgh and the *congregatio sancti Cuthberti*, but what this meant in practical terms is difficult to say. Even during the rule of the assertive eleventh-century Earls Siward and Tostig, it is likely that the House of Bamburgh retained a large measure of autonomy.[13]

The social and territorial structures of Cumbria and Northumbria were distinctive, reflecting the political independence of the region. The main features of northern society were resilient enough to withstand the imposition of the frontier along the line of the Tweed and Solway. The distinctive structure of northern society and its similarity with that of southern Scottish communities has long been realized.[14] It is argued that Cumbria and Northumbria shared an ancient tenurial structure and that their societies had more in common with

---

[10] M.O. Anderson, 'Lothian and the Early Scottish Kings', *SHR*, 39 (1960), 98–112.

[11] See B. Meehan, 'The Siege of Durham, the Battle of Carham and the Cession of Lothian' and A.A.M. Duncan, 'The Battle of Carham, 1018', *SHR*, 55 (1976), 1–19, 20–8.

[12] Gifts were made at the shrine of St Cuthbert by members of the Scottish, West Saxon and Norman royal houses. In 914 Ealdred of Bamburgh fought in alliance with Constantine king of the Scots against the Irish Norsemen. See Anderson, 'Lothian', 100.

[13] Dorothy Whitelock, 'The Dealings of the Kings of England with Northumbria in the Tenth and Eleventh Centuries', in P. Clemoes (ed.), *The Anglo-Saxons: Studies in Some Aspects of their History and Culture Presented to Bruce Dickins* (London, 1959), pp. 55–71.

[14] F.W. Maitland, 'Northumbrian Tenures', *EHR*, 5 (1890), 625–32.

those of the Welsh and the Scots, than with those of the English or Anglo-Scandinavians.[15] Cumbria, Northumbria and southern Scotland also shared a common culture. Thus, the Anglo-Scottish border established at the line of the Rivers Tweed and Solway was an artificial division. It hardly affected the languages spoken by the communities who lived on either side of it.[16] The addition of Norman French to the melting pot of Scandinavian, Northumbrian English, Cumbric and Gaelic did not change the composite nature of the region's language and there is substantial evidence for the survival of native families.[17] Despite the increasingly widespread distribution and intensity of Anglo-Norman settlement in northern England and southern Scotland it is possible to identify them. The family of Cospatric the earl of Northumbria deposed by the Conqueror in 1072, was given extensive lands centred on Dunbar in Lothian by Malcolm III, an arrangement sealed by the marriage of Malcolm's son, Duncan, to Cospatric's daughter, Uctreda.[18] Cospatric's son, Dolfin, seems to have been appointed as lord of Cumbria under Malcolm III and it was he who was driven out of Carlisle by Rufus in 1092.[19] In Northumbria the House of Bamburgh retained some influence in the government of the earldom at least until 1080 when Ligulf, who had acted as an adviser to Bishop Walcher of Durham then also acting as earl, was murdered by the bishop's relatives and retainers.[20] One of the most prominent northern families of the later Middle Ages, the Nevilles of Raby, were descended from a certain Dolfin son of Uchtred, a Northumbrian noble who was given, or

---

[15] See G.W.S Barrow, 'Northern English Society in the Twelfth and Thirteenth Centuries', *Northern History*, 4 (1969), 1–28.

[16] G.W.S. Barrow, *Kingship and Unity: Scotland 1000–1306* (London, 1981), p. 3; K.H. Jackson, 'Angles and Britons in Northumbria and Cumbria', in H. Lewis (ed.), *Angles and Britons: O'Donnell Lectures* (Cardiff, 1963), pp. 60–85.

[17] See Barrow, 'Northern English Society', 5.

[18] Barrow, 'Scots and the North', p. 238 and note 25.

[19] G.W.S. Barrow, *The Kingdom of the Scots* (London, 1973), pp. 143–4. But see also Kapelle, *Norman Conquest*, p. 151.

[20] T. Arnold (ed.), *Symeonis Monachi Opera Omnia*, Rolls Series (London, 1882–5), ii, pp. 208–9; W.M. Aird, 'St Cuthbert, the Scots and the Normans', *Anglo-Norman Studies*, 16 (1994), 15.

confirmed in possession of, estates in Staindropshire in 1131 by the prior of Durham.[21] In Cumbria native families can be found in possession of the baronies of Allerdale, Greystoke and Gilsland.[22]

There was, however, a significant change in the composition of the landholding classes of Cumbria and Northumbria in the late eleventh and twelfth centuries. Until 1092 it is unlikely that there had been much French settlement north of the Ribble or the Tyne. Although it is probable that Earl Robert de Mowbray created small baronies for some of his retainers along the Tyne valley in the early 1090s and that William Rufus established a lordship for Ivo Taillebois in Cumbria, it was not until the reign of Henry I that large-scale French immigration occurred.[23] The close relationship between Henry I and David I led to the creation of an aristocracy which held estates on both sides of the frontier, and which was as much a part of a common culture as the native Cumbrian and Northumbrian aristocracy which it eventually largely displaced. David drew upon the Anglo-Norman baronage, of which he himself was a member, to assist his development of royal power in Scotland.[24] David created an extensive estate for the Yorkshire baron, Robert de Brus, in Annandale just north of the border. Brus held this lordship on similar terms to those by which the Anglo-Norman baron Ranulf le Meschin held Carlisle from Henry I.[25] The Scots also imitated the English development of towns and coinage.[26] In these circumstances the border can have had little meaning for the inhabitants of those regions immediately to the north and south of it in the first half of the twelfth century. This regional identity made the Anglo-Scottish frontier permeable to the extent that it was almost negligible.

[21] See W. Greenwell (ed.), *Feodarium Prioratus Dunelmensis*, Surtees Soc., 58 (1872), p. 56 note 1; H.S. Offler (ed.), *Durham Episcopal Charters, 1071–1152*, Surtees Soc., 179 (1968), p. 76.

[22] G.W.S. Barrow, 'The Pattern of Lordship and Feudal Settlement in Cumbria', *Journal of Medieval History*, 1 (1975), 117–38.

[23] Judith A. Green, 'Aristocratic Loyalties on the Northern Frontier of England, c. 1100–1174', in Daniel Williams (ed.), *England in the Twelfth Century* (Woodbridge, 1990), pp. 83–100.

[24] G.W.S Barrow, *David I of Scotland (1124–1153): The Balance of New and Old*, The Stenton Lecture 1984 (University of Reading, 1985); Keith J. Stringer, *infra*, pp. 51–7, 61–2.

[25] A.C. Lawrie (ed.), *Early Scottish Charters Prior to A.D. 1153* (Glasgow, 1905), no. 54, pp. 48–9.

[26] Summerson, *Carlisle*, i, pp. 25–6, 28 and the references there.

The lack of resistance to the Scottish reoccupation of Carlisle and southern Cumbria and to the extension of Scottish claims to overlordship over Northumbria in Stephen's reign, must have owed something to this cross-border regional identity. This identity casts doubt on the assumption that border baronies were established primarily to shore up the frontier against Scottish invasion, as the border seems to have been ill-defended whenever the Scots attacked in the late eleventh and twelfth centuries.[27] It was only when the Scots attempted to extend their influence into the bishopric of Durham and Yorkshire that they encountered more concerted opposition. The site of the battle of the Standard, fought on Cowton Moor near Northallerton in North Yorkshire in 1138, perhaps marks the southern limits of those feelings of affinity with their northern neighbours which were felt by those living in the frontier region after Rufus's annexation of 1092. The government of Northumberland by David's son, Earl Henry, and the establishment of David's rule at Carlisle could be tolerated as long as good order was maintained, as it evidently was.[28] Any extension of this Scoto-Northumbrian realm further south would be opposed. However much the troubles of Stephen's reign allowed David I to realize the ambition of the Scottish kings to reunite under their authority Cumbria and Northumbria, the unrest could not wholly erase, especially in the mind of the kings of England, the memory of Rufus's frontier. By David's death in 1153 other developments had served to reinforce the notional division along the Tweed–Solway line. Increasing ecclesiastical divisions and the recognition of a separate identity for the church in Scotland ultimately facilitated Henry II's reimposition of the political frontier known to his grandfather, Henry I.

The parish of the church of St Cuthbert came to dominate the kingdom of Bernicia and reflected at its greatest extent the early medieval overlordship of the Northumbrian kings. The church of St Cuthbert enjoyed a continuous history from the early seventh to the twelfth century. Although the seat of the bishopric migrated from its original foundation on Lindisfarne to Chester-le-

---

[27] See M. Strickland, 'Securing the North: Invasion and Defence in Twelfth-Century Anglo-Scottish Warfare', in M. Strickland (ed.), *Anglo-Norman Warfare. Studies in Late Anglo-Saxon and Anglo-Norman Military Organization and Warfare* (Woodbridge, 1992), pp. 208–29.

[28] See Anderson, *Scottish Annals*, p. 221.

Street and then to Durham, the *congregatio sancti Cuthberti* managed to maintain control of a considerable landed endowment despite the Scandinavian attacks and settlement of the late ninth and tenth centuries. By the time of the introduction of the Rule of St Benedict to Durham in 1083, the heart of the patrimony of St Cuthbert was located in the estates lying between the Rivers Tyne and Tees, but there were also claims to lands and ecclesiastical jurisdiction in Lothian, Cumbria and north Durham.[29] During this period the bishop of Durham lost a certain amount of spiritual jurisdiction as the Scottish and English kings began to rationalize the ecclesiastical structure of northern England and southern Scotland to take account of the new political frontier.[30]

In the west, the British kingdom of Strathclyde/Cumbria was more or less coterminous with the parish of St Kentigern (or Mungo) whose episcopal seat was at Glasgow.[31] After the annexation of Carlisle and its region by Rufus, the Norman king found that ecclesiastical jurisdiction over it was claimed by the church of St Kentigern and the church of St Cuthbert. In the late eleventh century this posed no problem, but the reigns of Alexander I (1107–24) and David I (1124–53) saw the growth of the idea of the *ecclesia scotticana* and an attempt to separate the Church in Scotland from the provincial claims of the archbishopric of York.[32] The establishment of a separate ecclesiastical province for the Scottish kingdom was a symptom and a cause of the development of the *regnum scotie*.[33] Crucial in this regard was the foundation of the bishopric of Carlisle by Henry I and the loss of the church of St Cuthbert's spiritual jurisdiction in Lothian to the church of St Andrews.[34] Henry was anxious to

[29] North Durham refers to Norhamshire, Islandshire and Bedlingtonshire. For the lands of the church of St Cuthbert, see E. Craster, 'The Patrimony of St Cuthbert', *EHR*, 69 (1954), 177–99; W.M. Aird, *St Cuthbert and the Normans. The Church of Durham 1071–1153* (forthcoming).

[30] For Durham's jurisdictional claims, see F. Barlow, *Durham Jurisdictional Peculiars* (Oxford, 1950).

[31] R.K. Rose, 'Cumbrian Society and the Anglo-Norman Church', in S. Mews (ed.), *Religion and National Identity. Papers Read at the Nineteenth Summer Meeting and the Twentieth Winter Meeting of the Ecclesiastical History Society* (Oxford, 1982), pp. 119–35.

[32] Marinell Ash, 'The Diocese of St Andrews under its "Norman" Bishops', *SHR*, 55 (1976), 105–26; A.A.M. Duncan, *Scotland. The Making of the Kingdom* (Edinburgh, 1975), pp. 256–80.

[33] Duncan, *Scotland*, pp. 256–80.

[34] Barlow, *Jurisdictional Peculiars*, pp. 117–44; H.H.E. Craster, 'A Contemporary Record of the Pontificate of Ranulf Flambard', *Archaeologia Aeliana*, 4th ser., 7 (1930), 37–9.

reorganize the ecclesiastical structure of the region and the foundation of the Augustinian priory of St Mary and, later, the cathedral chapter at Carlisle was intended to provide a southward-looking ecclesiastical focus for English Cumbria.[35] Both the church of St Kentigern and the church of St Cuthbert lost out to Henry's foundation.[36] The effect of the establishment of the political frontier on the claims of the church of St Kentigern is demonstrated by an inquisition conducted by David I into the lands of the bishopric of Glasgow undertaken during the pontificate of Bishop John in 1122.[37] Despite the tradition developing at Glasgow that Kentigern's see had been coterminous with the kingdom of Cumbria, the places listed in the *inquisitio* all lay within Scottish territory as delimited by Rufus's frontier and there is only a vague phrase to suggest that Glasgow might have had any claims further south. The inquisitors included certain *Cumbrenses iudices* with names indicative of native origin, as well as a posse of David I's Anglo-Norman adherents such as Hugh de Morville, Robert Corbet and Gervase Ridel. Clearly the inquisition relied not only on the testimony of representatives of a recently settled Anglo-Norman and Scoto-Norman baronage but also on that of a regional aristocracy which had survived the annexation of Carlisle and the establishment of a new political frontier.

Although the redefinition of the border in 1092 prompted a reordering of the ecclesiastical structure of northern England and southern Scotland, ancient spiritual allegiances continued and new religious affiliations were established which also cut through the Tweed–Solway frontier. After 1092 Cumbrian society, both native and Anglo-Norman, continued to venerate Celtic saints such as Kentigern, Ninian, Bridget, Patrick, Cuthbert and Columba and their Northumbrian counterparts, Oswald, Hilda and Wilfrid. The continuation of interest in these regional saints was further stimulated in the twelfth century by hagiographical literature which presented these Celtic

---

[35] Rose, 'Cumbrian Society', pp. 124–5 and note 30.

[36] Summerson, *Carlisle*, i, pp. 30–8.

[37] *Early Scottish Charters*, no. 50; Barrow, *Kingdom*, p. 147.

figures in a palatably orthodox guise.[38] David I heads a list of the patrons of monasteries which established cross-border ties in this period by founding daughter houses on the opposite side of the political frontier. David established the Tironensian order at Selkirk, the Augustinians at Holyrood, Jedburgh and Cambuskenneth, and Melrose was colonized by the Cistercians of Rievaulx in 1136.[39] The traffic was not all south to north. For example, Holm Cultram in Cumberland was itself founded from Melrose in 1150 and a cell of Jedburgh was established at Liddel (Canonbie) by the Fleming Turgis of Rosedale.[40] The older religious orders also continued to enjoy the support of both Scots and Anglo-Normans. The Benedictines of St Cuthbert benefited from the patronage of the Scots royal family, especially at their cell at Coldingham in Lothian.[41] The Church in England also supplied personnel for the emerging Scottish episcopate, notably in the early twelfth century in the persons of Prior Turgot of Durham and Eadmer of Canterbury, successive bishops of St Andrews. Other forms of religious contact continued to permeate the border, and members of every stratum of Scottish society made their way on pilgrimage to the shrine of St Cuthbert at Durham.[42] There is also at least one example of a pilgrim from south of the border visiting a shrine in Scotland.[43]

David I's acquisition of Carlisle, southern Cumbria and the part of Northumbria to the north of the Tees in the years following 1136 seems to have met with very little local resistance. The generally good relations which had been maintained in the border region during the reign of Henry I continued throughout the period of Scottish government in the north of England.[44] There

---

[38] Rose, 'Cumbrian Society'.

[39] G.W.S. Barrow, 'Scottish Rulers and the Religious Orders, 1070–1153', *TRHS*, 5th ser., 3 (1953), 77–100; idem., *Kingdom*, pp. 188–211.

[40] Rose, 'Cumbrian Society', p. 133; Barrow, *Kingdom*, p. 146.

[41] See, for example, *Early Scottish Charters*, nos 18 (Edgar), 65, 89, 90, 174 (David) and 236 (Earl Henry).

[42] J. Stevenson (ed.), *Liber Vitae Ecclesie Dunelmensis nec non Obituaria duo eiusdem Ecclesie*, Surtees Soc., 13 (1841); G.W.S. Barrow, 'The Kings of Scotland and Durham', in David Rollason *et al.* (eds), *Anglo-Norman Durham 1093–1193* (Woodbridge, 1994), p. 322.

[43] Godric of Finchale visited St Andrews before *c.* 1110: Ash, 'Diocese of St Andrews', 107.

[44] One possible exception to this was the attempted usurpation of the bishopric of Durham by William Cumin, David I's chancellor, 1141–4: A. Young, *William Cumin: Border Politics and the Bishopric of Durham 1141–44*, Borthwick Paper, 54 (York, 1979).

had been a degree of cross-border contact and cooperation during the first half of the twelfth century even to the extent that, in 1134, David could call upon the Anglo-Norman barons of Cumberland to assist him in the suppression of a threat from the men of Galloway.[45]

Given the permeability of the Anglo-Scottish border it is necessary to identify when attitudes towards those living on the other side of the notional frontier line began to harden. The key events in this reorientation of sensibilities were the deaths of David I's son and heir, Earl Henry of Northumberland, in 1152 and the meetings of Malcolm IV and Henry II in 1157 and 1158.

Earl Henry's premature death followed in 1153 by the death of his father left the throne of Scotland in the hands of Malcolm, a boy of twelve or thirteen. It was doubly unfortunate that in 1154 Henry of Anjou succeeded to the throne of England determined to restore royal authority in England to the degree enjoyed by his grandfather, Henry I. Henry II's concept of the royal dignity would not allow the Scottish occupation of Cumbria and Northumbria as these territories had been part of his grandfather's sphere of lordship. In the summer of 1157 Malcolm IV was summoned to attend Henry's court. Malcolm and his entourage met Henry in Derbyshire and together they proceeded to Chester where, according to William of Newburgh, Henry II 'took care to announce to the king of Scots, who possessed as his proper right the northern districts of England, namely Northumbria and Cumberland and Westmorland . . . the king of England ought not to be defrauded of so great a part of his kingdom, nor could he patiently be deprived of it: it was just that that should be restored which had been acquired in his name.'[46] Henry argued that David I had occupied the north of England merely on his behalf and that it was not an excuse to found a Scoto-Northumbrian realm. Faced with the demand to return the north of England to Angevin control, the sixteen-year-old Malcolm, 'prudently considering that in this matter the king of England was superior to the merits of the case by the authority of might, although he could have

---

[45] Summerson, *Carlisle*, i, p. 30 and note 136.

[46] Anderson, *Scottish Annals*, p. 239.

adduced the oath which [Henry] was said to have given to David, his grandfather, when [Henry] received from him the belt of knighthood; when [Henry] asked them again [Malcolm] restored to him the aforementioned territories in their entirety, and received from him in return the earldom of Huntingdon, which belonged to him by ancient right.'[47] The *Chronicle of Melrose* added that Malcolm became Henry's vassal 'in the same way that his grandfather had been the vassal of the older King Henry'.[48] The validity of the assertion that David I had indeed done homage to Henry I for the kingdom of Scotland as well as for his English estates is unknown. The importance of the meeting at Chester was that Malcolm IV had been obliged to surrender a considerable portion of the southern part of his kingdom and, in doing so, had accepted the re-establishment of the Anglo-Scottish frontier along the line of the Rivers Tweed and Solway.

After the meeting at Chester Henry II spent the early part of 1158 consolidating his position in northern England. Having repaired the important border fortress at Wark, he went to Carlisle and again met the Scots king.[49] The two kings 'departed not well pacified on either side, and in such a manner that the king of Scots was not yet knighted'.[50] This can be interpreted as a snub for the Scottish monarch. If it is possible to assign the souring of relations between the kings of Scotland and England in the High Middle Ages to any particular event then this refusal by Henry II to admit Malcolm IV into the chivalric order must be a strong contender. The acquisition of the status of a knight was a necessary corollary of nobility and an essential component of the royal dignity. The Scottish king was summoned to attend his lord on campaign in Toulouse and perhaps the denial of knighthood was another method of reinforcing the Angevin's dominance in the relationship. Malcolm's acquiescence seems to have displeased the Scots magnates who besieged him at Perth on his return from France.[51]

[47] Ibid.

[48] A.O. Anderson, *Early Sources of Scottish History A.D. 500–1286* (Edinburgh, 1922; reprinted Stamford, 1990), ii, p. 235. See also R.R. Davies, *Domination and Conquest: The Experience of Ireland, Scotland and Wales 1100–1300* (Cambridge, 1990), p. 51.

[49] Barrow, *Kingdom*, pp. 285–6; idem *et al.* (eds), *Regesta Regum Scottorum 1153–1371* (Edinburgh, 1960–87), i, pp. 10–12.

[50] Anderson, *Early Sources*, ii, p. 235

[51] Barrow, *Kingdom*, pp. 285–6; *Reg. Regum Scott.* i, pp. 10–12.

In these circumstances it is not difficult to understand how a political frontier between the kingdoms of Scotland and England might begin to take on a real significance. Henry II saw the reacquisition of the northern counties as an essential component of his programme to restore the royal power which his grandfather had enjoyed. In so doing he destroyed the mutual respect which had characterized the relationship between David I and Henry I. Henry II's actions tended to inhibit the permeability of the frontier. He forced the inhabitants of this region to acknowledge the new tension between the kingdoms of England and Scotland and to reorientate their political affiliations accordingly. Hereafter English royal power was exercised more and more often in northern England at the expense of those communities which had hitherto seen their interests as straddling the frontier.[52] The ancient political divisions of Cumbria and Northumbria which had enjoyed a largely independent identity and existence were divided along an arbitrary line which had little rationale in social, economic or, at least initially, ecclesiastical terms. The period from the middle of the eleventh century to the middle of the twelfth century was crucial, therefore, in the creation of the region known as northern England. The inhabitants of Cumbria and Northumbria gradually lost an identity which was based on their central position between the kingdoms of Scotland and England, and had to acknowledge that from around 1157 they were on the peripheries of these two realms and liable to bear the brunt of any political tension between them. This period of marginalization saw the foundations of the distinctive collective psychology of the borderers. In other words, by 1157 the northern frontier of England had been pushed further north and the people of the border region had to recognize their remoteness from the centre of English power and their vulnerability in the face of their increasingly estranged neighbours across the Solway and the Tweed. Likewise, these neighbours were forced to reorientate their own political and cultural sensibilities.

---

[52] Barrow, *Kingship and Unity*, p. 47.

4

STATE-BUILDING IN TWELFTH-CENTURY BRITAIN: DAVID I, KING OF SCOTS, AND NORTHERN ENGLAND

Keith J. Stringer

State-making is once more at the focus of historical attention. This revival of interest is no doubt due partly to the recent breathtaking events in Eastern Europe, which have explosively demonstrated the inadequacies of the modern state. But the return of state-formation to centre stage also stems from a growing dissatisfaction with the Whiggish assumption that nation–states evolved simply and inexorably through linear processes of development. As Robin Frame has warned us: 'The states familiar to us . . . developed slowly and messily in competition with a range of possible alternatives.'[1] Since Bishop Stubbs's time, if not earlier, the exceptionally long continuity of England as a political community has been seen by English historians as comfortably agreeable and satisfying. Yet now that the apparent certainties of political geography seem rather less solid, it may be especially opportune to remind ourselves that the glorious progress of the English state was at times much more problematic than the perceptions of nationalist historiography have suggested.

This paper focuses on the struggle between the Scottish and English crowns during King Stephen's reign (1135–54). Understandably, historical treatments have generally concentrated on the wider contest between the Norman and Angevin power blocks, and how one 'empire' fell and another rose in its place. But it is nevertheless regrettable that in English historical consciousness King David's annexation of the far north (from his perspective, it was of course the 'near south') has normally been dismissed as an insignificant side-show or, at best, as hopelessly unrealistic and doomed to failure, the assumption being that

---

[1] R. Frame, *The Political Development of the British Isles 1100–1400* (Oxford, 1990), p. 3.

England was always bound to survive in its familiar form. That it is increasingly difficult to accept such conclusions is due primarily to Geoffrey Barrow's insights.[2] Indeed, Scottish expansionism made this period one of critical importance for the British political order, and what follows aims to reinforce our understanding of both David's policies and the extent of his achievement.

Scottish intervention in the disputed English succession fell into two main phases. The first involved massive Scottish offensives and, despite David's defeat in 1138 at the battle of the Standard (near Northallerton), successive territorial gains confirmed by formal treaties. The second phase (1141–53) saw the largely peaceful intensification of David's rule over much of the north to the Ribble and the Tees; and only in 1157 did Henry II manage to restore the border to the Tweed–Solway line. In all this, we have the opportunity to examine the state-building processes and problems involved in creating and maintaining a new polity, the reality of which, in point of fact, deeply impressed twelfth-century English historians such as John of Hexham and William of Newburgh. In particular, three issues will be addressed. Why did David go to war? What did the Scottish annexation of the far north actually involve? Did it rest on potentially lasting foundations?

David's war policy has sometimes been accounted for in terms of short-range causes, by stressing either his commitment to Empress Matilda as the rightful successor to the English throne, or else a predatory Scottish opportunism. Both approaches have their merits. Most obviously, few medieval states began wars expecting to lose; and if Stephen had been more secure, David would probably not have risked full-scale hostilities. Nor can it be doubted that Scottish political and strategic goals varied according to Stephen's changing fortunes and circumstances. But English dynastic troubles do not explain David's deeper motives. Crucial was his concern to uphold Scottish 'national' rights against the

---

[2] Most recently, G.W.S. Barrow, 'The Scots and the North of England', in E. King (ed.), *The Anarchy of King Stephen's Reign* (Oxford, 1994), pp. 231–53. See also P. Dalton, *Conquest, Anarchy and Lordship: Yorkshire, 1066–1154* (Cambridge, 1994), chapter 5; K.J. Stringer, *The Reign of Stephen: Kingship, Warfare and Government in Twelfth-Century England* (London, 1993), pp. 28–37; Summerson, *Carlisle*, i, pp. 38–44.

post-Conquest English monarchy's imperialist claims and triumphs, in part by asserting that the Scots realm was an independent entity and just as entitled to strengthen itself through territorial expansion. He thought, moreover, in terms of legitimate conquest.[3] Despite sustained periods of peace, control of the ancient 'middle kingdom' of Northumbria had been a long-standing source of competition between the Scots and English kings; and how the Scots perceived the status of 'northern England' after 1066 is of key importance. They knew that only the Conqueror's notorious harrying of 1069–70 had overcome northern resistance to Norman dominance; they believed that their historic claims to Northumberland, St Cuthbert's Land and even Yorkshire were no less valid – not least when renewed problems about the English succession meant that Stephen's credentials for kingship were widely questioned. Most of all, they bitterly resented William Rufus's conquest of Carlisle and its region in 1092, which had annexed territory for long belonging to Scotland, and whose recovery was David's primary aim. Just as dynastic right drove Empress Matilda, so it was uppermost for David, who likewise had little difficulty in justifying his actions. In fact, may not David (descended through his mother from the royal house of Wessex) have believed that he had a stronger claim than the usurper Stephen's to the English crown itself? As Sir Maurice Powicke put it many years ago, 'when a Scottish king invaded the lands of the king of England he was engaging in a . . . quarrel, about the rights of which even men who lived south of the Tweed might freely differ'.[4]

Another influential long-term factor was the tenuous nature of the relationship between the heartlands of the English state and its northern periphery. For all Henry I's work of political consolidation, 'England' north of the Ribble and the Tees remained far distant from the 'zone of palaces and councils' and beyond even that of 'uniform administration'.[5] It still had the appearance of a semi-autonomous appendage loosely tied to the remote

---

[3] Relevant issues are clarified in ibid., pp. 47–9; Barrow, 'Scots and the North', especially pp. 237–41, 245–6; and (concerning Yorkshire) Dalton, *Conquest*, pp. 197, 228–9.

[4] F.M. Powicke (ed.), *The Life of Ailred of Rievaulx by Walter Daniel* (London, 1950), p. xlii.

[5] J. Campbell, 'The United Kingdom of England: The Anglo-Saxon Achievement', in A. Grant and K.J. Stringer (eds), *Uniting the Kingdom? The Making of British History* (London, 1995), pp. 43–5.

Westminster-based core, and that gave David another good reason for deciding on war – the more so because the English monarchy's ability to project its power northwards depended heavily on Scottish cooperation and was therefore unlikely to last. Relatedly, willingness to challenge Stephen was increased by the fact that the Anglo-Scottish border was a porous frontier, penetrated by a network of socio-cultural and political ties evoking the former unity of Northumbria. The Normanization of what we now call the north-east had, it is true, brought in an Anglo-Norman 'court' party, most of whose members would resist the Scottish invasions. But Scottish influence was stronger in the relatively less Normanized north-west, where the still powerful native community had little sense of identification with England at all. That not only hardened David's resolve, but enabled him to destabilize English defences with maximum ease – his seizure of Carlisle in 1135 was unopposed, and so willing were the men of Cumbria to support Scottish war aims that in 1138 many fought on his side at the Standard.[6]

Finally, war was precipitated by medium-term power shifts of signal importance. Broadly speaking, it is possible to think in terms of Norman power rising spectacularly from the 1060s, then levelling out during Henry I's reign and, at some stage before 1135, beginning to lose its commanding lead over the resources of neighbouring states.[7] A loss of dynamic is indicated by the pre-1135 Angevin resurgence in France, and Scotland was the chief gainer in Britain, for it was under David's modernizing leadership from 1124 that the metamorphosis of the Scots kingdom into a European-style monarchy began. David 'increased his power', wrote Orderic Vitalis in the early 1130s, 'and was exalted above his predecessors'; or, as a Scottish source put it, 'wisely taking thought for the future, he furnished his kingdom with castles and weaponry'.[8] In consequence, in 1135 Stephen was confronted by a semi-Normanized Scottish state with a more formidable capacity to pursue its claims to the English north, and with David's new strength and confidence came war.

[6] Summerson, *Carlisle*, i, pp. 39–40.

[7] For a fuller discussion, see Stringer, *Stephen*, pp. 9–13.

[8] Quoted in G.W.S. Barrow, *Scotland and its Neighbours in the Middle Ages* (London, 1992), pp. 53, 64.

Let us look, briefly, at warfare as an instrument of Scottish state-building. Though David's Norman aristocracy furnished up-to-date military expertise and support, native Scots infantry (notably from Galloway and the Highlands) supplied the bulk of his fighting strength; their speciality was irregular warfare, and they were employed specifically to terrorize the north, or at least the north-east. As John Gillingham has stressed, English commentators regarded their incursions as exceptionally brutal, and what particularly repelled them was the systematic slave-hunt character of Celtic warfare.[9] So shocked was Archbishop Thurstan that he turned the defence of Yorkshire in 1138 into a holy war against barbarians.[10] Yet for David and his commanders, raiding and pillaging were not simply ends in themselves, but means of manipulating loyalties and imposing new patterns of power. Richard of Hexham's account of the fall of Norham in 1138 has David indicating to Bishop Geoffrey of Durham that 'if he would abandon Stephen . . . and swear fealty to his party, he would restore Norham to him, and make good the damage sustained'. Elsewhere, so undermined was Stephen's authority that Hexham and Tynemouth priories deserted him for safety from attack, both gaining charters from David and his son, Henry, which granted them immunity for as long as they accepted subjection to Scottish lordship.[11] Violence was not wholly gratuitous: accommodations were possible, otherwise terror would have brought few political gains.

Not until the 1140s, however, can the consolidation of a 'Scoto-Northumbrian kingdom'[12] begin to be clearly discerned. It has to be recalled that the second treaty of Durham (1139), though hardly entered into voluntarily by Stephen, took account of both English and Scottish interests. Stephen acknowledged the new power balance in the north, but also managed to restore Scottish conquests to English sovereignty. The evidence for Carlisle is not clear-

[9] Most recently, J. Gillingham, 'Foundations of a Disunited Kingdom', in *Uniting the Kingdom?*, pp. 56–7.

[10] D. Nicholl, *Thurstan, Archbishop of York (1114–1140)* (York, 1964), pp. 222ff.

[11] R. Howlett (ed.), *Chronicles of the Reigns of Stephen, Henry II, and Richard I*, Rolls Series (London, 1884–9), iii, pp. 154, 157; A.C. Lawrie (ed.), *Early Scottish Charters Prior to A.D. 1153* (Glasgow, 1905), no. 119.

[12] Barrow, *Scotland*, p. 64.

cut; but the earldom of Northumberland was unquestionably to be held, by Henry of Scotland, as part of the English kingdom.[13] For Stephen, the decisive struggle was taking place in southern England and in Normandy; to that extent, the northern marchlands were dispensable, and yet his concessions were not unconditional. Admittedly, his direct influence over the far north in 1139–40 was negligible, and it may be that Scottish power-building proceeded apace. But the evidence nevertheless suggests that, in the short term, the Scots did observe the 1139 treaty.[14] If so, what radically transformed the position was Stephen's capture at Lincoln in February 1141. During Empress Matilda's temporary ascendancy, the Scots began to encroach on Durham, and it was probably then that they took over north Lancashire and parts of west Yorkshire.[15] Though Stephen regained his freedom in November 1141, thereafter he concentrated almost exclusively on upholding his cause in southern England; the Scots dealt with the north largely on their own terms, and their attempts to reinforce their dominance from 1141 allow us to explore some of the more complex and variegated processes of medieval state-building.

For a successful union of the far north to Scotland the basic requirement was for David to hold his gains in full sovereignty. If he acknowledged Matilda as lady of the English at London in June 1141 – when he certainly recognized her royal authority over Durham[16] – he had abandoned her for good by mid-September. John of Hexham depicts Stephen making fruitless plans in 1142 for a northern campaign 'to restore the kingdom to its ancient dignity and integrity'.[17]

---

[13] Richard of Hexham details the terms concerning Northumberland: *Chron. of the Reigns*, iii, pp. 177–8. As regards Carlisle, for which Henry had done homage to Stephen under the first treaty of Durham (1136), coins in Stephen's name were struck there (and at Newcastle) possibly as late as 1141: M. Blackburn, 'Coinage and Currency', in *Anarchy*, pp. 192–3.

[14] For Henry's recognition of his obligations to Stephen in 1139–40, see K.J. Stringer, 'An Alleged Medieval Earl of Northumberland', *Archaeologia Aeliana*, 5th ser., 1 (1973), 133–6; H.A. Cronne and R.H.C. Davis (eds), *Regesta Regum Anglo-Normannorum 1066–1154, Volume III* (Oxford, 1968), nos. 410–11; and note 13, above.

[15] It has been argued (e.g., Dalton, *Conquest*, pp. 215, 227–8) that these annexations had taken place by 1138; but firm evidence is lacking.

[16] T. Arnold (ed.), *Symeonis Monachi Opera Omnia*, Rolls Series (London, 1882–5), i, p. 162.

[17] Ibid., ii, p. 312.

And how David himself saw matters was made very plain when in 1149 young Henry of Anjou (the future Henry II) arrived at the Scottish court in Carlisle, to be immediately confronted with demands to concede that the far north was and should remain sovereign Scottish territory. Thereupon, according to William of Newburgh, he solemnly promised that if he gained the English throne he would leave the Scots in possession of 'the lands that had passed from England into David's dominion'.[18] David further displayed his command by knighting Henry and rewarding one of his household, William Fitz Hamo, with a Scottish estate.[19] Moreover, when on the same occasion David bought off Earl Ranulf of Chester's claims to Carlisle with the grant of north Lancashire, Ranulf had to do homage not to Henry Plantagenet but to David himself, thus acknowledging that he held it as a feudal vassal under the Scots crown.[20]

Yet again, it was as 'king of Scots' that David issued charters for Northumberland and the north-west, and he directed his commands to northern magnates and local officials as if they were Scottish lieges and royal officers. Henry of Scotland, intimately involved as he was in the governance of the north, styled himself not merely 'earl [of Northumberland]', but 'son of the king of Scots', thus emphasizing his regal status as the Scottish king-designate. David and he shared a 'dual reign' in Scotland;[21] they also saw themselves as co-rulers who wielded a joint royal authority throughout the far north. For David's entire reign, 205 of their *acta* survive, and of these no fewer than fifty – twenty-four by David and twenty-six by Henry – were issued for northern English beneficiaries, the majority given no earlier than 1141.[22] The separateness of Northumberland, Cumberland, Westmorland and the honour of Lancaster was normally recognized; but a similar distinction was maintained between the original Scotia or Alba and David's other domains within the

---

[18] *Chron. of the Reigns*, i, p. 70.

[19] *Cartulaire des Iles Normandes* (Société Jersiaise, 1924), pp. 310–12. For William Fitz Hamo's attendance on Henry of Anjou in England in 1149, see *Reg. Regum Anglo-Normann.*, iii, no. 666.

[20] *Symeonis . . . Opera*, ii, p. 323.

[21] G.W.S. Barrow, 'The Charters of David I', *Anglo-Norman Studies*, 14 (1992), 34.

[22] The texts have been printed in *Early Scottish Charters*, and G.W.S. Barrow (ed.), *Regesta Regum Scottorum, I: The Acts of Malcolm IV King of Scots, 1153–1165* (Edinburgh, 1960). The fifty acts include those for Yorkshire beneficiaries, and for Durham Priory's cell at Coldingham (Berwickshire).

'composite' Scots kingdom proper. Furthermore, in a charter of 1153, confirming a grant of property in Northumberland (albeit a Tweed fishery belonging to Kelso Abbey), David addressed 'all the worthy men of his whole kingdom'.[23] Above all, father and son imposed their regal superiority in a strikingly systematic fashion. They dispensed royal justice, controlled the royal castles, towns, lands and forests, and appropriated royal revenues; they granted liberties and exemptions, inflicted occasional forfeitures, and used their rights of marriage to rework local power structures. They also took over the royal mints, whose coinages provide a specially graphic illustration of the affirmation of Scottish sovereignty. Up to *c.* 1141 coins issued in Northumberland and Cumbria seem normally to have born Stephen's name; thereafter they were struck in David's or Henry's name.[24]

It would, nonetheless, be wrong to conclude that from 1141 the far north was treated exactly like other Scottish dominions – it was far more accessible and governable than much of the territory north of the Forth and the Clyde. David and Henry held court at Newcastle and Carlisle probably as regularly as at royal centres in southern Scotland, with the sole exception of Edinburgh; and, certainly, each made his personal presence felt more than any king of England had ever done before. The replacement of English by Scottish sovereignty therefore involved an important *intensification* of regular royal oversight and control – symbolized by the fact that David himself died at Carlisle in 1153, attended by his full household, and equipped with his archives and treasure.[25] A strongly integrative administration is also indicated by the routine way in which Northumbrian affairs were dealt with from Scotland itself. Thus, at Haddington Henry confirmed Tynemouth Priory's liberties and endowments; at Roxburgh he confirmed to William son of Alfric the land of Dilston in Corbridge; at Jedburgh he ordered his constable to defend Durham Priory's possessions.[26]

[23] *Early Scottish Charters*, no. 259.

[24] I. Stewart, 'Scottish Mints', in R.A.G. Carson (ed.), *Mints, Dies and Currency* (London, 1971), pp. 195–6; R.P. Mack, 'Stephen and the Anarchy 1135–1154', *British Numismatic Journal*, 35 (1966), 99–100.

[25] Summerson, *Carlisle*, i, p. 44.

[26] *Reg. Regum Scott.*, i, nos. 22, 24; *Early Scottish Charters*, no. 257.

In 1141, however, the Scots still had to tighten their grip if a sustainable territorial union were to be forged. The centralizing activity of the royal courts was very important; yet that alone does not explain the increasing firmness of Scottish rule. Military lordship was another crucial ingredient of Scottish dominance – even more so when proper account is taken of the remarkable Scots castle-building programme at key strategic points: notably, the new castles at Warkworth and Tulketh near Preston, the massive stone keep still standing today at Carlisle, and (it can be argued) those at Bamburgh, Appleby and Lancaster.[27] Yet such masterful displays of Scottish might would further the new government's interests in only a qualified way – which brings us to the very heart of medieval state-building techniques. 'Domination', in Rees Davies's words, 'is a much more subtle, rich-textured and many-faceted process than an over-concentration on the military story line . . . might suggest.'[28] Not least, as David shrewdly realized, it was easier for rulers to cement territorial unions if they could legitimize their authority by ensuring adequate support locally. His policy towards the north thus entered an important new phase: coercion slipped into the background, making way for strategies of a different sort.

The processes involved were those that had already paid dividends for David in Scotland: cooperation with, and control of, the Church; aristocratic colonization; and cooption of powerful local families. All the main English border monasteries received charters of protection. In part, that reflected awareness that Scottish power was now more formidable and had to be recognized. But it also underlined that, as far as possible, David wanted to make amends for past excesses and treat the Church with respect. Even distant Shrewsbury Abbey obtained his confirmation of its possessions in north Lancashire, with David underlining his support for traditional rights by

---

[27] Warkworth: E. Bateson *et al.*, *A History of Northumberland* (Newcastle upon Tyne, 1893–1940), v, p. 21 and n. 1; Tulketh: Barrow, 'Charters of David I', 26; Carlisle (where the keep was possibly completed, not built from scratch): M.R. McCarthy, H.R.T. Summerson and R.G. Annis, *Carlisle Castle: A Survey and Documentary History* (London, 1990), pp. 119–20. Otherwise, see R.A. Brown, H.M. Colvin and A.J. Taylor, *The History of the King's Works, II: The Middle Ages* (London, 1963), pp. 553–5; A. Grant, *Lancaster Castle in the Middle Ages* (Lancaster, 1985).

[28] R.R. Davies, *Domination and Conquest: The Experience of Ireland, Scotland and Wales 1100–1300* (Cambridge, 1990), p. 24.

stipulating that the monks were to hold their property as they had best held it under his predecessors.[29] With Henry's active involvement, fresh endowments were provided for religious houses in Cumberland and the north-east on an impressively comprehensive scale. Here as elsewhere, there could be no doubt that David's intention was 'to supply the place previously filled by English kings'[30] and give enhanced legitimacy to his government.

As for the bishoprics of Carlisle and Durham, strenuous efforts were made to control them in the Scottish interest. Athelwold of Carlisle had regularly witnessed Stephen's charters between 1136 and 1140, for most of that time living an exile's life in the south. Thereafter, as Henry Summerson has argued, he 'appears to have accepted that David was his political master, and that his diocese lay within that master's kingdom'.[31] The princely bishopric of Durham presents a different story, as is well known from Alan Young's studies.[32] The ill-judged attempts of David's former chancellor, William Cumin, to secure the vacant see antagonized the Durham monks, and with Stephen's support they elected in 1143 their own candidate, William de Ste Barbe. David salvaged something by giving Ste Barbe sanctuary on Holy Island; and in 1144 Henry intervened to help him take possession of the see. They retained influence south of the Tyne – one measure of that influence being their apparent ability to draw revenues from Durham after 1144.[33] Even so, although Durham was subject to a form of Scottish overlordship, the Scots had only a restricted hold on it. The Durham mint struck coins in Stephen's name (1135–44?) and no Scottish issues;[34] and in 1153 the chapter unanimously elected as their next bishop Stephen's nephew, Hugh du Puiset. Durham drew the line at being

[29] *Early Scottish Charters*, nos. 138–9.

[30] G.W.S. Barrow, 'The Kings of Scotland and Durham', in D. Rollason, M. Harvey and M. Prestwich (eds), *Anglo-Norman Durham 1093–1193* (Woodbridge, 1994), pp. 317–18.

[31] Summerson, *Carlisle*, i, p. 41.

[32] A. Young, *William Cumin: Border Politics and the Bishopric of Durham 1141–1144*, Borthwick Paper, 54 (York, 1979); idem, 'The Bishopric of Durham in Stephen's Reign', in *Anglo-Norman Durham*, pp. 357ff.

[33] Ibid., pp. 358, 361.

[34] M. Allen, 'The Durham Mint before Boldon Book', in *Anglo-Norman Durham*, pp. 387–92, 396–7.

swallowed up by the Scottish monarchy and wanted to remain part of the English realm.

Evidently, from 1141 the transition to Scottish rule was not always smoothly achieved, but in general David consolidated his power speedily and thoroughly. The king's relations with the secular nobility largely bear this out. His superiority was given real substance through the insertion of a sizeable group of followers who, as lesser barons and sub-tenants, could be expected to further his control in detail: men like Ranulf Engaine, Ranulf de Lindsay, Uhtred son of Fergus of Galloway, William de Vieuxpont, and Edgar brother of Earl Cospatric of Dunbar (d. 1166) – the last, a leading plunderer of the north-east in 1138, achieved respectability as lord of Caistron (Northumberland) and a benefactor of Newminster Abbey.[35] David ensconced himself even more securely by installing in premier lordships two exceptionally loyal lieutenants. His constable, Hugh de Morville, already the lord of at least one first-class Scottish fief, gained the vast barony of Appleby (i.e. north Westmorland); he probably assumed superior lordship over Kentdale and, through his son Richard, may have controlled much of upper Lonsdale and Ribblesdale.[36] David's nephew, William son of King Duncan II – who in the 1130s had held the 'frontier' earldom of Moray – was entrusted with Allerdale and Copeland, and secured in addition the honour of Skipton and Craven. Just as Henry of Scotland dominated the north-east as earl of Northumberland, so these very experienced and capable courtiers acted as virtual governors of most of the north-west below the Wampool, including north-west Yorkshire.[37]

---

[35] W.P. Hedley, *Northumberland Families* (Newcastle upon Tyne, 1968–70), i, pp. 244–5.

[36] Appleby: G.W.S. Barrow, *The Anglo-Norman Era in Scottish History* (Oxford, 1980), p. 73; Kentdale: W. Farrer, 'On the Tenure of Westmorland Temp. Henry II', *TCWAAS*, n. s., 7 (1907), 100–1, 105–6; Lonsdale/Ribblesdale (where the Morvilles may not have become established until after 1157): K.J. Stringer, 'The Early Lords of Lauderdale, Dryburgh Abbey and St Andrew's Priory at Northampton', in K.J. Stringer (ed.), *Essays on the Nobility of Medieval Scotland* (Edinburgh, 1985), pp. 47–50.

[37] For William as earl of Moray to *c.* 1140, see G.W.S. Barrow, 'Macbeth and other Mormaers of Moray', in L. Maclean (ed.), *The Hub of the Highlands* (Inverness, 1975), p. 119. See also Dalton, *Conquest*, pp. 190, 244–6, for the reality of his power in Yorkshire.

Yet it is of utmost significance that all this was achieved without embarking on any wholesale displacement of established nobles, and that enabled David to give his regime strength in depth by harnessing their loyalties. Security of tenure was offered in return for allegiance, and in general great care was taken not to upset vested interests unnecessarily. Inheritance conventions were undeniably stretched in the build up of William Fitz Duncan's power base;[38] but even in dealing with northerners who had earlier opposed him, David did not pursue a vindictive course. At Appleby, hostility to a powerful newcomer's arrival was minimized because Hugh de Morville took over a lordship that had been vacant since c. 1120; elsewhere, new men were almost invariably fitted in alongside the traditional elites by means of marriage alliances – 'one of the easiest . . . and most comfortable routes to domination'.[39]

In such ways, David prudently reassured local power holders that they had little to fear from Scottish rule. More positively, loyalty was rewarded by favour, as for example in the case of the Umfravilles of Prudhoe and Redesdale: Gilbert de Umfraville became Henry of Scotland's constable, gained estates in East Lothian and Stirlingshire, and remained in Scottish royal service until he died in c. 1180.[40] The sympathies of the native northern thegns had probably lain with David all along. Conversely, Anglo-Norman barons had a keener sense of allegiance to the English crown, and their acceptance of Scottish lordship was less unanimous and spontaneous. The mighty Walter Espec refused an accommodation and withdrew from his Northumberland barony of Wark on Tweed (which was promptly confiscated) to his Yorkshire estates.[41] But Espec's attitude was in fact exceptional. Virtually to a man the border nobles submitted and, to a greater or lesser degree, identified themselves with Scottish interests.

From 1141 David thus asserted his sovereignty as a powerful but peaceful monarch who dealt with old and new subjects on more or less equal terms.

[38] Ibid., pp. 207, 213–14.

[39] Davies, *Domination*, p. 5.

[40] *Liber S. Marie de Calchou* (Bannatyne Club, 1846), i, no. 92; *Registrum Monasterii S. Marie de Cambuskenneth* (Grampian Club, 1872), nos. 80, 86; G.W.S. Barrow (ed.), *Regesta Regum Scottorum, II: The Acts of William I King of Scots, 1165–1214* (Edinburgh, 1971), no. 292.

[41] Wark's forfeiture can be inferred from the details given in G.W.S. Barrow, *The Kingdom of the Scots* (London, 1973), p. 34.

Technically, a ruler could do what he pleased with his conquests; but David never saw matters in that light. Quite apart from other considerations, uncompromising policies would have been completely at variance with his view that the far north was rightfully his and he was now its lawful ruler; and his concern to make Scottish government acceptable, even advantageous, goes far to explain his success in forging a new polity which, by the standards of twelfth-century Europe, was a relatively stable entity. It had its weak points, Durham providing the most obvious example. Yet, for the moment, we need to take fuller stock of its strengths and viability.

Central to the coherence of any state forged through territorial union is the loyalty of its new subjects. To Scottish royal clerks, the northerners were as much David's *probi homines* as were his lieges of the Scots kingdom proper. But just how committed were the northerners – in particular the Anglo-Norman 'establishment' – to David personally? As recent research has emphasized, within contemporary English landed society the ordinary nobility had essentially localized interests and ambitions, and nowhere was that pattern more pronounced than in the far north.[42] This played directly into David's hands, for it enabled him to monopolize loyalties the more effectively. Some of the greater lords, however, were landowners on an inter-regional scale. Accustomed as they were to playing a fuller role in English political life, their allegiances were more complex, ambiguous and flexible. We cannot ignore Eustace Fitz John's important 'external' lordships and his closeness to Ranulf of Chester, with whom he temporarily submitted to Stephen in 1146. Nevertheless, Eustace helped to enforce Scottish authority over Durham in the early 1140s, and remained firmly rooted in Northumberland, where he founded Alnwick Abbey in 1147.[43] Even the Balliols and Bolbecs were lured into the Scottish obedience. Bernard de Balliol, one of Stephen's chief military captains,

---

[42] D. Crouch, 'Normans and Anglo-Normans: A Divided Aristocracy?', in D. Bates and A. Curry (eds), *England and Normandy in the Middle Ages* (London, 1994), pp. 51–67; J.A. Green, 'Aristocratic Loyalties on the Northern Frontier of England, *c.* 1100–1174', in D. Williams (ed.), *England in the Twelfth Century* (Woodbridge, 1990), pp. 91–4.

[43] Young, 'Bishopric of Durham', pp. 357–8; H.M. Colvin, *The White Canons in England* (Oxford, 1951), pp. 54–5.

had distinguished himself at both the Standard and Lincoln – perhaps that explains why Stephen never deprived him of his Hertfordshire estates. But Bernard's main attachment after 1141 was apparently to David's court, and in 1153 he endowed Kelso Abbey specifically for the benefit of Henry of Scotland's soul. The Bolbecs split their estates in *c.* 1141: Hugh took Whitchurch barony (Buckinghamshire) and gave his allegiance to Stephen; his brother, Walter, took Styford barony (Northumberland) and gave his allegiance to David. Similarly, the Brus family partitioned their lands at the Tees.[44] Both these houses pragmatically accepted the new political realities and divided their loyalties accordingly.

Furthermore, if, as John Gillingham contends, the Celtic 'barbarity' of the 1130s had helped to develop a heightened sense of Englishness,[45] in the changed conditions of the 1140s national loyalty was no doubt less of a force. Arguably, personal protection and advancement counted for more, especially if we bear in mind David Crouch's recent stress on the 'volatility' of lordship ties in twelfth-century England: men followed 'the leader who offered . . . most, whether in terms of security or lands'.[46] Here the key point is that Anglo-Norman nobles, and churchmen, probably accepted Scottish dominance all the more readily because David's stewardship was manifestly preferable to Stephen's. Such were Stephen's failings as a feudal suzerain that he had effectively abandoned the northerners. By contrast, David was to be trusted and respected because he gave good lordship of the kind that, in the 1140s, the English crown was incapable of providing almost anywhere north of Watford. Even the earl of Chester was appeased when he gained north Lancashire, originally granted to him by Stephen in 1146, but wholly ineffectively; and even William de Ste Barbe must have felt some obligation to David. To gain entry to

[44] Balliol: *Reg. Regum Anglo-Normann.*, iii, nos. 859–60; *Early Scottish Charters*, nos. 258–9; Bolbecs: Hedley, *Northumberland Families*, i, p. 25; *Reg. Regum Anglo-Normann.*, iii, nos. 4, 874, 958; *Early Scottish Charters*, nos. 133, 184; *Reg. Regum Scott.*, i, no. 13; Brus: Frame, *Political Development*, p. 59.

[45] Gillingham, 'Foundations of a Disunited Kingdom', pp. 54ff.

[46] D. Crouch, 'A Norman "Conventio" and Bonds of Lordship in the Middle Ages', in G. Garnett and J. Hudson (eds), *Law and Government in Medieval England and Normandy* (Cambridge, 1994), p. 315.

Durham, he had after all relied on the Scots rather than on Stephen, who had been powerless to assist. A strong impression of David's overall success in ensuring political allegiance and even affection is certainly gained from the distinctly pro-Scottish tone adopted by the chief northern English chroniclers in their assessments of his governance. Ailred of Rievaulx and John of Hexham, both great admirers of Henry of Scotland, were still more effusive in their praise of David. Ailred stressed his desire to be loved rather than feared; John saluted him because 'he tempered the fierceness of his barbarous nation', and thought that no contemporary king had greater virtues. For his part, William of Newburgh believed that peace and stability were the hallmarks of David's regime in the north.[47]

The disturbances reported in Furness and Cravenshire were indeed short-lived, and did not affect other areas; even at Durham, the accounts of William Cumin's oppressions may well have been exaggerated.[48] An administrative system based on sheriffs, justices and other agents remained in place and, significantly, the identifiable office-holders are all local men.[49] That the provincial elite, native and Anglo-Norman alike, retained a degree of continuing 'self-government' highlights David's sensitivity to local interests. But such cooperation in governance, and the public peace it helped to foster, also provide striking testimony of the extent to which David's authority was perceived as acceptable and legitimate. The animosities of the pre-1141 period were gradually replaced by a pattern of trust and dependence; and in general David created the harmonious conditions that made this territorial union intrinsically workable.

But a ruler anxious to incorporate new acquisitions successfully had more concrete measures at his disposal. Of course, protected as it now was from the onslaughts of Scotland's Gaelic world, Northumbrian society renewed its

---

[47] W.M. Metcalfe (ed.), *Pinkerton's Lives of the Scottish Saints* (Paisley, 1889), ii, p. 271; *Symeonis . . . Opera*, ii, pp. 327, 330; *Chron. of the Reigns*, i, p. 70.

[48] Ibid., p. 75; *Symeonis . . . Opera*, ii, p. 326; D. Whitelock, M. Brett and C.N.L. Brooke (eds), *Councils and Synods . . . Relating to the English Church, I* (Oxford, 1981), pt 2, p. 797.

[49] Hedley, *Northumberland Families*, i, p. 191; P. Dalton, 'Scottish Influence on Durham 1066–1214', in *Anglo-Norman Durham*, p. 350.

contacts with that other Scotland, the Normanized Lowlands which were becoming increasingly 'civilized' due to David's modernization and reform. Within this context, geographical contiguity, institutional similarities and other forms of convergence all made for a structurally well-grounded union. Yet what specific policies of integration did David pursue? At the topmost level, David's and Henry's courts were vital unifying agents, not least because of their frequent presence in the far north. Prominent northerners were also given an active role in them. Some appeared infrequently; but the critical point was that, collectively, they had a greater 'voice' there than they had ever had at the remote English court. The Scottish courts thus became potent sources of identification overriding former attachments, and gave the provincial elite a stronger sense of loyalty as subjects of the Scots king. Indeed, just as Scottish notables attended David and Henry south of the Tweed, so northerners came to courts held north of the Tweed. As early as *c.* 1141, five members of the Norman baronage of Northumberland joined David at Selkirk, and even Richard (prior) of Hexham – the most outspoken critic of the Scots at war – witnessed for Henry at Jedburgh in *c.* 1150.[50]

Scoto-Northumbrian links were further strengthened by monetary union when, in the late 1140s, David introduced a standardized royal coinage struck at Carlisle, Roxburgh, Berwick, Perth and Aberdeen, with Carlisle itself effectively acting as the 'principal mint of the Scottish kingdom'.[51] More important was the careful fostering of closer cohesion through the intermarriage of nobilities. A pivotal figure was Alan son of Waltheof of Allerdale, who could already count William Fitz Duncan and the earl of Dunbar among his cousins, and whose sisters went on to marry into the Lindsay and Galloway houses.[52] More important still, political union was given greater stability by the encouragement of property ownership across the former Tweed–Solway border – a topic that would repay more detailed attention than it can be given here. Even before

---

[50] *Reg. Regum Scott.*, i, no. 11; *Early Scottish Charters*, no. 257.

[51] Stewart, 'Scottish Mints', pp. 183, 195; I. Stewart, 'The Volume of Early Scottish Coinage', in D.M. Metcalf (ed.), *Coinage in Medieval Scotland (1100–1600)*, British Archaeological Reports, 45 (Oxford, 1977), p. 67.

[52] Hedley, *Northumberland Families*, i, p. 239.

1135 the Brus lords of Annandale, the Dunbars and Durham Priory had accumulated important 'cross-border' estates. But, clearly, a significant expansion of such linkages can be attributed to the period 1141–57, when the ranks of those with property straddling the old frontier were swelled by, among others, the abbeys of Dunfermline and Kelso, and the Northumberland priories of Brinkburn and Holystone. In addition, Jedburgh Abbey's important gains in Cumberland had probably been secured by 1157. Even the hermit Godric of Finchale, nearly done to death by Scottish raiders in 1138, acquired a small estate in Lothian, perhaps as belated compensation for his sufferings. And, yet more remarkably, tiny Harehope hospital near Alnwick received from David lands in Edinburgh and the church of St Giles – a mark of signal favour.[53] As regards secular proprietors, we might mention Roger Bertram of Mitford, who gained some standing in Berwickshire; Countess Ada de Warenne, Henry of Scotland's wife, whose lands included property near Hexham, and who provided Scottish estates for members of the Northumberland 'gentry'; William de Vieuxpont, who obtained extensive concerns in Tynedale and an estate at Warkworth, within a day's ride of his land at Horndean (Berwickshire); or – though their Anglo-Scottish interests may have originated before 1141 – the native lords Uhtred son of Liulf, a Cumberland proprietor, who became lord of Mow (Roxburghshire), and whose heir, Eschina, was joint founder of the house of Stewart; and Alan son of Waltheof's bastard brother, Cospatric, also a Cumberland landowner, who held Dalmeny (West Lothian) and Inverkeithing (Fife).[54] But pride of place must surely go to Hugh de Morville, whose lordships

---

[53] Jedburgh: Barrow, *Kingdom*, p. 146; Godric: J. Stevenson (ed.), *Libellus de Vita et Miraculis S. Godrici*, Surtees Soc., 20 (1847), pp. 114–16, 346; Harehope: I.B. Cowan, 'The Early Ecclesiastical History of Edinburgh', *Innes Review*, 23 (1972), 18.

[54] Bertram: Stringer, 'Lords of Lauderdale', p. 50; Warenne: V. Chandler, 'Ada de Warenne, Queen Mother of Scotland, *c.* 1123–1178', *SHR*, 60 (1981), 125–6, 128, 136–9; Vieuxpont: *Reg. Regum Scott.*, ii, no. 84; J.T. Fowler (ed.), *Chartularium Abbathiae de Novo Monasterio*, Surtees Soc., 66 (1878), p. 213; J. Raine, *The History and Antiquities of North Durham* (London, 1852), Appendix, nos. 155–6; Uhtred: Barrow, 'Scotland and Durham', p. 322; Cospatric: *Reg. Regum Scott.*, i, no. 126. Waltheof, Cospatric's son, granted the churches of Bassenthwaite (Cumberland) and Dalmeny to Jedburgh Abbey (J. Bain *et al.* (eds), *Calendar of Documents relating to Scotland* (Edinburgh, 1881–1986), i, no. 429; Scottish Record Office, Edinburgh, Register House Charters, RH6/34).

of Appleby, Lauderdale in Berwickshire and (probably) Cunningham in Ayrshire gave him a very powerful stake on both sides of the old border. It was he who in 1150 founded Dryburgh Abbey (Berwickshire) as a daughter-house of Alnwick; and Dryburgh's initial endowment included assets at Great Asby and Maulds Meaburn (Westmorland).[55] Evidently, territorial integration was becoming increasingly a reality, and most of the proprietors just mentioned would have been deeply committed unionists. The chief exception was Durham Priory; even so, the extensive properties held by St Cuthbert's monks in Berwickshire – where their estate office at Coldingham was developing into a fully fledged religious house[56] – helped to ensure that their attitude towards David never degenerated into outright hostility.

Against this broad backdrop of Scottish power-building, it is easier to see why even Henry of Anjou apparently accepted in 1149 that the far north had become part of an extended Scottish state. It was, indeed, as if what we now regard as the English border region was bound more tightly to Scotland than it had ever been bound to England. On this line of argument, the new Scoto-Northumbrian polity was in principle as viable as any other kingdom in twelfth-century Europe, and – at least in today's Borders – perhaps more cohesive than most.

Though the unifying forces outweighed those of disunity and division, David was nevertheless not satisfied that he had created a perfect union. He hoped to make his position even stronger, and that was why, in 1149, he formed an alliance with Henry Plantagenet and Ranulf of Chester for an advance on York. He was also supported by Henry Murdac, archbishop of York (1147–53), whom Stephen had disowned and was keeping from his see. This episode has normally been discussed in the context of Angevin strategic aims rather than Scottish ones; but the latter were clearly paramount, as recent studies have indicated,[57] and they deserve closer examination.

Ideally, a medieval state needed well-defined boundaries. In this regard David could settle for ruling an expanded kingdom that extended on the east to the

---

[55] Stringer, 'Lords of Lauderdale', p. 51.

[56] Barrow, 'Scotland and Durham', p. 319.

[57] Stringer, *Stephen*, pp. 36–7; Dalton, *Conquest*, pp. 226–8.

Tyne, thus writing off Durham and the problems associated with it. But one difficulty was that the estates of leading northerners included enclaves south of the Tyne and of the Tees as well. Leaving those interests outside Scottish frontiers was not fatal to effective state-building, especially if the English crown remained weak, but it could lead to complications. Another argument for pushing the border further south stemmed from the fact that political and ecclesiastical boundaries did not coincide. Not only did the York archbishopric have jurisdiction over Carlisle and Durham, but it challenged David's supremacy by claiming metropolitan authority over the Scottish Church itself, which had no archbishopric of its own. Again, this was not an insuperable difficulty – York's prestige was at a low ebb in the 1140s and, in any case, Scots kings and bishops were very experienced in rebuffing its claims – but the *potential* threat York posed to Scottish sovereignty could not be ignored.

Now, as Paul Dalton has underlined, English royal power in Yorkshire was much reduced by 1149, and David had already made important inroads – indeed, his Yorkshire clientage was apparently far more extensive than Stephen's, and he had especially close personal ties with Henry Murdac's main allies, the Cistercian and Augustinian reformers.[58] We have, however, still to address the point that it was a very serious step for Murdac and his faction to ally themselves politically with the Scots, thus escalating an election dispute into a conflict about English unity. Yet, as Mary Cheney has stressed, York had earlier put its rights before the 'national interest' by securing in 1120 explicit papal recognition of its freedom from Canterbury's primacy, in defiance of the express wishes of Henry I, who regarded York's subjection to Canterbury as a vital counter to northern separatism. The independent-minded Murdac was himself a great champion of York's privileged status, and as recently as 1148 Rome had reaffirmed its autonomy.[59] Here, then, was an English archbishop who claimed to rule the Scottish Church, but who rejected Canterbury's authority, refused to obey Stephen, and had not even sworn fealty to the

[58] Ibid., pp. 174–5, 211ff.

[59] M. Cheney, 'Some Observations on a Papal Privilege of 1120 for the Archbishops of York', *Journal of Ecclesiastical History*, 31 (1980), 429–39; A. Morey and C.N.L. Brooke, *Gilbert Foliot and His Letters* (Cambridge, 1965), p. 91.

English crown.[60] There was, therefore, a good deal of common political ground between Murdac and David. Nor would the willingness of Murdac's party to ally with David have been uninfluenced by the practical consideration that in Northumberland and Cumbria he controlled endowments belonging to many Yorkshire monasteries and, not least, to the archbishopric itself – the liberty of Hexhamshire being one of its most valuable possessions.

The stage was set for the extension of Scottish control over the entire north. On the one hand, if David could install Murdac as his own metropolitan archbishop, he would effectively govern a kingdom with its twin capitals at Edinburgh and York and simultaneously reinforce his control over church affairs throughout his domains. On the other, under Scottish rule York would satisfy its ambitions by both realizing its claims in north Britain and putting beyond doubt its cherished autonomy from Canterbury. But at this critical juncture Stephen made a rare foray north and arrived unexpectedly at York in sufficient strength to force David to back down: 'So when the king of Scotland and his allies saw that King Stephen's forces were stronger . . . they lost heart . . . and, dispersing in different directions, returned home individually.'[61] On any reckoning, the year 1149 must surely rank as one of the most decisive dates in British history, and Stephen (with whom Murdac was reconciled in 1151) deserves full credit for preventing an expansion of Scottish dominance that may have left 'England' permanently confined to the Midlands and the south.

Despite this major setback, the Scots remained firmly entrenched in the far north, and no one could yet have confidently predicted that its future would not lie with some kind of 'greater Scotland'. In 1150 Henry of Scotland founded a Cistercian monastery at Holm Cultram (Cumberland) as a daughter-house of the great abbey of Melrose. At about the same time, David granted to the Corbets the lordship of Yetholm (Roxburghshire), which included as an integral part of it lands previously belonging to Walter Espec's barony of Wark on Tweed.[62] Both actions strongly indicate that the union with Scotland was still

---

[60] As was stressed by William of Newburgh: *Chron. of the Reigns*, i, p. 56.

[61] K.R. Potter and R.H.C. Davis (eds), *Gesta Stephani* (Oxford, 1976), p. 217.

[62] *Early Scottish Charters*, no. 244; Barrow, *Kingdom*, p. 34.

expected to last; and the structure of the Corbets' estate, embracing as it did the old border line itself, vividly symbolized the reality of that union.

In 1157, however, the Scots were ousted by Henry II, who contrary to his promise of 1149 insisted that, in Newburgh's telling phrase, he 'ought not to be defrauded of so great a part of his kingdom'.[63] Was this the inevitable outcome after all? There was in fact nothing 'natural' or unavoidable about it.[64] English weakness was of course basic to Scottish success. To that extent, the supremacy David achieved was artificial; but to assume that it was also fundamentally flawed presupposes that an English resurgence was a foregone conclusion. This rested, however, to a remarkable degree on chance.

First of all, but for Stephen's defence of York in 1149, made possible only by a lucky easing of his military commitments elsewhere, combined, perhaps, with Welsh advances that distracted Ranulf of Chester,[65] all Yorkshire could well have been lost, and that would have made the Scots much harder to dislodge. Hugh du Puiset would probably not have become bishop of Durham; and the alliance with the Chesters – in 1149 Ranulf had agreed to marry his son into the Scots royal house[66] – might have continued, thus bringing most of the north Midlands within the Scottish orbit, however indirectly. More crucial was the premature death, in his early thirties, of Henry of Scotland in 1152. Henry's second son, the nine-year-old William, was installed (with some understandable difficulty) as earl of Northumberland, and when David himself died in May 1153 he was succeeded by Henry's eldest son, Malcolm IV, who was only twelve. Had Henry, like David, survived into his seventies, the Scots would obviously have been in a much stronger position. In the event, firm leadership lapsed, and in Scotland the boy-king's rule was immediately challenged by Hebridean sea-kings and Highland warlords. Another critical blow was the ability of Stephen and Henry Plantagenet to agree a settlement five months after David's death, a turn of events which also owed much to contingency – the sudden death in August 1153 of Stephen's son, Eustace, in his early twenties. As

---

[63] *Chron. of the Reigns*, i, p. 105.

[64] As Geoffrey Barrow was the first to emphasize: Barrow, *Scotland*, p. 65.

[65] D. Crouch, 'The March and the Welsh Kings', in *Anarchy*, p. 279.

[66] *Symeonis . . . Opera*, ii, p. 323.

Graeme White has indicated, the Anarchy would almost certainly have continued had Eustace lived.[67] Henry II's uncontested succession was therefore by no means predestined; but it was of course the smooth transfer of power in 1153–4 which above all transformed the political scene – and, unsurprisingly, brought Eustace Fitz John and Bishop Athelwold scurrying to the English court.[68] Yet if events had not played so generously into Henry II's hands, it does not seem too far-fetched to suppose that, instead of political structures returning to their familiar patterns, a greater Scottish polity, perhaps reaching even to the Humber, would have developed into a mature and fully established state; and while further speculation must be resisted, it is sufficiently clear that the consequences for the future history of Britain would have been profound.

As it was, although David's successes in Scotland obviously did not rest solely on his control of the far north, the short-lived Scottish occupation had a very real, long-term impact on the power and authority of the Scots monarchy. David's state-building at Stephen's expense naturally enhanced his prestige, and helps to explain why, in the 1140s, Anglo-Norman adventurers flocked into his service from every quarter.[69] Again, 'English' resources were used to contain challenges from Scotland's 'Celtic fringe' – to buy off trouble-makers, as in the case of Bishop Wimund of the Isles (who pressed claims to the Scots throne);[70] or to reinforce loyalties, as in the case of William Fitz Duncan (who, despite his royal descent, never pressed such claims). Possession of Carlisle also enabled David to impose himself on Fergus lord, or 'king', of Galloway. All this allows us to understand more clearly why his modernizing programme was not seriously disrupted by traditional Scottish interest groups in the 1140s and early 1150s; indeed, it is notable that Fergus did not join the opposition to Malcolm IV until after Carlisle had been surrendered.[71] Moreover, Ian Blanchard has stressed

---

[67] G.J. White, 'The End of Stephen's Reign', *History*, 75 (1990), 10–11.

[68] *Reg. Regum Anglo-Normann.*, iii, nos. 664, 993; Summerson, *Carlisle*, i, p. 46.

[69] Barrow, *Anglo-Norman Era*, passim.

[70] He was granted the province of Furness, where eventually he fell foul of the local nobility, who had him blinded and emasculated 'for the peace of the kingdom of Scots': *Chron. of the Reigns*, i, pp. 75–6.

[71] D. Brooke, 'Fergus of Galloway', *Transactions of the Dumfriesshire and Galloway Natural History and Antiquarian Society*, 3rd ser., 66 (1991), 47–56.

that the annexation of the far north involved a major redistribution of economic power to Scotland's enduring advantage.[72] Crucial here was David's control of the immensely rich silver mines on Alston Moor, for Pennine silver not only gave Scotland its first national coinage, but generated boom conditions in the Lowlands which maximized crown revenues, gained a self-sustaining momentum, and guaranteed the wealth on which any state's strength ultimately depends. In particular, this helps to account for the ability of David and his successors to finance castles, cathedrals and monasteries, and to reward incomers on attractive terms. In sum, southern expansion served to accelerate modernization, and enabled the twelfth-century Scots kingdom to develop more swiftly than would otherwise have been the case. So, while from 1154 there was no gainsaying the very real disparity of resources between the Scottish and Angevin kings, the superior power of English kingship was less great than it might have been; and the emergence of Scotland as a self-confident medieval state can be fully understood only by recognizing the vital role that control of the far north, however temporary, played in its development.

---

[72] I. Blanchard, 'Lothian and Beyond: The Economy of the "English Empire" of David I' (forthcoming). My thanks to Ian Blanchard for kindly supplying a copy of his essay prior to its publication.

5

DAMAGE AND 'WASTE' IN YORKSHIRE AND THE NORTH MIDLANDS IN THE REIGN OF STEPHEN*

Graeme White

The pioneering work on the Danegeld returns for 'waste' in the 1156 pipe roll was published by H.W.C. Davis, in an attempt to shed light on the amounts of suffering and devastation endured by different parts of England during Stephen's reign. His interpretation was generally accepted until the 1980s, when stress came to be laid upon the administrative difficulties faced by those responsible for levying the tax after 1154. The entries for 'waste' were seen as amounts written off on various grounds, of which physical damage was only one.[1] This view was challenged in 1991 when Emilie Amt defended the traditional interpretation advanced by Davis and interpreted 'waste' as a result of real damage rather than of administrative or political problems. Amt argued that several of the administrative difficulties in levying Danegeld which have been seen as covered by the write-offs for 'waste', were handled by the exchequer in ways demonstrable from the pipe rolls. In other words the exchequer was competent to deal with its accounting problems and did not need to take

---

* I am grateful to Professors Edmund King and Thomas Keefe for commenting on an earlier draft of this paper.

[1] H.W.C. Davis, 'The Anarchy of Stephen's Reign', *EHR*, 18 (1903), 630–41; J.A. Green, 'The Last Century of Danegeld', *EHR*, 96 (1981), 241–58; Edmund King, 'The Anarchy of King Stephen's Reign', *TRHS*, 5th ser., 34 (1984), 133–53; G.J. White, 'Were the Midlands "Wasted" During Stephen's Reign?', *Midland History*, 10 (1985), 26–46.

refuge in the convenient fiction of 'waste'.[2] This paper takes account of Amt's important contribution, but restates the case for regarding the 1156 Danegeld accounts as evidence for administrative as well as economic dislocation.

Yorkshire deserves close attention in this context, as a shire with abundant evidence of physical damage to property during Stephen's reign, but only 7 per cent of its Danegeld liability written off as 'waste'.[3] One reason for this may be that, as England's largest shire, it was manifestly under-assessed for Danegeld, ranking only thirteenth in terms of total liability to the levy of 1156. The exchequer's recognition of this under-assessment came in the form of the other major tax raised in 1156, the county assize (or *donum comitatus*), Yorkshire's liability to which was pitched at 500 silver marks, a far larger sum than for any other shire.[4] If Yorkshire was lightly burdened with Danegeld, landholders presumably retained a capacity to pay their tax in full despite severe damage to their property. Put another way, it needed more physical devastation in Yorkshire to make an impact on the Danegeld figures for 'waste' than was the case in more heavily assessed shires. This suggestion, based on a relationship between Danegeld 'waste' and the economic condition of landholders' estates, is a point in favour of Amt's hypothesis. But close scrutiny of the pipe rolls, for Yorkshire and elsewhere, indicates that this is only part of the answer.

Yorkshire's Danegeld accounts as a whole have much in common with those of other shires, particularly when we set the figures for 1156 in the context of the two other levies recorded in detail, those of 1130 and 1162 (See Tables 1 and 2). The total liability appears to have been the same in 1156 as in 1130, but to have fallen by a round sum in 1162: a pattern consistent with that in eight other shires. The implication is that Henry II's exchequer was working to assessments current under Henry I, but in 1162 deliberately wrote off several

---

[2] E. Amt, 'The Meaning of Waste in the Early Pipe Rolls of Henry II', *Economic History Review*, 44 (1991), 240–8; idem, *The Accession of Henry II in England: Royal Government Restored, 1149–1159* (Woodbridge, 1993), pp. 133–43.

[3] Paul Dalton, *Conquest, Anarchy and Lordship: Yorkshire, 1066–1154* (Cambridge, 1994), pp. 145–95; T. Callahan, 'The Impact of Anarchy on English Monasticism, 1135–1154', *Albion*, 6 (1974), 218–32.

[4] On exchequer policy in determining the sums for each shire, see F.W. Maitland, *Domesday Book and Beyond* (Cambridge, 1897), pp. 545–6.

Table 1

YORKSHIRE DANEGELD RETURNS 1156

In treasury	£124 10s. 10d.
And in pardons by King's writ	
Monks of Rievaulx	13s. 4d.
Richard de Camville	4s. 0d.
Henry d'Oilli	20s. 0d.
Knights of the Temple	4s. 6d.
Earl of Leicester	6d.
King's demesne of Doncaster	9s. 0d.
King's demesne of Tickhill	4s. 0d.
King's demesne of Wighton	27s. 0d.
In 'waste forest'	40s. 0d.
Chancellor	57s. 0d.
Bertram de Bulmer	40s. 0d.
Total	£10 19s. 4d.
And in waste	£11 1s. 8d.
Owes	£18 17s. 7d.

(Total liability: £165 9s. 5d.)

Source: *Pipe Roll 2 Henry II*, p. 27.

pounds, whether as an undeclared remission to the shire or as a tacit allowance to the sheriff. In a further six shires, although the shortfall in 1162 is not to be found, the total liabilities in 1130 and 1156 are again identical; in most of the remainder, they are sufficiently close to reinforce the impression that pre-civil war assessments continued to determine the totals due.

The categories of people formally pardoned Danegeld in Yorkshire are also typical of those across the country. In 1130, the list included the king's servants and favourites, a religious house (St Oswald's Priory, Nostell), odd portions of royal demesne and 'waste forest', plus a number of tenants-in-chief not known to

Table 2

SUMMARY OF YORKSHIRE DANEGELD RETURNS, 1130 AND 1162

1130

In treasury	£114 0s. 4d.
In pardons by king's writ	£51 19s. 2d.
Quit	
(Total liability: £165 19s. 6d.)	

1162

In treasury	£101 10s. 0d.
In pardons by king's writ	£33 13s.10d.
Owes	£7 3s. 7d.
In soltis	
(repayment of advance expenditure)	£3 2s. 0d.

(Total liability: £145 9s. 5d.)

Sum left owing continued as a debt until 1166, when £7 paid.

Source: *Pipe Roll 31 Henry I*, p. 34; *Pipe Roll 8 Henry II*, p. 52.

have been royal officials. The sum pardoned amounted to almost a third of the shire's total liability to Danegeld.[5] In 1156, in Yorkshire as elsewhere, a more stringent policy towards official exemption applied. Royal officials were pardoned, as were the Templars and the monks of Rievaulx, and allowances were also made for 'waste forest' and portions of royal demesne. Further pardons

---

[5] The explanation of waste in C. Johnson *et al.* (eds), *Dialogus de Scaccario* (Oxford, 1983), pp. 60–1, is unconvincing in explaining Danegeld pardons on account of 'waste forest'. In the *Dialogus* a man who wasted forests was said to commit 'an offence . . . so serious that he can in no way be quit of it by his session at the exchequer but must . . . suffer a money penalty', clearly no justification for the remission of taxes.

were granted in 1157 on lands held by the king of Scots and by four religious houses.[6] As was usual in 1156, however, the tenants-in-chief were largely absent from the pardons list. Their apparent obligation to pay, here as elsewhere, meant that, despite the inclusion of the item for 'waste', the total paid into the treasury nationally in 1156 was only a little less than in 1130, and in ten shires, including Yorkshire, it was actually higher.[7] In 1162, again in line with the pattern in the rest of the country, there was an increase in the total sum pardoned, but the categories of those enjoying exemption remained the same. More religious houses found a place on the list, but tenants-in-chief were still excluded, unless (like Bertram de Bulmer) they were also royal favourites or officials.

Comparison with accounts from north Midland shires shows that these Yorkshire Danegeld figures followed the norm. In Staffordshire, the Danegeld liability was identical in 1130 and 1156, and £2 lower in 1162. The number of pardons fell from twenty-two in 1130, when tenants-in-chief featured on the list, to eight in 1156, when they were restricted to the sheriff and other royal officials, the Templars, and portions of escheated demesne and 'waste forest'. The amounts paid into the treasury from Staffordshire in 1130 and 1156 were similar, despite a figure for 'waste' in 1156 which represented about 19 per cent of the total Danegeld liability. Six years later, the pardons list here was augmented by further religious houses, but continued to exclude many tenants-in-chief. In Nottinghamshire and Derbyshire, accounted for together, the number of pardons followed the customary trend, from twenty-three in 1130, when tenants-in-chief were included, to seven in 1156 when they were not, and twenty-two in 1162, when several religious houses appeared for the first time. In this case, however, the total written off as 'waste' in 1156 was 52 per cent of the shires' total, the second highest figure in the country behind Warwickshire, and the sum paid into the treasury fell to half that recorded in 1130.[8]

These statistics may be interpreted as follows.[9] Faced with a shortage of cash,

[6] *Pipe Roll 3 Henry II*, p. 86.

[7] White, 'Were the Midlands "Wasted"?', 43–5.

[8] *Pipe Roll 31 Henry I*, pp. 11–12, 76; *Pipe Roll 2 Henry II*, pp. 29–30, 39; *Pipe Roll 8 Henry II*, pp. 29, 33.

[9] See White, 'Were the Midlands "Wasted"?'; V.H. Galbraith and J.Tait (eds), *Herefordshire Domesday*, Pipe Roll Soc., n. s., 25 (London, 1950), pp. 75, 77; *Dialogus*, p. 105.

Henry II's exchequer was prepared in 1155–6 to levy Danegeld even though its records had become outdated during Stephen's reign. It knew the total liabilities to danegeld for each shire, but individual assessments of hides and carucates had fallen into disarray following changes of tenure, some of them disputed. The *Herefordshire Domesday* shows that Henry II's early exchequer was aware of the total Danegeld liability for the shire but was endeavouring to bring its record of landholders and hidages up-to-date. Meanwhile, the application of a restrictive policy on pardons would almost certainly have led to some resistance towards paying the tax, whether from tenants-in-chief accustomed to exemption as in 1130, or from religious houses holding charters promising quittance from Danegeld. In these circumstances, sheriffs must have faced great difficulties in 1156 in collecting what was due. The exchequer chose not to pursue them over these shortfalls. Of the debts entered as 'owing' in 1156, nearly all were pardoned in the following year, and none was carried forward any further. Instead, the exchequer wrote off any discrepancy as 'waste', the sums entered against these headings in the pipe roll frequently being precisely what were required to make shires' total liabilities match those of 1130. Such action might seem indulgent, but in the circumstances of 1156 the Danegeld had achieved its objective in raising almost as much for the treasury as in 1130. None of this is to deny that economic dislocation and physical damage to property might have been among the reasons for sheriffs' failure to collect all the Danegeld due; but given the adverse circumstances in which they levied the tax, there are many other possible explanations for the exchequer's resort to the term 'waste' .

Amt has challenged this interpretation on several grounds, one of which is that the distribution of Danegeld 'waste' is not incompatible with the known impact of warfare in different parts of the country. However, much depends on which areas one focuses upon. The high 'waste' levels in Notting-hamshire–Derbyshire, where the boroughs also had half their *auxilium* remitted as 'waste', and there was a substantial sum spent on restocking the royal demesne, could possibly be explained by the efforts of Ranulf II earl of Chester to consolidate his territorial control of the north Midlands. But more sophisticated arguments are needed for Yorkshire, where the tide of civil war ran high but the pipe roll figure was low. The amount collected for Shropshire, vulnerable to the resurgent Welsh, also defies a simple explanation, for here

Danegeld 'waste' was only 5 per cent of the total liability. Amt also cites cases in Henry II's early pipe rolls in which 'waste' refers to physical destruction, but these are taken from accounts of pleas or, more usually, farms. There are occasional remissions for 'waste' in the Danegeld accounts of 1130 and 1162, probably referring to devastated land, but these are all embraced within the list of pardons, as items contributing to the pardons totals for the relevant shires.[10] The treatment of Danegeld 'waste' in 1156, as a separate category after the pardons total and before the statement of quittance or outstanding debt, is exceptional. This suggests that the term has a significance specific to these accounts.

More substantial is Amt's argument that 'waste' should not be regarded as a polite fiction to cover disputed liability, because the exchequer already had procedures for handling issues of this kind. In the Danegeld accounts of 1156, the sums due from nineteen religious houses, from Stephen's surviving son William de Warenne, from William earl of Gloucester, William de Chesney, Ralph of Hastings and various other laymen, were entered as owing, only for the debts to be pardoned in the following year, apparently after their claims to exemption had been acknowledged. In these cases the exchequer knew the sum due from the landholder concerned at Michaelmas 1156, but preferred that this was carried forward as 'owing' until the question of payment or pardon was resolved. The reasons for delay appear to be political in some cases, notably those of William de Warenne and William earl of Gloucester where the official pardons seem to have been delayed until *rapprochements* with the king, and may have been procedural in others, possibly arising from failures to produce the relevant charters, or from disputes over their authenticity. Instances such as these are taken to suggest that the exchequer had no need of recourse to 'waste' in order to cover Danegeld which it was uncertain whether to collect or to pardon. But in all these cases the precise sums involved were known, hence their initial inclusion within the category 'owing'. There is no reason to believe

[10] In 1130 under Oxfordshire, plus an old account for 1128 under Middlesex; in 1162 under Essex, Herefordshire, Hertfordshire, Northamptonshire and Nottinghamshire–Derbyshire: *Pipe Roll 31 Henry I*, pp. 6, 151; *Pipe Roll 8 Henry II*, pp. 8, 33, 59, 71–2.

that every instance of contested liability was dealt with in this way. The Yorkshire Danegeld entries throw light on the issue.

One landholder cited in this connection is Stephen's son, William de Warenne. Of him, we read that 'instead of writing off his obligations as "waste" in 1156, the exchequer consistently deferred action (whether collection or pardon) on William's Danegeld and other taxes that year. Then, in the spring of 1157 . . . the king and the earl came to terms. At Michaelmas that year, when the next pipe roll was written, William was pardoned his various tax obligations from 1156.'[11] There was certainly a meeting between Henry II and William de Warenne in May 1157, as a result of which William surrendered his castles, together with his acquisitions under the peace terms of 1153, but retained the baronial lands his father had held in 1135 plus the Warenne honour in right of his wife.[12] But the position on tax exemption was not so clear-cut. In Norfolk the Danegeld due from his lands in 1156 was 'postponed by the king's writ until the close of Pentecost', but elsewhere only that from Cambridgeshire, Surrey and Sussex was recorded as owing, to be pardoned in the following year. William's lands in various other shires, some inherited from Stephen, others held by previous Warenne earls such as the Yorkshire barony of Conisbrough, received no formal Danegeld pardon in 1156 or 1157. In some cases, the *donum comitatus* due from Warenne in 1156 was left owing and then pardoned in 1157 (Essex, Somerset, Yorkshire), in other cases his first entry against a pardon came with the *donum* of 1158 (Buckinghamshire–Bedfordshire, Leicestershire, Lincolnshire, Rutland, Staffordshire). Conversely, he enjoyed remission of the county assize on his 'new land' in Norfolk and Suffolk as early as 1156; elsewhere, he appears to have missed out on a pardon, as for example in Hertfordshire.[13] If there is a pattern to all this, it is hard to detect. It is tempting

[11] Amt, 'Meaning of Waste', 243.

[12] H.A. Cronne and R.H.C. Davis (eds), *Regesta Regum Anglo-Normannorum 1066–1154, Volume III* (Oxford, 1968), no. 272; R. Howlett (ed.), *Chronicles of the Reigns of Stephen, Henry II, and Richard I*, Rolls Series (London, 1884–9), iv, pp. 192–3.

[13] *Pipe Roll 2 Henry II*, pp. 7, 9, 10; *Pipe Roll 3 Henry II*, pp. 73, 79, 86, 94, 96, 98; *Pipe Roll 4 Henry II*, pp. 137, 140, 145, 161, 183; *Pipe Roll 8 Henry II*, p. 72.

to see the 1157 Danegeld pardons on the Warenne lands in eastern and south-eastern England as confined to 'new land' gained under the peace settlement and restored to Henry II in that year. He surrendered holdings in Norfolk and Surrey at this time; it is possible that the pardon in Cambridgeshire covers outlying parts of his acquisition in Norfolk, while that in Sussex relates to the barony of Pevensey. But this cannot be proved. All that can be said is that the general picture is one of diversity: of William de Warenne making good his claims to exemption on some of the tax due, on some of his holdings, in some parts of the country, at different times. The impression is of sheriffs and exchequer struggling to cope with the requirement to levy the taxes, from a magnate whose landed wealth had been derived from various sources, some recently acquired, and who may not have been disposed fully to cooperate with the new regime. This is the context in which there might well have been *ad hoc* solutions to problems as they arose, and a pragmatic readiness to write off as 'waste' what could neither be collected nor accounted for.

There was similar variability in the treatment of other individual landholders. Although Richard de Lucy, John Marshal, Hugh de Gundeville and Walter de Dunstanville were among those to receive a pardon in 1157 on Danegeld left owing in 1156, these were not the only entries against their names; other Danegeld pardons were granted to them first time around in 1156.[14] Even William earl of Gloucester, whose pardons were repeatedly deferred until 1157, does not seem to have been dealt with entirely consistently, for his lands in Devon and Somerset, which merited pardons for the *donum comitatus* in 1158, were omitted from the Danegeld pardons of 1156 and 1157.[15] Either he paid on these lands, and evidently no others, or he enjoyed similar remissions to those in other shires, hidden here within the overall figures for 'waste'. One of the best examples in favour of Amt's hypothesis does in fact come from Yorkshire, where the lands of the king of Scots were pardoned Danegeld in 1157, again following a debt recorded in 1156. The entry presumably relates, in large part, to holdings in the south of the county, based upon Hallam. Malcolm IV did not do

[14] See, for example, *Pipe Roll 2 Henry II*, pp. 17, 20, 34. See also *Pipe Roll 3 Henry II*, pp. 81, 89, 98.
[15] *Pipe Roll 4 Henry II*, pp. 122, 159.

homage to Henry II, by surrendering his lands in northern England, until May 1157. Accordingly, the Danegeld due from his Yorkshire holdings was not collected in 1156, but in this case, rather than write it off as 'waste' the exchequer evidently decided to enter the sum as 'owing' pending a settlement with the king. In the event, the property was given up to Henry as part of the agreement of May 1157, so the sum due 'in the land of the king of Scots' was formally pardoned the following Michaelmas.[16] Here we do appear to have an instance in which the exchequer, faced with a clear problem in enforcing the payment due, opted to carry the item forward instead of having recourse to the convenient cover of 'waste'. But practice in a high-profile case such as this cannot be taken as illustrative of general exchequer policy.

The Yorkshire folios also illustrate the exchequer's handling of religious communities. While Rievaulx Abbey and the Templars received Danegeld pardons in 1156, the houses at Fountains, Thornton and Watton were not pardoned until 1157, on sums left owing in the previous year. Several other communities were subsequently entered against Danegeld pardons for the first time in 1162. There were many reasons for this variability. The Templars were the beneficiaries of the new king's special favour.[17] It is possible that some failures to obtain immediate exemption were related to the rule explained in the *Dialogus de Scaccario*. Here, it is stated that pardons from particular impositions were only granted if charters specified them, general quittances from every exaction being insufficient.[18] Yet Fountains had received a charter from Henry II dated to the early summer of 1155, in which the monks' holdings had been confirmed, with quittances specifically including Danegeld.[19] We can only speculate on why this charter did not immediately entitle Fountains to the pardon due in 1156. As significant is the failure of Meaux Abbey to receive a pardon until 1162, despite receiving charters specifying Danegeld exemption from both Stephen and Henry

---

[16] *Chron. of the Reigns*, i, pp. 105–6.

[17] *Pipe Roll 2 Henry II*, pp. 3, 6, 7, 8, 10, 13, 14, 16.

[18] *Dialogus*, p. 106.

[19] W. Farrer (ed.), *Early Yorkshire Charters* (Edinburgh, 1914–16), i, nos. 76–7.

in January 1154.[20] The abbey's mistake may have been to rely on charters issued before Henry's accession as king. Yet there is a similar case among the Nottinghamshire–Derbyshire accounts, where Rufford Abbey, despite a confirmation charter from Henry II mentioning quittance from Danegeld, and a writ to royal officers in Nottinghamshire ordering that the charter be observed, did not figure among the pardons until 1162.[21] If religious communities had gone to the trouble of obtaining confirmation charters at the outset of the new reign, it would be surprising if they had not used them to claim the tax exemptions which were evidently their due. And if the monks of Rufford, Meaux and elsewhere were expected to pay Danegeld in 1156, despite holding charters which authorised their exemption from the tax, there would doubtless have been resistance. In that resistance may well lie one of the explanations for the exchequer's resort to 'waste' to cover uncollected tax.

Amt's third argument in favour of a literal meaning of 'waste' in the 1156 Danegeld accounts involves comparison with the other taxes levied in that year, the *auxilium* on boroughs and the *donum comitatus*. Amt points out that the total amount of 'waste' entered for the *auxilium* was significantly less in percentage terms than for the Danegeld, and that the *donum* had no 'waste' recorded at all. Her interpretation of these figures is that, as extraordinary taxes newly assessed, *auxilium* and *donum* ought to have excited more resistance than the Danegeld; the fact that they apparently did not weakens the case for regarding administrative difficulties as in any way relevant to the question of 'waste' and takes us back to a physical explanation of the term. But this argument is open to challenge because these taxes were, in fact, well established. *Auxilia* on boroughs had been levied annually under Henry I, for the same amounts as under Henry II, and there had been occasional impositions of *auxilia* and *dona* on shire communities as well.[22] A contrast is certainly apparent between the 'waste' figures for Danegeld and those for the *auxilium* in 1156, but the explanation lies elsewhere.

The sums entered as Danegeld 'waste' in 1156 were counted to the last

---

[20] *Regesta*, nos 583–4.

[21] C.J. Holdsworth (ed.), *Rufford Charters*, Thoroton Soc., 30 (1974), ii, nos. 662, 664; the writ was issued in February 1156.

[22] Judith A. Green, *The Government of England Under Henry I* (Cambridge, 1986), pp. 75–6.

penny, while those relating to *auxilia* involved round sums representing a clear proportion of the total due.[23] This suggests that in handling Danegeld, the exchequer was inserting into its accounts whatever sum was necessary to match the predetermined total liability, which (being based on precise, if outdated, hidage assessments) was itself rarely in neat round figures. With the *auxilium*, a customary lump sum in a round number of pounds had traditionally been imposed by the exchequer on each borough, and it was the responsibility of the local community to apportion the individual contributions. The sheriff and exchequer were thus spared the difficulties posed by outdated hidage records, tenurial disputes and dubious claims to exemption. But pleas of poverty from a borough community were certainly heeded, and the response was to slice off a neat fraction of the total sum due. This happened in 1130, when Hertford had £5 of its £10 *auxilium* pardoned 'for poverty', and two boroughs in Dorset were pardoned £4 out of the £15 due for the same reason.[24] In writing off lump sums as 'waste' in 1156, the exchequer was surely doing likewise. The *auxilia* figures, in other words, can be interpreted as indicators of physical damage or economic dislocation; they represented the exchequer's attempt to acknowledge the problems certain boroughs faced in meeting the traditional impositions in the aftermath of war. But the clear difference between the *auxilium* figures for 'waste', and those for the Danegeld, reinforces the point that the same explanation will not do for both.

The *donum comitatus* was assessed in a similar way to the borough *auxilium*. The *Dialogus de Scaccario*, which refers to the *donum* by the alternative name of 'common assize', describes the process clearly enough: 'the sum demanded from the county being known, it is apportioned in common, at so much a hide, by those who have lands in the county, so that nothing of it may be lacking when the exchequer comes at which it is due.'[25] Again, therefore, the landholders of the shire, on the evidence of the pipe rolls the tenants-in-chief, were supposed to take responsibility for allocating the contributions due, within an overall sum

---

[23] White, 'Were the Midlands "Wasted"?', 45–6.

[24] *Pipe Roll 31 Henry I*, pp. 16, 63.

[25] *Dialogus*, pp. 47–8.

which was invariably imposed in round numbers of silver marks: 500 marks in Yorkshire in both 1156 and 1158, 40 and 50 marks respectively in Staffordshire, 80 and 140 marks in Nottinghamshire–Derbyshire. One likely explanation for the absence of 'waste' from the *donum* pardons is that, since the total Danegeld liability was fixed but that of the *donum* could be raised or lowered from one levy to the next, a shire's economic circumstances could be taken into account when the lump sum was imposed. In a small majority of shires, the total *donum* was increased from 1156 to 1158, which may indicate a recognition of improving economic circumstances as the civil war receded. Amt does have a point, however, in suggesting that any shortfalls in *donum* collected or otherwise accounted for in 1156 may have been transferred to the same shire's Danegeld accounts, where it contributed to the total for 'waste'. There was not a shire in England where there had not been some conflict or other during the civil war, and it is beyond belief that all over the country the tenants-in-chief would have apportioned their *donum* contributions as harmonious shire communities, in the manner suggested by the *Dialogus*. Where disputes and resistance meant that sheriffs did not collect all the *donum* due, they may well have been credited with full payments into the treasury, only for their Danegeld 'waste' to be inflated accordingly. But this argument only reinforces an administrative, rather than an economic, explanation for the figures.

In summary, the Danegeld of 1156 was levied at a time when Henry II's exchequer faced major difficulties. Assessments would have become outdated as a result of the upheavals of Stephen's reign. Resistance was to be expected, given the attempt to raise more than had been levied under Henry I by cutting down on exemptions. Although some individual cases of disputed liability, often involving prominent political figures, could be deferred for further consideration, and the relevant sums collected or pardoned in 1157, many problems would surely have defied quick solutions. In these circumstances, the write-offs for 'waste' were a convenient means to close the sheriffs' accounts. But what, then, should we make of the disparities in the amounts of Danegeld 'waste' entered for different shires? In those with high levels, such as Nottinghamshire–Derbyshire, the severe impact of civil war seems undeniable, but it took the form not only of physical and economic damage but also of a breakdown in the administrative machinery which left sheriff and exchequer ill-equipped at the outset of Henry II's reign to levy more than a fraction of the Danegeld due. Yorkshire, by contrast, was not so impoverished in 1156 that it could not meet nearly all its Danegeld liability, and sheriff and exchequer had the means to enforce most of the payment expected. This suggests the maintenance during Stephen's reign of reasonably accurate records of landholders and their carucate assessments, and possibly the continuation of a taxpaying tradition in the shire, which duly bore fruit in the low level of Yorkshire's Danegeld 'waste' in 1156. Given the largely independent line pursued by William of Aumale as Stephen's earl of York, it may well be to comital rather than royal government that we must look for this measure of administrative continuity.[26]

[26] Dalton, *Conquest*, p. 160.

6

THE NORTH AND ANGLO-SCOTTISH RELATIONS IN THE THIRTEENTH CENTURY

Alan Young

The north had been more central to the policies of Scottish rulers than English rulers in the eleventh and twelfth centuries. A claim to northern England was a feature of Scottish royal policy in this period, especially during Stephen's reign when David I exercised wide control in the region.[1] York was, for a time, an isolated outpost of English influence.[2] The near achievement of a Scoto-Northumbrian realm in the 1140s influenced Scottish political attitudes thereafter. When civil war broke out in England at the end of John's reign, Alexander II reasserted Scottish control of Cumbria and in 1216 claimed Northumbria and received the homage of its barons.[3]

In contrast, English kings until 1204 had tended to see the 'outer perimeter' of England as expendable.[4] Henry I, Stephen, Henry of Anjou and Richard I all offered northern territory to the Scots as a response to political crises in England and Normandy.[5] However, the loss of Normandy in 1204 meant an

[1] G.W.S Barrow, 'The Scots and the North of England', in E. King (ed.), *The Anarchy of King Stephen's Reign* (Oxford, 1994), pp. 245–51.

[2] Paul Dalton, *Conquest, Anarchy and Lordship: Yorkshire 1066–1154* (Cambridge, 1994), pp. 211–27.

[3] Chronicle of Melrose, cited in A.O. Anderson, *Early Sources of Scottish History A.D. 500–1286* (Edinburgh, 1922; reprinted Stamford, 1990), ii, p. 406.

[4] For the useful definitions of the north's 'outer perimeter', that is the four border counties, and the 'inner core', that is Yorkshire, which I have followed, see Frank Musgrove, *The North of England: A History from Roman Times to the Present* (Oxford, 1990), pp. 75–9.

[5] Helen M. Jewell, *The North–South Divide: The Origins of Northern Consciousness in England* (Manchester, 1994), p 37. For details, see A. Young, 'The Bishopric of Durham in Stephen's Reign', in David Rollason *et al.* (eds), *Anglo-Norman Durham 1093–1193* (Woodbridge, 1994), p. 356; Barrow, 'Scots and the North', p. 251; idem, 'The Reign of William the Lion', in his *Scotland and its Neighbours in the Middle Ages* (London, 1992), pp. 81–2.

end to absentee kingship in England, a greater awareness of the north as an underexploited financial resource and a more forceful attempt by King John to integrate the north administratively into the English kingdom. John's military success against Scotland in 1209, when he took an army to Norham, had shown the same superiority of resources as Henry II had demonstrated to Malcolm IV in 1157.[6] The 1209 episode, if taken alongside similar military success in Ireland in 1210 and Wales in 1211, indicated that an English overlordship or 'superoverlordship' of the British Isles was possible.[7]

At the beginning of the thirteenth century control of northern England remained a contentious issue in Anglo-Scottish relations. John's aggression seemed an unlikely prelude to the period 1217–96, recognized as one of the most sustained periods of Anglo-Scottish harmony in the Middle Ages.[8] During this period the Treaty of York (1237) has been generally credited with resolving the chief difficulty in Anglo-Scottish relations – Alexander II relinquished Scottish claims to the English northern counties.[9] Yet in 1244 there was a serious confrontation between English and Scottish armies at the border, and again in 1255 Henry III brought an army to the border. These later episodes show that Anglo-Scottish relations remained fraught with tension, and warn us to be wary of exaggerating the significance of the Treaty of York and of making too vivid a contrast between these relations in the twelfth and thirteenth centuries.

Recent research has emphasized that there were strong vested interests in the well-being of both sides of the border and for peace in Anglo-Scottish relations.

---

[6] Roger of Wendover cited in A.O. Anderson, *Scottish Annals from English Chroniclers, A.D. 500–1286* (London, 1908; reprinted Stamford, 1991), pp. 328–9; R. Howlett (ed.), *Chronicles of the Reigns of Stephen, Henry II, and Richard I*, Rolls Series (London, 1884–9), i, p. 105.

[7] R.R. Davies, *Domination and Conquest: The Experience of Ireland, Scotland and Wales 1100–1300* (Cambridge, 1990), p. 81.

[8] Keith J. Stringer, 'Identities in Thirteenth-Century England: Frontier Society in the Far North', in Claus Bjorn *et al.* (eds), *Social and Political Identities in Western History* (Copenhagen, 1994), p. 32; G.W.S. Barrow, 'The Anglo-Scottish Border: Growth and Structure in the Middle Ages', in W. Haubrichs and R. Schneider (eds), *Grenzen und Grenzregionen (Borders and Border Regions)* (Saarbrücken, 1994), p. 206.

[9] J.A. Tuck, 'War and Society in the Medieval North', *Northern History*, 11 (1985), 34–5; Richard Lomas, *North-East England in the Middle Ages* (Edinburgh, 1992), p. 41.

The recent impressive scholarship of Dr Stringer, in particular, has developed a comprehensive picture of the strong social, economic and religious networks binding the north of England to the south of Scotland in the twelfth and thirteenth centuries, making this area a distinct region in its own right.[10] Scottish kings had long-established roles in northern society. The liberty of Tynedale gave the Scottish king authority deep into northern England – forty-two miles southwards, in fact, from the Kielder Gap to Cross Fell overlooking Appleby – from c. 1139 to 1286.[11] From 1242 to 1286, a sizeable chunk of south-east Cumberland, the honour of Penrith, was under Scottish control. Marriages between the English and Scottish royal houses, in 1221 between Alexander II of Scotland and Henry III's sister, Joan, and in 1251 between the young Alexander III and Henry III's daughter Margaret, took place at York and led to good social relationships between the two royal families. Many meetings and journeys across the border took place. A significant number of magnates, holding land on both sides of the border, reinforced these royal links. The most powerful baronial family in thirteenth-century Scotland, the Comyns, held land in Tynedale from the mid-twelfth century and received royal confirmation of this from Henry III in 1262. In addition, John Comyn, having served Henry III in 1264 and 1265 against the king's baronial opposition in England, was given licence to fortify his manor house of Tarset in Tynedale in 1267.[12]

An ecclesiastical network also illustrates the social unity of the region comprising northern England and southern Scotland. The abbeys of Jedburgh, Melrose and Kelso had strong links with northern England. Many northern houses were property owners in southern Scotland. The general picture is further reinforced in the north-west by the firm economic ties linking Carlisle

[10] G.W.S. Barrow, *The Anglo-Norman Era in Scottish History* (Oxford, 1980); Keith J. Stringer, *Earl David of Huntingdon, 1152–1219: A Study in Anglo-Scottish History* (Edinburgh, 1985), chapter 9; Summerson, *Carlisle*, i; Keith J. Stringer, 'The Scottish Foundations: Thirteenth-Century Perspectives', in A. Grant and K.J. Stringer (eds), *Uniting the Kingdom? The Making of British History* (London, 1995). I am grateful to Dr Stringer for letting me see the latter prior to publication.

[11] Barrow, 'Scots and the North', p. 253.

[12] *Calendar of Charter Rolls 1257–1300* (London, 1903–19), ii, pp. 40–1; *Calendar of Patent Rolls 1266–72* (London, 1893–), p. 178.

and Cumberland with southern Scotland.[13] While most of the social, economic and religious links which have been mentioned were between the north's 'outer perimeter' and southern Scotland, there were certainly contacts between Scotland and Yorkshire too.[14] Yorkshire's migration to southern Scotland, as Professor Barrow has illustrated, began early in the twelfth century, continued late in the thirteenth century and included such important families as Brus, Balliol and Mowbray. Rievaulx Abbey in north Yorkshire, the mission centre for the spread of the Cistercian order in Britain, included in its religious network two houses in southern Scotland, Melrose and Dundrennan.

All of these social, economic and religious ties linking northern England to southern Scotland represented powerful forces for peaceful political relationships between England and Scotland. The weight of evidence necessitates that Anglo-Scottish relations are 'set in the context of growing cross-border contacts especially in the ecclesiastical sphere and in the families of the lay aristocracy'.[15] Yet English and Scottish policy towards the north was affected by other, sometimes less rational, forces. One historian has observed that 'Good relations and diplomatic niceties are only part of the story'.[16] Indeed, policy towards the north was ultimately dependent on changing political circumstances which affected the priorities of Scottish and English rulers. The whims of individual rulers should not be discounted. Barrow has referred to Henry III's 'fit of paranoia which nearly pitched him into all out war' in 1244.[17] When assessing Scottish policy towards the north of England in the thirteenth century the need for the strengthening of Scottish royal authority in the north of their kingdom after rebellions in 1211–12 and 1229 and in the west against the Norwegians in the 1260s needs to be taken into account. The minority of Alexander III from 1249 to 1258 was obviously a major influence

[13] Summerson, *Carlisle*, i, pp. 140–3.

[14] Barrow, *Anglo-Norman Era*, pp. 106–17.

[15] Judith A. Green, 'Anglo-Scottish Relations, 1066–1174', in Michael Jones and Malcolm Vale (eds), *England and Her Neighbours, 1066–1453: Essays in Honour of Pierre Chaplais* (London, 1989), pp. 53–4.

[16] Davies, *Domination*, p. 84.

[17] G.W.S. Barrow, 'Frontier and Settlement: Which Influenced Which? England and Scotland, 1100–1300', in Robert Bartlett and Angus MacKay (eds), *Medieval Frontier Societies* (Oxford, 1989), p. 11.

on Scottish policy. Similarly, in England, civil war at the end of John's reign, the minority of Henry III, and the Baron's War 1258–65 affected English policies. English kings throughout the thirteenth century had continental ambitions and commitments. They also had increasing financial problems. All of these factors should be placed alongside cross-border links as influences on policy towards the north of England. A combination of political circumstances contributed to the thirteenth century being such a peaceful one, and it would be misleading to give particular weight to any particular one.

The impact of those with cross-border links and strong vested interests in peace in the north is difficult to judge. Those who favoured peace were unable to prevent the battle of the Standard taking place when David I invaded Yorkshire in 1138.[18] They did not stop the invasion of William the Lion in 1174. Nor were they primarily responsible for the military success of King John against the Scots being short-lived. It does seem, however, that the nobility, including some no doubt with Anglo-Scottish interests, played a part in preventing the border confrontation between English and Scottish armies in 1244 from breaking out into war.[19] Opposition in England and defeat abroad rather than vested interests for peace probably made John's military success against the Scots in 1209 so short-lived. Cross-border links could be used to encourage aggressive alliances. Thus the northern nobility who opposed King John sought to take advantage of these links to ally with Alexander II in 1215 and instigate war between Scotland and England.[20] Suspicion of the northern baronage remained a factor for Henry III, though he was grateful for the military support of northern and Anglo-Scottish barons against Simon de Montfort in 1264.[21] Similarly, the king of Scots benefited in 1275 from the military leadership provided by another northern and Anglo-Scottish baron, John de Vescy, in an expedition to the Isle of Man.[22] Marriage alliances too could have a variable impact on Anglo-Scottish relations. Even after the marriage of

---

[18] Young, 'Bishopric of Durham', pp 356–7 and n. 26.

[19] Matthew Paris, *Chronica Majora*, ed. H.R. Luard, Rolls Series (London, 1872–83), iv, pp. 360–1; Anderson, *Early Sources*, ii, p. 538.

[20] Chronicle of Melrose, cited in Anderson, *Early Sources*, ii, pp. 405–6.

[21] Paris, *Chronica Majora*, v, pp. 137, 569; *Calendar of Close Rolls 1261–64* (London, 1892–), pp. 381–2.

[22] *Chron. of the Reigns*, ii, pp. 570–1.

Alexander II to Henry III's sister, Joan, and that of Hubert de Burgh, the English justiciar, to the Scottish king's sister in 1221, Alexander's claims to the northern counties were not seriously checked.[23]

The loss of Normandy was significant for Angevin policy in northern England though its immediate impact should not be exaggerated. Thus John sought to increase royal authority in the north as a means to exploit the relatively untapped resources of that area. He found jobs for his displaced Norman followers such as Robert de Vieuxpont who became custodian of Appleby and Brough Castles and sheriff of Westmorland, and Brian de Lisle who became custodian of Bolsover and Knaresborough.[24] Increased administrative attention to the north was not matched, however, by the same commitment to border defence against Scotland. Most of the £15,000 John spent on royal castles was used to fortify Yorkshire fortresses.[25] It is a reflection of John's political priorities in England that while his spending on castles was large – a total of £15,000 was spent on twenty-five castles – most of the money was spent on the Yorkshire castles of Scarborough, Pickering, Knaresborough, Pontefract and Tickhill. Indeed, three of these castles, Scarborough, Knaresborough and Tickhill, consumed £3,800 while only £670 was spent on three border castles at Norham, Newcastle and Wark which were in the front-line of defence against Scotland. Investment in royal castle-building seems to have been aimed at opposition to John from prominent Yorkshire nobles, at protection of royal authority in the north's 'inner core' rather than in its 'outer perimeter'. The twelfth century had shown that there was no adequate defence system beyond the Tees, suggesting that the peaceful and social nature of the Norman 'invasion' of southern Scotland did not require a heavily fortified frontier and that the far north was not a priority for military expenditure.[26]

For the English, Durham, York and Carlisle remained key channels for royal influence in the thirteenth century. After the northern rebellion against John,

---

[23] Paris, *Chronica Majora*, iii, pp. 66–7.

[24] Musgrove, *North of England*, pp. 113–14.

[25] Ibid., p. 104; R. Allen Brown, 'Royal Castle-Building in England 1154–1216', *EHR*, 70 (1955), 357–8, 361.

[26] Barrow, 'Anglo-Scottish Border', pp. 201–2.

Eustace de Vescy's honour of Alnwick was given to Richard de Marisco, bishop of Durham, in 1217.[27] From 1217 to 1226 Richard, a former royal chancellor, reasserted royal influence in north-eastern England which John had achieved during the vacancy at Durham between 1208 and 1217. It is hardly surprising that Henry III tried to extend this influence by trying to force his chaplain on the monks of Durham as their bishop in 1226.[28] The monks reacted against this by electing William Scot of Stichil (Roxburghshire). Henry refused him and when the appeal went to Rome, the king's lawyers argued against a Scot being appointed to a see on the border.[29] The continuing importance of the need to have a loyal bishop of Durham is evident in the bishop of Lincoln's attempt to persuade Nicholas of Farnham to accept the see in 1241 on the grounds that, 'the castles of Norham and Durham are in that part of England the bulwarks against the assaults of our enemies'.[30] In practice, these castles could be said to be relatively poor bulwarks during the Scottish invasions of 1138 and 1173–4, but it cannot be denied that the income of the bishops of Durham was considerable and highly prized. The income of the bishopric was in the region of £2,600 per year, the land of the archbishop of York being worth only half of this. In 1249, after Nicholas, bishop of Durham resigned, 'the king was not slow to take into his charge the property of that see'.[31]

Financial exactions rather than military expenditure were the key to Angevin policy in the north. The bishopric of Carlisle was in the hands of royal civil servants between 1223 and 1254.[32] Taxes were taken but the castle of Carlisle was given few resources. In 1250 Geoffrey Langley, a royal bailiff and forest inquisitor extorted immense sums of money from nobles in northern England.[33] According to Paris, this exploitation originated in John's hatred of northern

---

[27] Anderson, *Early Sources*, ii, p. 410; G.W.S. Barrow, 'The Kings of Scotland and Durham', in *Anglo-Norman Durham*, p. 321.

[28] Simon Taylor *et al.* (eds), *Scotichronicon by Walter Bower* (Aberdeen, 1990), v, pp. 139, 255.

[29] Ibid.

[30] Paris, *Chronica Majora*, iv, p. 190.

[31] G.V. Scammell, *Hugh du Puiset, Bishop of Durham* (Cambridge, 1956), pp. 193–4: Paris, *Chronica Majora*, v, p. 90.

[32] Summerson, *Carlisle*, i, pp. 121–2.

[33] Paris, *Chronica Majora*, v, p. 137.

baronial resistance.[34] Later in the thirteenth century, Anthony Bek, one of Edward I's chief counsellors, immediately prior to being elected bishop of Durham was despatched to negotiate a subsidy from an assembly of the northern shires at York.[35]

The Treaty of York has sometimes been seen as a definitive resolution of Anglo-Scottish tension in the north. The seriousness of this tension and its escalation in the 1230s is evident in Pope Gregory's injunction to maintain the peace in 1235; in Alexander II's threat to use 'the edge of the sword' to support his claim that he had been promised the hand of John's daughter, Joan; and in the proposed alliance between the Scottish king and one of Henry III's rebels and enemies Gilbert Marshal, 'who had united himself in wedlock with Alexander's third sister, Margaret'.[36] By the Treaty of York, Alexander quitclaimed to Henry the counties of Northumberland, Cumberland and Westmorland in return for £200 of land in Northumberland and Cumberland.[37] The treaty can be seen as stabilizing the border and Anglo-Scottish relations at minimal cost.

Henry III, like John, begrudged spending money on border defence. On 28 February 1237 he ordered expenditure on the castles of Bamburgh and Newcastle to be reduced.[38] Financial constraints and continental ambitions caused Henry III to compromise with northern security in 1237 and the years afterwards. But the events of 1242 to 1244 showed how risky such a policy was. In 1242 Henry crossed the sea to pursue his ambitions on the Continent.[39] Contemporary chroniclers note that 'he had prepared for this attempt by establishing good relations with Scotland . . . and had committed the defence of the northern counties . . . to the Scottish king.'[40] This approach to the north did

[34] Ibid., pp. 137, 569.

[35] C.M. Fraser, *A History of Antony Bek* (Oxford, 1957), p. 25.

[36] E.L.G. Stones (ed.), *Anglo-Scottish Relations 1174–1328* (Oxford, 1965), pp. 35–7; Paris, *Chronica Majora*, iii, pp. 372–3.

[37] *Anglo-Scottish Relations*, pp. 39–53.

[38] J. Bain *et al.* (eds), *Calendar of Documents Relating to Scotland* (Edinburgh 1881–1985), i, no. 1362; v, no. 12.

[39] Anderson, *Early Sources*, ii, p. 530; Paris, *Chronica Majora*, iv, pp. 192–3.

[40] Ibid.

not work. From 1242 to 1244 a range of issues emerged which had the potential to provoke tension in the north and in Anglo-Scottish relations. One of these issues was northern disloyalty, real or imagined; Henry instructed the archbishop of York, whom he regarded as a key figure in the guardianship of England, to confiscate the lands of traitors on the Continent, especially those of William de Ros and other northern nobles. Other issues included the relationship between England and Scotland, the dangers of a Franco-Scottish alliance and the building of fortifications on the border. These issues led to a confrontation between Scottish and English armies in Northumberland in 1244.[41] According to Paris, 'The king of Scots had saucily sent a message to him that he did not hold the least particle of Scotland from him, the king of England. The friendship between the two kings had become very much lessened since the king of Scotland had formed a matrimonial alliance with the daughter of Engelram de Courcy. The king of Scots also fortified castles on the confines of England and earnestly begged the assistance of the nobles, his relatives and neighbours against the king of England who was plotting against him.'[42] The castles sanctioned by the Scottish king seem to have been Caerlaverock, by the mouth of the Nidd, built by the Maxwells, Hermitage in Liddesdale built by Nicholas de Soules, Tarset Castle in Northumberland which had been fortified by Walter Comyn, earl of Menteith, and Dally in Tynedale which owed its construction to the Lindsays.[43] The English view of the latter castle was that 'once it is finished and furnished with weapons . . . (de Lindsay) plans to garrison it with men who wish evil to the kingdom of England and especially Northumberland. If such men come from the north, this house will be an excellent refuge for them and a great nuisance to the king's land'. King Henry's response was to reassert superior English military power, 'that he might not appear to reply in a lukewarm way to the message and insolence of the king of Scots'.[44]

[41] Ibid., pp. 358–9.

[42] Ibid., pp. 360–1, 380; *Scotichronicon*, v, p. 185.

[43] Barrow, 'Frontier and Settlement', p. 11; *Calendar of Close Rolls 1242–47*, p. 222; *Calendar of Documents*, v, no. 12.

[44] Paris, *Chronica Majora*, iv, pp. 358–9.

The Close Rolls of 1244 record that Henry wrote to the sheriffs of Yorkshire, Westmorland, Cumberland and Lancashire commanding them to 'permit no foreigner to pass through their territories towards Scotland. If such a foreigner should be found carrying arms, or letters of which there could be suspicion, they were to arrest him and send him without delay to the king'.[45] The sheriffs were also ordered to send provisions to Newcastle. The king of Scots was reported to be leading an army of one thousand knights and men-at-arms. War was averted partly because of 'the wise and prudent intervention of some of the nobles on both sides', and partly because the powerful Scottish force was a deterrent to the English.[46]

The seriousness of the 1244 crisis has been understated in most accounts of Anglo-Scottish relations. It was a national emergency. It showed that stability in the north was dependent not just on the good relationship between the Scottish and English royal houses, but on diplomatic needs. The real fear of a French marriage alliance with the Scots had been a preoccupation of Henry III since 1238 when his sister Joan, queen of Scotland, died and Alexander II married the daughter of a French nobleman. Henry's aggressive stance in 1244 forestalled another French marriage alliance with the future Alexander III. Instead such an alliance was made between Alexander and Henry's daughter, Margaret.[47]

Following Alexander II's death in 1249, Scotland was faced with a minority crisis. The wedding of Alexander III and Margaret at York on Christmas Day 1251 had a special significance for Anglo-Scottish relations and the north. Henry III used this occasion to raise the issue of the Scottish king owing homage to the English king for Scotland.[48] He also made changes in the Scottish government by depriving the chancellor, justiciar and chamberlain of their offices.[49] In addition, two prominent cross-border nobles, John Balliol and

---

[45] *Calendar of Documents*, i, no. 1631.

[46] G.W.S. Barrow, 'The Army of Alexander III, Scotland', in N. Reid (ed.), *Scotland in the Reign of Alexander III 1249–1286* (Edinburgh, 1990), p. 133.

[47] Paris, *Chronica Majora*, iv, p. 380–5; Anderson, *Early Sources*, ii, p. 538n.

[48] Paris, *Chronica Majora*, iv, pp. 266–70.

[49] D.E.R. Watt, 'The Minority of Alexander III of Scotland', *TRHS*, 5th ser., 21 (1971), 10–11; A. Young, 'The Political Role of Walter Comyn, Earl of Menteith, During the Minority of Alexander III of Scotland', in K. J. Stringer (ed.), *Essays on the Nobility of Medieval Scotland* (Edinburgh, 1985), pp. 135–6; Anderson, *Early Sources*, ii, p. 562.

Robert de Ros, were given responsibility for the young king and queen of Scotland, and probably for the administration of the kingdom. Balliol and Ros were punished for not being effective enough agents of the English king, and their northern lands were confiscated.[50] On this occasion Henry exploited both cross-border links and Anglo-Scottish marriages for his political ends.

Henry was active on the borders in his supervision of Scottish affairs between 1251 and 1258. He supported the overthrow of the Comyn-led Scottish government which had acted a little too independently of Henry's two agents between 1251 and 1255.[51] Henry and his queen travelled to Wark on Tweed with an armed force to supervise a change in Scottish government in 1255, when a new seven-year guardianship was established.[52] In 1256 and 1257 when the Comyn family rebelled against the new Scottish government, Henry again made his presence felt on the borders. In 1256 he ordered the sheriffs of Yorkshire, Northumberland, and Westmorland to assist the Scottish king against his rebels.[53] The situation in Scotland became more serious in 1257 when the Comyn party kidnapped the young Scottish king and queen. The years 1257 and 1258 saw Henry activate all his northern officials to restore order in Scotland. In 1257 he commanded Robert de Neville, sheriff of Northumberland, and William Latimer, sheriff of Yorkshire, to be in readiness with their forces.[54] The bishop of Durham and archbishop of York were also sent to Scotland to settle the dispute. In 1258 the sheriff of Yorkshire and Robert de Neville were commanded to ensure that the Scottish queen had necessary solace and succour.[55] In the same year, at the king's request 'on account of the war and disturbance of Scotland' William, bishop of Durham, delivered Norham Castle to be occupied and provisioned by the sheriff of Northumberland for the king. Provision was also to be made for Alan Durward and Walter de Moray, two nobles deprived of office by the Comyn 'coup', to

---

[50] Ibid., pp. 501–7, 569.

[51] Young, 'The Political Role of Walter Comyn', p. 139.

[52] Ibid.; Paris, *Chronica Majora*, v, pp. 504–6; Anderson, *Early Sources*, ii, pp. 581–2.

[53] *Calendar of Documents*, i, no. 2058.

[54] Ibid., nos. 2102, 2113.

[55] Ibid., nos. 2090, 2128.

have safe retreats at Norham and Wark.[56] The Melrose Chronicle voiced concern that Henry's interference in Scottish affairs 'might result in the dishonour of the king and kingdom', although the nationalist fourteenth-century chronicler John of Fordun praised this interference for stabilizing Scottish affairs.[57]

It can be argued that border disputes have always been a normal part of life for neighbouring kingdoms. In the case of England and Scotland, there were occasional practical difficulties in defining specific parts of the border. These were evident in 1245, when a meeting of perambulators ended in deadlock, in 1246 and again in 1248 and 1249.[58] Such meetings to resolve difficulties reveal the presence of long-established Marcher law but also the continuing expansion of English royal administration in the north. It is noticeable that complaints by the Scots about English administration in the north increased in frequency, especially after 1275.[59] The involvement of English officials in the Scottish liberty of Tynedale was a particular cause of complaint. This reflects the growth of English administration in the north. The main purpose behind this was financial, as the political priorities of English kings remained focused south of the Channel. When these priorities changed with their growing interest in Scottish affairs by the middle of the thirteenth century, this northern administration could be used for political ends.

The thirteenth century has rightly been singled out as a particularly peaceful one in the history of Anglo-Scottish relations. As one historian has stated, 'only a serious misreading of history can represent England and Scotland as inveterate enemies before the end of the thirteenth century'.[60] Yet it would be

---

[56] Ibid., nos. 2118, 2121.

[57] Chronicle of Melrose in Anderson, *Early Sources*, ii, p. 583; W.F. Skene (ed.), *Johannes de Fordun, Chronica Gentis Scottorum* (Edinburgh, 1871–2), i, p. 296.

[58] Barrow, 'The Anglo-Scottish Border', pp. 205–6; William W. Scott, 'The March Laws Reconsidered', in Alexander Grant and Keith J. Stringer (eds), *Medieval Scotland . . .* (Edinburgh, 1993), pp. 114–31; H. Summerson, 'The Early Development of the Laws of the Anglo-Scottish Marches 1249–1448', in W.M. Gordon (ed.), *Legal History in the Making* (Glasgow, 1991), pp. 29–32.

[59] *Calendar of Documents*, ii, nos. 59, 62, 82, 90, 97, 111, 152, 154, 160, 241; v, no. 38.

[60] William Ferguson, *Scotland's Relations with England; A Survey to 1707* (Edinburgh, 1977), p. 22.

equally misleading either to simplify the reasons for peace or to underestimate the sources of tension. Undoubtedly the many cross-border social, economic and religious links represented strong vested interests for stability in the north and friendly relationships between England and Scotland. They prospered because of peace, but were only one of many factors influencing the political relationship between the neighbouring kingdoms.

The north's role in Anglo-Scottish relations was dependent on the varying priorities of the Scottish and English rulers as their kingdoms were affected by changing internal or external political circumstances. The crisis of 1244 showed how unpredictable these relations could be. A variety of personal, local, national and international issues combined to bring Scotland and England close to war and destroy the north's stability. The political equilibrium was, perhaps, more precarious than is sometimes realized.[61] The thirteenth century saw a significant shift in the attitudes of English and Scottish kings to the north. The region was a main focus for Scottish policy for the first three decades of the century, whereas English rulers, despite John's aggressive military gesture in 1209, were content to adopt a low-key, low-expenditure policy at the same time as trying to bring the north more fully into the country's administrative framework. They were, above all, adjusting to the loss of Normandy. The year 1244, rather than that of 1237 in which the Treaty of York was agreed, marked a turning point in Anglo-Scottish relations. The north acquired a greater strategic importance in English eyes as Henry III, in the 1240s and 1250s, gave closer attention to Scottish affairs. The minority of Alexander III gave Henry the opportunity to adopt a more pro-active policy and exercise greater influence over Scotland than had been feasible for John after 1209. A policy of establishing English overlordship over Scotland using the north as a base does not seem to have been in Henry's mind, as even Scottish nationalist chroniclers such as John of Fordun recognized. Yet Henry's actions in 1244 and his supervision of Scottish affairs from the north in the 1250s established a precedent in Anglo-Scottish relations which was to have a strong influence on the policy of Edward I.

---

[61] See Keith J. Stringer, 'Scottish Foundations: Thirteenth-Century Perspectives', in *Uniting the Kingdom?*, p. 86.

7

THE GOVERNMENT OF THIRTEENTH-CENTURY YORKSHIRE

Barbara English

In the 1270s a jury complained that 'Earl Warenne unjustly obstructs justice, because his men of Fishlake and Thorne used to be geldable and now withdraw themselves, who in the last eyre of the justices presented all the pleas of the crown with the wapentake.'[1] This paper discusses the territorial courts of Yorkshire; the problem of who owed suit to the courts; the link between suit of court and 'the geldable land'; the late thirteenth-century concept of 'the geldable county'; and the franchise of return of writs, which acted as a hinge between the geldable and non-geldable lands. The evidence is mainly drawn from the last quarter of the thirteenth century: the analysis is less relevant to the earlier years, when many aspects of local government were still evolving.

Yorkshire had by *c.* 1200 become a clearly defined area. The major subdivisions, the three thirds or 'ridings' (East, North and West), were first named in Domesday Book, but were undoubtedly formed earlier. Although they were very different in size, in 1086 the tax assessments (the carucage for geld) of the three ridings were very similar, almost exactly 3,200 carucates each, which suggests that when the carucage was first assessed on the shire in the tenth century the ridings had been deemed to have either an equivalent number of people, or an equivalent wealth within each third.

The administrative subdivisions of the three ridings were the wapentakes. At the time of the hundred inquiries, 1274–5, the East Riding contained five wapentakes, plus a similar unit, Howdenshire; the West Riding contained twelve; and the North Riding eight plus a similar unit, Allertonshire. The

---

[1] B. English (ed.), *Yorkshire Hundred and Quo Warranto Rolls*, Yorks. Arch. Soc. Record Series, 151 (1996), p. 93.

division of the ridings into six, twelve and nine units respectively, with the echo of the northern duodecimal system which was recorded in this county by the Domesday clerks, suggests that the number of the divisions was the result of planning rather than evolution. The number of wapentakes in each riding reflects the sizes of the ridings rather than their value. Wapentakes, however, were very unequal in both size and wealth.

Below the wapentake were the vills and townships, both rural and urban (the boroughs and the one city, York). Shire administration operated through these units, although operations were complicated by the existence of pockets of privileged land, the liberties or franchises, which had greater or lesser degrees of exemption from shire administration. All the units had their administrative role and all except the vills had territorial courts and jurisdictions.

Alongside the territorial units of government, the Normans introduced other units of seignorial or feudal government, each with their own officials and courts. The 'territorial' courts overlapped in jurisdiction with some of the 'feudal' courts, and often the distinction was blurred: for instance, a private wapentake court could function as the court of a liberty. In the same way many vills were coterminous with manors, and although rural vills did not have their own courts, the business of the (territorial) vill might be conducted in the (feudal) manor court.

The chief officer in thirteenth-century Yorkshire was the sheriff. All orders of central government were processed by him. The sheriff was responsible for collecting royal revenues and accounting for them to the exchequer. He or his deputy presided over the county court. After c. 1200 some of the sheriff's work was devolved upon coroners and escheators, but the sheriff remained ultimately responsible for local government.

The sheriff's staff in Yorkshire included his clerks, his bailiffs, the under-sheriff and the under-sheriff's clerk, and a receiver. There is a reference early in the thirteenth century to a man who kept the seal of the county of York by inheritance, whose ancestors had additionally looked after the benches upon which the court sat.[2] There was a sheriff's archive at York, in the treasurer's

---

[2] D.M. Stenton (ed.), *Rolls of the Justices in Eyre for Yorkshire 1218–19*, Selden Soc., 56 (1937), no. 1147; R.C. Palmer, *The County Courts of Medieval England* (Princeton, 1982), p. 20.

remembrancer's office.[3] It seems likely that the jailer of York Castle was also on the sheriff's staff, for the sheriff was responsible for the prisoners kept there.[4]

Below the sheriffs and their staff were the bailiffs of the ridings and the wapentakes, each with their own staff. Yorkshiremen were not always clear about the rank of the officials and often called them all 'bailiffs'. Jurors described both Henry de Kirkby and Richard de Vescy as sheriffs, when it appears that they were never more than under-sheriffs.[5] Occasionally the term chief-bailiff or under-bailiff was used. A man could hold several posts simultaneously. For example, John de Octon, Yorkshire sheriff in 1260–1 and again in 1265, combined the post with that of seneschal to the bishop of Durham, and was also seneschal to the king's brother.[6] The sheriffs seemed unconcerned about their title. A Langbargh wapentake charter of 1207, almost certainly made in the county court, was attested by the constable of Chester, who was the sheriff of Yorkshire but did not use the title on this occasion, and the deputy sheriff, who attested as sheriff.[7]

All the territorial divisions of Yorkshire had courts. The Yorkshire county court met at York Castle, on Mondays, following a six-week schedule.[8] During the thirteenth century the county court session which was held after Michaelmas, called the 'general' or 'great' court, became the principal court of the year. Those who actually performed suit of court and acted as judges of the county court seem to have been the seneschals of the major lords of the county. The archbishop of York in the 1290s owed suit by his seneschal for all his lands in Yorkshire, and it was to be performed throughout the year. Mowbray, the earl of Lincoln, Wake, Maulay, Everingham and Ros, sent their seneschals to every

---

[3] R.H. Skaife (ed.), *The Survey of the County of York . . . called Kirkby's Inquest*, Surtees Soc., 49 (1867), p. 148.

[4] W.A. Morris, *The Medieval English Sheriff* (Manchester, 1927), p. 231.

[5] *Yorkshire Hundred and QW*, pp. 71, 94.

[6] Palmer, *County Courts*, pp. 41–2.

[7] W. Brown (ed.), *Cartularium de Gyseburne*, Surtees Soc., 86 (1889), i, pp. 92–4; *Pipe Roll 9 John* p. 70.

[8] Palmer, *County Courts*, pp. 307–13.

county court.[9] However, some leading Yorkshiremen such as Stuteville, Vavasour and Percy in the 1290s owed only one suit to the county each year. Some tenants in chief owed no county suit. Earl Warenne and all his tenants claimed to be free of county courts, as did the men of the honours of Chester and of Eye, the prior of Durham, the Benedictine and Cistercian abbots and a handful of lesser barons.[10]

Little is known of the riding courts. They were represented in the county court in some way, perhaps having to report there, as well as meeting within their divisions. In one case of 1218–19 the county court, asked to provide a record of an earlier proceeding, replied that two ridings of the county were absent and so obtained an adjournment.[11] Another case of c. 1260 before the justices in eyre was adjourned because no one from the West Riding was present.[12] Although the ridings seem to have been the least important of the Yorkshire territorial courts, nevertheless it was worthwhile for men to bid for a riding at a higher farm than any of the wapentakes, so that they must have produced a reasonable revenue.[13] Suits to the riding were generally due at the next court after Michaelmas, but no record has been found of suitors actually appearing at the riding court.

During the thirteenth century the wapentake divisions remained significant, as the unit for many functions of local government. The wapentake courts were less active. Only one session of the wapentake court, the meeting that followed Michaelmas, appeared to have had any suitors, and by the 1290s it was being called the general wapentake court.[14] Unlike

---

[9] *Yorkshire Hundred and QW*, pp. 131, 140, 147, 149, 159, 163–5, 173, 235; J.C. Holt, *The Northerners: A Study in the Reign of King John* (2nd edn, Oxford, 1992), p. xxviii; H.M. Thomas, 'The Knights of the County Court in 1212', in E.B. King and S.J. Ridyard (eds), *Law in Medieval Life and Thought* (Sewanee, 1990), pp. 137–50; P.R. Coss, 'Knighthood and the Early Thirteenth Century County Court', *Thirteenth-Century England*, 2 (1988), 45–57.

[10] *Yorkshire Hundred and QW*, pp. 131–2, 140, 149, 164–5, 176–7, 221, 275; W. Brown (ed.), *Yorkshire Inquisitions*, Yorks. Arch. Soc. Record Series, 12 (1892–1906), i, p. 118.

[11] *Rolls of the Justices in Eyre*, no. 744.

[12] C.T. Clay (ed.), *Three Yorkshire Assize Rolls*, Yorks. Arch. Soc. Record Series, 44 (1911), p. 99.

[13] W.W. Shirley (ed.), *Royal Letters II*, Rolls Series (London, 1866), p. 325.

[14] *Yorkshire Hundred and QW*, pp. 234–5, 241; *Yorkshire Inquisitions*, i, p. 25.

southern England, there was no sheriff's tourn or frankpledge in Yorkshire.[15] The obligation to pay suit to the wapentake court was inherent in the land itself, so that if the land changed hands the suit followed. In its simplest form, as was reported to the king in 1251 of the wapentake of Ewcross, the great landholders (a baron and two knights) together with all the free tenants of the nine vills that lay within the wapentake owed suit to the wapentake court.[16] But in practice that simple form was unusual, and many areas of land (or their tenants) were free from suit.

The survey of 1284–5 known as Kirkby's Inquest, which is primarily a list of military services, records wapentake suits and the concomitant fines in lieu of suit for about half the wapentakes. Within those areas some vills or parts of vills owed suits or fines, others did not. In Ainsty wapentake, for instance, thirty-seven vills were described. For a quarter of them the clerk wrote that the court services were not mentioned in the inquisitions, which may indicate that they owed nothing. For seven vills where land was held in frankalmoign or from the honour of Eye, together with some of the lands held from the honours of Mowbray and Paynel, he wrote that no service or fine was due; and for twenty-seven vills or parts of vills, wapentake fines ranging from twelve pence to four shillings were listed, but no county or riding fines.[17] Only two suits to the wapentake (as opposed to fines) are mentioned among all the wapentake tenants of Ainsty. In Halikeld wapentake there were thirty-four vills. Of the military tenants in the vills, most but not all owed wapentake fines. Those that were exempt included St Leonard's, York, the Knights Templar and the heirs of the Percys. No suits of court were mentioned. Within Skyrack wapentake there were forty-eight vills. Most of these vills paid wapentake fine to the bailiff of Skyrack, but only one person in the wapentake owed suit to any territorial court. His obligation was to attend once a year at the county court, once at the riding and once at the wapentake. It seems that although wapentake fines in lieu of suit were not uncommon, many territorial courts were almost entirely without suitors. In the wapentake of Ouse and Derwent, however, most vills

---

[15] *Kirkby's Inquest*, p. 68.

[16] *Yorkshire Inquisitions*, i, p. 25.

[17] *Kirkby's Inquest*, pp. 22–9.

owed suit at the first county and the first wapentake after Michaelmas, and most paid fines for the remaining suits of the year.[18]

The opening phrase of this paper suggests a connection between the obligation to suit of court (or payment in lieu) and the status of geldability. Thirteenth-century records refer to the 'geldable county', a phrase covering the land directly under the sheriff's control, responsible to the king through the sheriff, while outside the geldable county the privileged landholders had some degree of autonomy.

What was meant by the 'geldable county' in the later thirteenth century, when Danegeld was no longer collected? By the end of the twelfth century, Danegeld and geld were two distinctive taxes. Green suggested cautiously that the geld to which Becket objected in 1163 might have been sheriff's aid, and certainly the geld due from some but not all areas of the county in the thirteenth century seems more closely linked to the sheriff and his jurisdiction than to the ancient royal tax of Danegeld.[19] The Yorkshire hundred rolls and *quo warranto* inquiries provide forty-nine references to geldable areas of land, vills or manors, and, exceptionally, geldable men. The references are generally in reply to article seven of the hundred inquiries, 'Concerning ancient suits, customs, service and other things withdrawn from the king', and include comments on land that used to be geldable, which had subsequently been withdrawn from the common payments to which those who owed suit of court were liable.[20] Although 'geldable' is never defined in the Yorkshire hundred or *quo warranto* rolls, there is a persistent connection with suit to the territorial courts, or fine in lieu of suit.[21]

In 1290–1 an inquiry was held to discover whether or not the king should have the 'service called geldable' from the lands and tenements of Roger de Mowbray's barony of Kirkby Malzeard in the wapentake of Claro. It was found that the lands and tenements were geldable to the king, but that the bailiff of Richmondshire had appropriated the king's rights by holding the wapentake

[18] Ibid., pp. 60–9.

[19] J.A. Green, 'The Last Century of Danegeld', *EHR*, 96 (1981), 255–7.

[20] Some references to 'geldable' are found under articles 10 and 14.

[21] *Yorkshire Hundred and QW*, pp. 42, 89, 93, 216.

courts of Hang (part of the liberty of Richmondshire) within the boundaries of Claro, distraining a particular royal tenant from Claro to come to the wapentake of Hang in its new location.[22] Geldable service was, in this instance, tied to suit to the territorial court.

In a *quo warranto* case of 1293–4 the abbot of Selby was found guilty of subtracting 'the suit or appearance and a fine' for some of his holdings. The court decreed that 'the holdings of the abbot which in the time of King Richard and after used to be geldable shall remain geldable and the abbot shall contribute common fines and amercements for those holdings.'[23] This offers a late thirteenth-century definition of what was implied by 'geldable'. If the landholder was fully part of the community of the territorial court he and his tenants were liable to contribute to customary payments, administrative expenses such as sheriff's aid, livery for bailiffs, and to the communal fines levied on the community. Men on geldable land were also obliged to act as jurors for inquiries and assizes, and to follow the hue and cry.[24] The concept of the 'geldable county' is recorded in the hundred rolls all across England, but seems to have been little noticed by historians.[25] It is tempting from the evidence to treat suit owed to a territorial court as synonymous with being geldable in that territory; but there are ambiguities and exceptions. In Lancashire in 1292, for instance, a jury found that the abbey land of Cockersand did not owe suit to county or hundred, but was geldable, obliged to contribute to common fines and amercements. The abbot had claimed a double exemption, perhaps indicating their close connection in the opinion of franchise holders.[26]

Landholders often claimed a general range of exemptions, rolled up together in phrases like 'gelds and Danegeld, sheriff's aids and suits of counties, ridings

---

[22] W. Brown (ed.), *Yorkshire Inquisitions*, Yorks. Arch. Soc. Record Series, 23 (1898), ii, pp. 99–102.

[23] *Yorkshire Hundred and QW*, pp. 235–6.

[24] *Three Yorkshire Assize Rolls*, pp. 126–7; Morris, *Medieval Sheriff*, p. 246.

[25] See W. Illingworth (ed.), *Rotuli Hundredorum Temp. Hen. III & Edw. I in Turr' Lond' et in Curia Receptae Scaccarii Westm. Asservati* (London, 1812–18); H.M. Cam, *Liberties and Communities in Medieval England* (London, 1963), pp. 117, 208; *VCH Wiltshire*, v, p. 71.

[26] A. Cantle (ed.), *The Pleas of Quo Warranto for the County of Lancaster*, Chetham Soc., n. s., 98 (1937), pp. 101–2.

and hundreds, and common fines and amercements'. It is possible that at some time in the pre-Conquest past *all* the land had owed these dues; but already by the Conquest exemptions had been granted, and many more were to be granted post-Conquest.

From the earliest records some land was free of geld and some was free of suit of court. In Domesday Book, for instance, it was written that 'Beverley was always free of the king's geld'. Beverley claimed exemption from suit of court from the time of King Athelstan. The bishop of Durham also claimed this from the time of St Cuthbert or from that of the Norman Conquest. Thomas de Furnivall in Hallamshire claimed exemption from suit of court from the time of the Conquest, and Hugh Fitz Henry, with lands in the far west, owed suit to the wapentakes that formed Richmondshire, but claimed his ancestors had never owed suit to the county court.[27]

Later grants created other immunities. After the Conquest much land was granted to abbeys in frankalmoign, free of any tax or service, and abbeys sometimes (illegally) extended these exemptions to properties acquired in later years. The king could free land from taxation and services by his direct grant. His barons could free land by promising to pay the taxes and to do the service themselves, at least until the 1279 statute of mortmain impeded this. So at the end of a list of grants, recorded in the hundred rolls for Strafford wapentake, grants which resulted in those who were enfeoffed neither paying geld nor doing suit, the jurors added that 'all the enfeoffers or their heirs defend all the holdings and do services for the rest of the holding which they hold'. In other words, they carried the additional services on their own land.[28]

The mixture of geldable and non-geldable county can be thought of as a random patchwork of pieces of land, with boundaries not evident to outsiders, but known to the people of the district. In a case of 1293–4 the crown prosecutor asked if Richard de Malebisse, who had legal privileges in three vills, but apparently only gallows in one, should be allowed to continue his practice of leading felons from one of his vills 'through the middle of the geldable

---

[27] *Yorkshire Hundred and QW*, pp. 125, 155.
[28] Ibid., p. 43.

county' to another vill to be hanged.[29] The archbishop of York could reclaim any prisoner arrested in the geldable county, who had come from, or had committed a felony within, his liberties of Beverley or Ripon.[30] Somewhere between Malebisse and the archbishop in privilege of this kind is the abbot of Selby, who had certain rights over thieves caught in his liberty for a theft made in 'the geldable county outside the power and fief of the abbot'; he might condemn them if they pleaded guilty, and if they asked for a jury, the abbot could hold the inquiry with his own men.[31] In these cases, it seems clear that the local jurors would be expected to know the privileges appertaining to every small piece of land. Possibly the sheriff's office or wapentake bailiffs kept some sort of written record, for the precise extent of a liberty was difficult to remember. The Pontefract case, cited below, demonstrates that there could be differences of opinion about what was, and what was not, geldable county.

The mosaic of geldable and non-geldable land can be seen in Kirkby's Inquest. For Langbargh, for instance, the ninety-seven vills within the wapentake were listed, and then a note was appended that all the vills were geldable except one which was in the liberty of the Templars, and two which were in the liberty of the abbey of Whitby; and except Rudby, which the jurors had thought was geldable, but on closer examination found it was not, because it was the demesne (*dominicalis*) of the church of Rudby.[32] Langbargh had almost no ungeldable land, even though it was itself a private wapentake; an apparent contradiction which is puzzling.[33] Ryedale wapentake, with forty-seven vills, had much more ungeldable land, and many individual vills within Ryedale contained a mixture of geldable and ungeldable. The same patchwork of exemptions existed within York where 'men of religion' acquired houses and buildings within the city, the tenants of which used to contribute with the city,

---

[29] Ibid., p. 221.

[30] Ibid., pp. 254–5.

[31] Ibid., pp. 233–4.

[32] *Kirkby's Inquest*, p. 125.

[33] A possible explanation could be that it was more difficult to abstract service or fine in lieu from a private wapentake under a vigilant baron than to abstract it from the king and his overworked sheriff.

but after the property passed to the Church the contributions ceased. A margin note in the hundred rolls adds 'not geldable because men of religion occupy them'.[34]

Some Yorkshiremen apparently found it worthwhile to put themselves into the protection of the highly privileged lords of the county. One man had withdrawn himself from suit, assizes and all other things, by the protection of his lord the earl of Cornwall for which he paid six pence for three years.[35] A general complaint was that many men of the county put themselves into the protection of Templars, Hospitallers or prebendaries, to be withdrawn from watch, assizes, inquisitions and 'that sort of thing'.[36]

The piecemeal operation of privilege included exempt areas as small as one bovate that belonged to great lords or favoured religious orders, the three Malebisse vills cited above, manors that were or had been ancient demesne, and large areas such as whole wapentakes. There were many varieties of privilege within the various areas. Franchises could be restricted to minor rights such as the assizes of bread and ale, or extended to cover most of the sheriff's powers within a wapentake. At what point in the scale of privilege land became 'ungeldable' is never defined. It might seem logical that private wapentakes, of which there were fifteen in Yorkshire out of a total of twenty-seven, were *ipso facto* ungeldable, but it is clear in the case of Langbargh, cited above, that this was not so.[37]

Private wapentakes, or smaller franchised areas, obstructed royal power by slowing down fiscal and legal processes, as well as by offering safe-haven. Many wapentake juries complained about the effect of liberties and the obstruction of the private bailiffs. In the wapentake of Bulmer, for example, a complaint was made that the liberties granted to the cathedral, the abbeys, the military orders and the citizens of York obstructed justice because felons and thieves were received in the liberties where the king's officers dared not enter to arrest

---

[34] *Yorkshire Hundred and QW*, p. 75.

[35] Ibid., p. 62.

[36] Ibid., p. 48.

[37] H.M. Cam, *The Hundred and the Hundred Rolls* (London, 1930), pp. 284–5.

them.[38] The Howden jury enlarged on this, by reporting that neither the cathedral canons of York nor their tenants would answer anyone with or without a writ except in the cathedral church itself; tenants of St Mary's Abbey, York, would only answer at the door of the abbey church; and the Templars would only answer before the king himself or the justices' eyre.[39] The lord of Hallamshire did not allow any of the king's bailiffs to enter his lands, and claimed that from the time of the Conquest royal orders within Hallamshire had to be passed by the king's bailiffs to the Hallamshire bailiffs, who carried out the instructions and reported back, and that the king's bailiffs could only enter if those of Hallamshire failed in their duty.[40] In 1269 the king's bailiffs tried to collect some exchequer debts in the Pontefract area, and the Pontefract bailiffs with almost all of the able-bodied men of the district attacked them, wounded them and imprisoned them in Pontefract Castle. The locals apparently believed the king's bailiffs had entered Pontefract liberty, but the jurors reported that the debt-collecting attempt took place on land 'that is geldable to the king'.[41]

The hinge between the sheriff's control of the geldable county and the liberties in the later thirteenth century was the return of writs.[42] Some twenty Yorkshire landholders exercised this privilege according to the hundred and *quo warranto* rolls, including the archbishop, the bishop of Durham, the major abbots, laymen with great honours, York and Scarborough.

The royal courts and the exchequer could issue writs, but the vast majority came from chancery. Their number for Yorkshire can be assumed to be great, for a surviving register for Bedfordshire and Buckinghamshire shows that in seventeen months of 1333 and 1334 almost two thousand writs were received.[43] Yorkshire writs were delivered to the sheriff and were then distributed. For

---

[38] *Yorkshire Hundred and QW*, pp. 67–8.

[39] Ibid., p. 102.

[40] Ibid., p. 124.

[41] *Yorkshire Inquisitions*, i, pp. 109–10.

[42] T.F.T. Plucknett, *Legislation of Edward I* (Oxford, 1949), chapter 2; M.T. Clanchy, 'The Franchise of the Return of Writs', *TRHS*, 4th ser., 17 (1967), 1–32.

[43] W.A. Morris *et al.* (eds), *English Government at Work* (Cambridge, Mass., 1947), ii, p. 65.

matters within the sheriff's domain, they were sent to the wapentake bailiffs, and for liberties with return of writs, which are first mentioned in John's reign, they were delivered according to an established protocol. Some lords of franchises had to send to York to receive their writs, and in other cases the sheriff's staff took them to a convenient point. The archbishop of York, as lord of Beverley, had writs delivered to him at the Mile Cross, Beverley's outer boundary.[44] A hundred years later, in 1375, the duchy of Lancaster's bailiffs from six Yorkshire wapentakes went each week to York Castle to collect the writs for their wapentakes.[45] In most cases the bailiffs received a copy of the writ and the sheriff kept the original.[46] But in the case of Richmondshire, the franchise holder claimed to have the right to the original writ. This claim caused trouble from at least 1218–19.[47] In the 1250s an inquisition set out in more detail the difficulties caused by the bailiffs of Richmondshire:

They will not permit the king's bailiffs to enter within the limits of Richmondshire to do the king's business, nor will they permit anyone from Richmondshire to come before the sheriffs or his bailiffs outside Richmondshire. They will not do anything unless they have the king's original writ, just as it was sent to the sheriff of Yorkshire; and if a writ of right is sent to anyone in Richmondshire, the bailiffs will not make the summons unless the original writ of right comes into the court of Richmond, just as in the county court.[48]

It was ultimately the sheriff's responsibility to see the writs were obeyed throughout his shire, no matter how privileged the liberty. Action taken in response was recorded on the back of each writ. Failure to act led to the issue of a further writ of *non omittas propter libertatem* (do not omit on account of the

[44] *Yorkshire Hundred and QW*, p. 256.

[45] *English Government at Work* (Cambridge, Mass., 1950), iii, p. 148.

[46] See W.T. Lancaster and W.P. Baildon (eds), *Coucher Book of the Cistercian Abbey of Kirkstall*, Thoresby Soc., 8 (1904), pp. 31–3.

[47] *Rolls of the Justices in Eyre*, no. 744.

[48] *Yorkshire Inquisitions*, i, p. 34.

liberty), and after 1275 the law was amended by the statute of Westminster so that the sheriff could enter the liberty without further delay if the bailiffs failed to act.

It was sometimes difficult for the sheriff to deliver the writ, and often difficult for him to obtain a response. In Holderness there were many recorded occasions when the bailiff did not execute the writs properly. In 1266 the sheriff of Yorkshire received a writ ordering him to attach a Holderness man accused of trespass and theft. The writ was passed on to the seignorial sheriff of Holderness, who refused to act and would not allow the sheriff of York to enter his bailiwick. A writ *non omittas* came for the sheriff of York, still without effect. On the back of the second writ is written the sheriff's reply that the sheriff of Holderness and his bailiff will not allow the sheriff or bailiff of the king to enter the wapentake, with or without a writ. 'So', concludes the endorsement, 'concerning your writs applying to Holderness we can in no way answer in the proper manner until a remedy is provided by the king and his council.' The remedy was not recorded in this case, but frequently it was temporary confiscation of the liberty.[49]

Not everyone took the extreme line of the bailiffs of Richmond or Holderness, and these clashes with the sheriff's staff were not characteristic of the business of the shire. Local government in Yorkshire was reasonably effective in the thirteenth century, both within and without the geldable county. As the thirteenth century grew older, royal lawyers tried to establish royal origins for all liberties. Most lords recognised, as did the lord of Hallamshire, that the king, or the sheriff his officer had an ultimate right over any liberty, however great; that pleas of the crown belonged to the crown in the last resort, and that the production of the royal writ *non omittas* could force entry into even the archbishop of York's highly privileged towns. As the abbot of Selby conceded in 1293–4:

When the king's bailiff ought to exercise any office in Selby he comes to the abbot's bailiff and commits to him anything that has to be executed;

---

[49] B. English, *The Lords of Holderness* (Oxford, 1979), pp. 105–6.

and the abbot's bailiff testifies to the king's bailiff that it has been carried out. If the abbot's bailiff were to be negligent, then it is fully allowed for the king's bailiff, on account of the default of the abbot's bailiff, to do this kind of execution and on this condition were the abbot and his predecessors seised.[50]

The recognition of the king's supremacy in the last resort linked the liberties to the geldable county, and so made the conduct of local government possible.

[50] *Yorkshire Hundred and QW*, p. 233.

8

YORKSHIRE NUNNERIES IN THE MIDDLE AGES: RECRUITMENT AND RESOURCES

Janet Burton

T he rapid expansion of monasteries for men which began in Yorkshire after the Norman Conquest and accelerated in the early twelfth century was matched, from around 1125, by a growth in houses for women. By 1215 the number of monasteries was fairly evenly matched. There were twenty-eight male and twenty-five female houses.[1] Other features stood in sharp contrast. Whereas male houses could be identified by the congregation or order to which they belonged, the nature of the affiliation or self-identity of female houses was less clearly defined. There was a contrast, too, in the size of communities. Although the evidence is limited it suggests that numbers in the nunneries of the north were smaller than in most of its monasteries. There is an even greater divergence between the valuation of male and female houses. Apart from the double Gilbertine house of Watton, which was exceptional both in size and wealth, female houses were generally poorer than their male counterparts. The *Taxatio Ecclesiastica* (1291) and the *Valor Ecclesiasticus* (1535), the two fixed points of comparison which we have, although they may be deficient in some respects, nevertheless give us an index of monastic wealth and poverty. They show northern female houses lagging unequivocally behind male monasteries. In 1535, out of the twenty-four female houses then in Yorkshire, only Watton was assessed at over the value of £200 a year needed to avoid closure. Of the remaining twenty-three houses only Swine Priory had an annual gross value of over £100. Ten were valued at less than £25 per annum, gross. This is to be contrasted with the figures for male houses, the richest of which, St Mary's, York,

---

[1] See D. Knowles and R.N. Hadcock, *Medieval Religious Houses: England and Wales* (London, 1971).

was valued at over £3,000, and only a handful of houses at less than £200. This paper will explore two themes which have a bearing on these general points: recruitment and resources. It will consider how these are linked and what they reveal about attitudes towards women in the monastic life, their spiritual and social functions, as well as the place of nunneries within local society.

These communities were not only less wealthy than male houses but also generally smaller in terms of the number of their inhabitants. The glimpses which we have of the composition of the Yorkshire nunneries suggest that they rarely numbered more than twenty nuns and sometimes fewer. Rosedale had five or six nuns in 1322 and eight in 1378/9.[2] At Nun Monkton there were fifteen in 1376 and the same number in 1424.[3] In 1497 a prioress came from Basedale to rule the eight nuns at Keldholme.[4] The clearest figures come at the Dissolution, and these show the smallest convent to have been Nunburnholme with only three nuns. Rosedale had the same number as in 1378/9, while the others ranged through nine (Yedingham and Moxby), to nineteen (Nun Monkton), and twenty (Swine).

Why were the numbers in female houses apparently smaller than in male houses? Was it that fewer women than men were drawn to the monastic life? Or were the number of places inadequate for the women who wanted to enter northern nunneries? One thing that seems to suggest the latter is that limits were frequently placed on recruitment. From the thirteenth century onwards archbishops of York tried to control the inflow of female postulants. Recruitment was closely tied to resources. A visitation of Swine Priory in 1268, for instance, found that the house 'cannot maintain more nuns or sisters than are there now, because those that there are, are badly provided for at table . . . and the house remains in debt to the sum of 140 marks at least. On this account the lord archbishop has decreed that from now on no nun or sister should be

[2] R.M.T. Hill and D. Robinson (eds), *The Register of William Melton, Archbishop of York, 1317–1340*, Canterbury and York Soc., 70–1, 76 (1977–88), ii, pp. 84, 89; *VCH Yorkshire*, iii, p. 175.

[3] A. Hamilton Thompson, 'The Registers of the Archdeaconry of Richmond', *Yorks. Arch. Journal*, 25 (1920), 129–268, esp. 183, 209.

[4] E.E. Barker (ed.), *The Register of Thomas Rotherham, Archbishop of York, 1480–1500*, Canterbury and York Soc., 69 (1976), i, p. 152.

received without his consent.'[5] In 1281 no one was to be admitted as a nun or sister at Nun Appleton, or even to stay in the monastery except by special licence. Similar injunctions were laid down for Hampole in 1268 and 1308, at Nun Appleton again in 1290 and 1346, at Thicket in 1309, 1315 and 1319, and at Esholt in 1319.[6] A number of these injunctions date from the early fourteenth century when those houses in particular, both female and male, which found themselves in the path of the Scottish armies, were in financial distress. However, attempts to control recruitment to female houses occur throughout their history.[7]

This policy of restricting entry had a number of consequences. First, recruitment may have become susceptible to pressure from patrons and their lords. When Avice de Rumilly confirmed the foundation of Arthington Priory, established by her tenant Peter, she stipulated that one nun should be nominated by her, and that privilege was to be transmitted to her heirs in perpetuity.[8] Patrons might therefore add to the problems of recruitment by reserving for themselves the right to nominate a nun at a vacancy. Concrete examples are few, but suggest a strong involvement between the priory and its patron. In 1472 Joan Ward, nun of Esholt, received dispensation to hold the office of prioress at the nunnery. Ward was the name of the family of the patron, and Joan was most likely to have been an illegitimate offspring. Not only was she secured a place at Esholt, but in the years after 1472 she displaced the prioress, Elizabeth Lasenby. When Joan herself resigned in 1497 Elizabeth

[5] W. Brown (ed.), *The Register of Walter Giffard, Lord Archbishop of York, 1266–1279*, Surtees Soc., 109 (1904), p. 148.

[6] Ibid., pp. 20–1; idem (ed.), *The Register of William Wickwane, Lord Archbishop of York, 1279–1285*, Surtees Soc, 114 (1907), pp. 140–1; idem (ed.), *The Register of John le Romeyn, Lord Archbishop of York, 1286–1296*, Surtees Soc., 123, 128 (1913–17), i, p. 96; idem and A. Hamilton Thompson (eds), *The Register of William Greenfield, Lord Archbishop of York, 1306–1315*, Surtees Soc., 145, 149, 151–3 (1931–40), iii, pp. 41, 100, 139; *Register of William Melton*, ii, pp. 37–40; BI, Register 10 (Register Zouche), f. 14v.

[7] See, for example, 'Visitations in the Diocese of York Holden by Archbishop Edward Lee (AD 1534–5)', *Yorks. Arch. Journal*, 16 (1912), 424–58, esp. 441.

[8] Janet Burton, *The Yorkshire Nunneries in the Twelfth and Thirteenth Centuries*, Borthwick Paper, 56 (York, 1979), p. 25.

Lasenby was returned to rule the house.[9] Other cases are also suggestive of patronal pressure, or at least indicate that the nunnery provided a place of refuge for the female kin of the extended family of the patron. The daughter of the founder of Sinningthwaite, Bertram Haget, became a nun there, and the connection persisted, for in the thirteenth and fourteenth centuries descendants of Bertram Haget are to be found among the Sinningthwaite nuns.[10] Such examples indicate that a patron was not detached, but might exercise his or her power to aid the entry of a female relative or protégé.

Pressure might also come from local gentry and clergy. A cluster of instances occurs at Hampole Priory during the early fourteenth century.[11] In 1310 the archbishop ordered an enquiry as to whether Elena, daughter of Reyner Sperry, late citizen of York, was fitted by reason of age and character to be received as a nun, and asked that should she prove worthy she should be received even though the house was suffering from poverty. Two years later Hampole was reported to have received two novices despite an injunction from the archbishop to receive no more postulants. One was a young child named Matilda de Dreffield, the niece of the abbot of Roche, a Cistercian house to which Hampole was the nearest nunnery. The other was Jonetta, daughter of Sir Hugh de Cressy, who was the brother of the then prioress of Hampole, Custance de Cressy. In 1313 Hampole had licence to receive as a nun twelve-year-old Matilda, daughter of William Fitz William of nearby Emley and Sprotborough. Accordingly, within three years the nuns of Hampole had been allowed to receive four nuns, one the niece of the prioress, one related to a local ecclesiastic, and one a member of a local gentry family. Such instances, which could be multiplied, demonstrate that where entry into a nunnery was restricted, the path of a prospective nun was eased by patronage, the sponsorship of a local gentry or clergy family.

The impression that patrons were prepared to influence recruitment is reinforced by the clustering of families in certain houses. The control of

---

[9] BI, Register 22 (Register Neville), f. 150r; *Register of Thomas Rotherham*, pp. 126–7.

[10] For example, Agnes de Bedale (1286), Elizabeth de Waleys (1320).

[11] *Register of William Greenfield*, ii, pp. 92, 124–5, 152.

recruitment, and the scarcity of places, meant that a vacancy might not occur often. The presence, therefore, of nuns of the same name in the same priory suggests a certain stranglehold by local families. When Archbishop Giffard visited Swine Priory in 1268 he noted that the presence of three 'sisters of the flesh' led to discord as they formed a faction within the nunnery.[12] At Arden in the early fourteenth century there were two members of the Punchardon family, and in 1397 the house had two women of the Darell family of Sessay, Christina and Elizabeth.[13] Several members of the Calverley family entered the house of Esholt, and the local gentry family of Ryther produced three prioresses for Nun Appleton. Nun Monkton was evidently one of the refuges of the Fairfax women. In his will of 1393 John Fairfax, rector of Prescott, mentioned his sister, Margaret, prioress of Nun Monkton, and Elizabeth Fairfax, a nun there.[14] A few years later we find another Fairfax nun at Nun Monkton.[15] Something of the secular family was evidently carried over into the monastic household.

Documentary sources identify only a tiny proportion of the women who entered the Yorkshire nunneries. We know some of their names from charters and leases, from mandates issued by archbishops, from visitation returns, occasionally from the lists of those who elected a prioress, and from probate records, but often the names are first names only, and tell us nothing of the geographical or social origins of the nuns. However, my research into the identities of the women who entered Yorkshire nunneries has shown that a substantial number seem to have been of gentry origins, both the upper and the parish gentry. A word of caution must be sounded here. Many of the names we have are those of prioresses, and they may have been of a higher social status than nuns. Although the monastic community was theoretically one of equality, there may have been a tendency to carry over social status from the secular world. Moreover, nuns whose names are known to us because they received

---

[12] *Register of Walter Giffard*, p. 147.

[13] *Register of William Greenfield*, iii, p. 6; *Register of William Melton*, ii, p. 64; BI, Register 5A (*Sede Vacante* Register), ff., 228r, 229r, printed imperfectly in J. Raine (ed.), *Testamenta Eboracensia*, pt 1, Surtees Soc., 4 (1836), pp. 283n–5n.

[14] Ibid., pp. 186–90.

[15] See BL, Add. Charter 1782, summarized in *VCH Yorkshire*, iii, p. 123.

bequests are likely to belong to the class of person who had property and goods to leave. So it is with some reservations that any suggestions may be made. The seeming preponderance of nuns from the gentry classes raises a number of questions. Was entry *restricted* to the gentry and clerical families of the county? Was it possible for a poor woman to become a nun? Might the number of gentry nuns indicate an economic factor, that is, might there have existed a link between payment and entry into a female religious house? Evidence from twelfth-century charters suggests that on occasion a grant of land was linked to the entry of a female relative into the house.[16] One interpretation could be that this was a free-will gift, made out of charity. In this case it was something which the Church allowed. However, another interpretation could be that it was simony, the buying of an ecclesiastical office, and therefore something to be avoided, indeed, something against which the Church legislated. It is for this reason that we may suspect that the practice was more widespread than the records make out, for charters might mask the link between a grant of land or money as a dowry and recruitment. The archbishops of York frequently warned against the practice. Arden Priory was one of those warned by Archbishop Greenfield not to receive novices 'for money . . . or by any pact . . . but on the instincts of charity'.[17] Archbishop Lee in his 1535 injunctions to Sinningthwaite ordered 'the saide prioresse, and euery oon of the said covent, that they make no graunt to eny persone to be admitted or receved a nune or a conuerse of that house, for money or odre pleasure or advauntage, by reason of a couenant or pacte made for the same purpose, for such admissions be dampnable and be plane simonye'.[18] He did not, however, forbid them to accept a gift made freely, out of love, by a sister on her admission as long as it was given 'without pacte, couenaunt or bargeyn'.

Mandates like this are difficult to interpret. Were the archbishops reprimanding nuns for real sins, or anticipated ones? Historians have debated the frequency of dowry grants, and Gilchrist and Oliva have suggested recently

[16] Burton, *Yorkshire Nunneries*, pp. 20–3.
[17] *Register of William Greenfield*, iii, p. 8.
[18] 'Visitations in the Diocese of York', 442.

that in East Anglia they were not common.[19] From Yorkshire several pieces of evidence suggest that entry into a nunnery may not have been free. In 1430 Richard Fairfax made arrangements for his daughter Elan to become a nun of Nun Monkton. She was to receive 40s. a year from the income of certain lands, and 19s. for making her a nun.[20] The nunnery accordingly received a lump sum and an annual income. In her will Elizabeth Sewardby left her namesake £6 13s. 4d. if she became a nun at Nun Monkton.[21] There survives in her probate inventory a list of the expenses in making Elizabeth Sewardby a nun there in 1470. These amounted to £10 7s. 11½d., rather more than the £6 13s. 4d. bequeathed to her. We have a breakdown of the expenses. They comprised the fee of £3 *customarily demanded* from each novice, £3 13s. 7½d. for her habit and bed, £3 11s. 4d. for entertaining her friends who visited, presumably for her profession, and 2s. to John Homylton for a sermon for the occasion. Taken together the fee, habit and bed amounted to £6 13s. 7½d., roughly the same sum as had been bequeathed. That same amount, £6 13s. 4d., was left by William Vavasour of Gunby to make his daughter a nun of Swine (1495), and by William Hungate of North Dalton to his daughter Lucy as her dowry to be a nun of Watton (1535).[22] In 1345 Robert de Playce, rector of Brompton, left 100s. to help his niece become a nun at Wykeham, Yedingham or Nun Monkton.[23] Robert's specification of three nunneries as possible destinations for his niece is further evidence that entry might not be easy. This evidence indicates that in the fifteenth century, on being professed at Nun Monkton, a nun might be expected to make a payment, *customarily* £3, and that the full expenses, including the fee and the provision of her habit and bed, were expected to be £6 13s. 4d., or 10 marks, a sum paralleled at Swine and Watton. These payments were in effect dowries, and they raise the question of whether entry was restricted to the better off. Jeremy Goldberg has pointed to instances

---

[19] Roberta Gilchrist and Marilyn Oliva, *Religious Women in Medieval East Anglia*, Studies in East Anglian History, 1 (University of East Anglia, 1993), pp. 51–2.

[20] See above, note 15.

[21] *Testamenta Eboracensia*, pt 3, Surtees Soc., 45 (1865), p. 165.

[22] Ibid., pt 4, Surtees Soc., 53 (1869), pp. 90–1; C. Cross, *The End of Medieval Monasticism in the East Riding of Yorkshire*, East Yorkshire Local History Soc. (1993), p. 9.

[23] *Testamenta Eboracensia*, pt 1, pp. 9–12, from BI, Register 10 (Register Zouche), f. 302.

in the fifteenth century where among the upper rural peasantry of Yorkshire a marriage dowry appears to have been between 20 and 25 marks (an average of £15).[24] So, crudely speaking, entry into a nunnery was a cheaper economic option than marriage and not limited to gentry. It was within the means of the upper peasantry and freeholders, and indeed provision of a sum of money for a daughter, or a number of daughters, to enter a nunnery might be an acceptable alternative to a marriage dowry. Nevertheless, some clearly expected the cost of entry into a nunnery to be higher than 10 marks. The will of Thomas de Walleworth, canon of York, left 40 marks (£24 13s. 4d.) to a relative named Agnes de Aclom as her marriage portion or to enter religion.[25]

The picture that emerges is one in which small monastic houses for women, poorly resourced, were compelled to restrict the number of professed nuns. The results were pressure from gentry and clerical families to secure entry for their female relatives, and possibly financial demands on recruits.[26] Although this could lead to a close connection between certain houses and local families, the occurrence of nuns from the same family in different houses across the county suggests that because of the restrictions on places, recruits were forced sometimes to go where places were available. The limitation on the number of places served to disrupt the geographical pattern of recruitment, which otherwise appears to have been fairly local.

The small size and limited economic resources of the Yorkshire nunneries therefore restricted recruitment. However, pressure did not just come from nuns, the principal inhabitants of the nunneries, but also from the demands of other individuals on the financial resources of the nunneries, those who sought education, hospitality, and retirement within their confines. These were some of the socio-religious functions which nunneries (just as male houses) were expected to perform but which could cost them dearly both financially and in terms of disruption of regular discipline. Time and again the archbishops attempted to stem the financial drain which these seculars placed on the nuns.

---

[24] P.J.P. Goldberg, *Women, Work and Life Cycle in a Medieval Economy* (Oxford, 1992), pp. 245–6.

[25] *Testamenta Eboracensia*, pt 1, pp. 353–6.

[26] Though not to the extent suggested by Eileen Power in her classic treatment, *Medieval English Nunneries c. 1275–1535* (Cambridge, 1922).

When in 1535 Archbishop Lee forbad new nuns or sisters at Sinningthwaite he included in that prohibition 'any seculer or spirituall persons to suggiorne or dwell within the precinct of that monasterie'.[27] This command was one of the last of a long line of such prohibitions.

Some visitors and boarders, however, brought money with them, and could provide much needed revenue, which introduces the second theme of this paper, the question of how nunneries were resourced. The traditional source of revenue for monastic houses was land, and nunneries were landowners in the same way as monasteries, though on a smaller scale. Some avenues open to male religious, such as the provision of spiritual services, were closed to nuns. But their revenue might be supplemented in other ways, by alms and gifts in the form of money. Often evidence emerges only when there were complaints about mismanagement. We discover, for instance, that when Arden Priory was visited in 1397 it was in a poor financial state despite Prioress Eleanor having received £19 6s. 8d. in alms and gifts.[28] The granting of corrodies, board and lodging in return for a payment, was another source of income, though a hazardous one which archbishops occasionally tried to curtail. In 1352 the nuns of Yedingham granted to a woman named Emma Hart, for the payment of a sum of money, the position of dairywoman. She was to receive the food allowance of a nun, a share in the small pittances of the nuns, and a building called 'le chesehouse'. When she was too old to work she was to be allowed a place in 'le sisterhouse'. In 1524 Alice, widow of William Berre, paid £12 to the nuns of Arden for 'mett and drynke as their convent hath', 'an honest chamber with sufficient fyer att all tyme' and clothing. Alice was still living in 1536 when her corrody was commuted to a money payment.[29]

In the later Middle Ages, however, it was through testamentary bequests that nunneries might frequently supplement their resources. A testator might leave a legacy to a nunnery in the form of goods, or money, expressed either as a total or in terms of a certain amount per nun. Some testators left bequests to a single

[27] 'Visitations in the Diocese of York', 441.

[28] *Testamenta Eboracensia*, pt 1, p. 283n.

[29] Quoted in *VCH Yorkshire*, iii, pp. 115, 128.

house, others to a number of houses; some favoured only female or only male house, while others made legacies to both.[30] In 1402 Sir John Depeden left his body to be buried at the Augustinian house of Healaugh Park, a legacy to his parish church and a bequest of 20s. to each of twelve nunneries 'to pray for my soul and that of Elizabeth my wife and the souls of all the faithful departed'.[31]

Testators such as Sir John Depeden specified that a legacy was made to secure the prayers of the nuns. In other cases, however, the interests of testators in nunneries may have been dictated by family considerations. Nuns did not leave the world and family behind them, and testators made bequests to members of their kin and to female acquaintances who were nuns. Their wills show a mixture of money gifts and material goods, some of which were practical and some ceremonial. Walter Percehay bequeathed to Joan his daughter, a nun of Yedingham, and to Agnes, his daughter, a nun of Watton, 40s. each. Two years later his widow Agnes made an identical bequest but in addition left to the daughter who was by then prioress of Yedingham, two robes with mantles.[32] Roger de Moreton, citizen and mercer of York, left money appropriately to purchase black flannel for his daughter, Isabella, a nun of St Clement's, where Roger's sister was also a nun.[33] Sir Thomas Redness, knight of Whitgift, left his daughter Alice, a nun of Hampole, a cow and a fatted pig and 20s., and to the convent 23s.[34] When John Fairfax made his will in 1393 he remembered the convent of Nun Monkton, bequeathing 6s. 8d. to each nun and 3s. 4d. to each sister, his white robe with gold stars on it, the gilded cross with Mary and John in silver, and a gilded chalice. But his main bequests were to a range of individual female religious. To his sister Margaret, the prioress, he gave 13s. 4d., a silver cup, a mazer, a pix for spices, six silver spoons, a cloak of black cloth trimmed with fur; to Elizabeth Fairfax, 26s. 8d.; to another nun of Monkton, Margaret de Pickering, a platter of silver with the head of a deer carved on the

---

[30] See, for instance, the will of Agnes Stapleton (1448), in J.W. Clay, *North Country Wills*, Surtees Soc., 116 (1908), pp. 48–9.

[31] *Testamenta Eboracensia*, pt 1, pp. 294–9.

[32] Ibid., pp. 6, 53–4.

[33] Ibid., pp. 133–4.

[34] Ibid., pp. 348–9.

base, and 20s.; and to Margaret de Cotam, nun, 13s. 4d. Fairfax also named as beneficiaries individual nuns of Marrick and Nun Appleton and a female recluse of Richmond.[35]

These wills suggest a strong link persisting between the secular family and the professed nun. The examples quoted raise the question of whether the bequests made to nuns were retained by them as personal financial resources and property. Members of the monastic orders were vowed to personal poverty and were forbidden to own property. It is likely, therefore, that when a testator bequeathed a sum of money to each nun, it was not to be used personally. Rather it was intended that religious houses receive a sum commensurate with the size of the community. Moreover, goods bequeathed to individuals could have been intended for communal use, or for entertaining visitors to a house. Despite this there were clearly some lapses in monastic practice. Sir John Depeden, in addition to his bequests to twelve nunneries, left to Elizabeth, daughter of John Fitz Richard, a nun of Appleton *for her own use* 6s. 8d., and to each nun *for her own use* 2s. This is not an isolated example, and it is instructive to note that in 1411 Archbishop Bowet warned the nuns of Hampole that any of them who received gifts or legacies were to reveal them to the prioress.[36]

Nunneries seem to have been heavily dependent on such gifts. The Yorkshire nunneries were indeed poor on paper, that is in terms of income from property and rents. Their economy probably depended on irregular bequests of money to supplement their regular income from land. The evidence shows legacies not only providing money for both general and specific use, such as repairs to the fabric, but also clothing for the nuns, beds and bedding for the dormitory, domestic utensils for refectory, kitchen and guesthouse, books for the library, and service books and ornaments for the altars. The fine quality of some of the goods which the nuns received need not suggest that they lived in luxury; rather, their poverty meant that such goods would have been put to practical use.[37] Nevertheless there may have been an ironic discrepancy between the poverty of the houses and the seemingly rich surroundings and furnishings of some of them.

[35] See above, note 14.

[36] BI, Register 18 (Register Bowet), f. 101.

[37] A point made by John H. Tillotson, *Marrick Priory: A Nunnery in Late Medieval Yorkshire*, Borthwick Paper, 75 (York, 1989), p. 13, to counteract views of Power, *Medieval English Nunneries* and M.G.A. Vale, *Piety, Charity and Literacy among the Yorkshire Gentry*, Borthwick Paper, 50 (York, 1976).

Despite the geographical remoteness of the Yorkshire nunneries their nuns were in many ways enmeshed in local society. Certainly the evidence of the wills suggests that a number of their members remained a perceived part of a secular family. Their kin continued to have contact with, and in some respect, responsibilities for, women who were now members of a monastic family. When Archbishop Greenfield ordered the nuns of Hampole to examine Elena Sperry, a prospective nun, he allowed them, if they decided to accept her, to be 'helped and relieved by her friends' so long as there was no suspicion of simony.[38] In 1319 Archbishop Melton noted the poverty of Sinningthwaite, and ordered that those nuns who had no elders or relatives or friends and who lacked clothes were to be provided with clothes from the funds of the house.[39] Clearly it was expected that the secular family had a financial responsibility for their nuns. Members of the family were among those who from time to time were entertained in the priory guest houses. In 1318 Moxby was found to be in debt, and as a means to alleviate this it was ordered that relatives of nuns were not to visit for longer than two days, which implies that extended visits by kin were a normal feature of monastic life there.[40] When Archbishop Lee ordered the prioress of Sinningthwaite to ensure that no seculars had 'resort or recurse' to her or any of her nuns, he excepted fathers and mothers or near kin.[41] Finally, it is clear that nuns expected to be able to visit their families, as in 1306 when the archbishop gave licence for Mary de Ros, prioress of Rosedale, to leave her priory twice a year for the purposes of visiting her father, Sir William de Ros of Ingmanthorpe.[42]

The nunneries of the north were small and poor institutions, but they still had the power to attract gentry recruits like Mary de Ros, and other members of her family. It is evident that at certain points in their history female religious houses

---

[38] *Register of William Greenfield*, ii, p. 92.

[39] BI, Register 9 (Register Melton), f. 164 (new foliation); *VCH Yorkshire*, iii, p. 117.

[40] *Register of William Melton*, ii, pp. 12–14.

[41] 'Visitations in the Diocese of York', 441.

[42] *Register of William Greenfield*, iii, pp. 12–13.

in the north were under financial pressure which led to the number of nuns being restricted in order that recruits and resources be balanced. To raise the question of why, when the level of demand was evidently high, nunneries were not larger and better endowed, is to open another avenue which is beyond the scope of this paper. One consequence, however, was that nunneries remained an integral part of local society. They provided an outlet for female vocation, a place of education for the young, a place of retirement for widows. They needed, more than the large male houses, the financial support of the local community in order to fulfil their various functions, both spiritual and social.

9

ABUSE OR EXPEDIENCY? PLURALISM AND NON-RESIDENCE IN NORTHERN ENGLAND IN THE LATE MIDDLE AGES

A.D.M. Barrell

The late medieval Church is frequently castigated for its tolerance, indeed encouragement, of the abuses of pluralism and non-residence among clergy. Pluralism, the holding of several benefices simultaneously by the same individual, has often been seen as the means whereby avaricious churchmen accumulated great personal wealth at the expense of their less fortunate or well-connected brethren and without regard to the spiritual needs of parishioners to whom they had a duty to minister. Pluralism implied absenteeism from one or more of the benefices held; and even some who were not pluralists were still non-resident and therefore inattentive to the concerns of their flock. When these absentees and pluralists were, in addition, based outside England, especially if they were foreigners unacquainted with the language of the common people, the scandal was so much the greater. The pre-Reformation Church, we are frequently led to believe, was riddled with greed and corruption, and the hierarchy from the papacy downwards either connived at or even actively stimulated widespread pluralism and non-residence.

This summary of the traditional hostility directed towards the late medieval Church may be simplistic, but the attitude encapsulated in it continues to be widely prevalent. It has, of course, a basis in contemporary evidence. Parliaments frequently complained about the influence in England of greedy, non-resident papal appointees who saw their English benefices merely as a source of profit; they resented the draining of treasure from the realm; they bemoaned the difficulties experienced by local men who wished to advance in the ecclesiastical hierarchy; and, for good measure, they pointed out how pastoral work, almsgiving, and hospitality suffered from the absenteeism of churchmen. Chroniclers drew attention to what they saw as the rapacity of the papacy and remarked upon the scandalous promotion of unlettered and unsuitable clerics; and popular sermons and vernacular literature also offered acerbic comments on the beneficed clergy and drew unflattering comparisons between them and their less well-heeled colleagues.

Some of these claims can be corroborated by more sober, documentary evidence, drawn from the records of both the Church itself and the English state; and it is the purpose of this paper to offer some observations on pluralism and non-residence on the basis of sources which do not have the polemical slant of parliamentary petitions and of chroniclers and preachers who often had personal grievances to air. Those of us looking back across many centuries must also be aware that the role of the Church and the function of churchmen (as broadly defined) have shifted noticeably since pre-Reformation days. In the Middle Ages, for instance, education was largely an ecclesiastical preserve. Those teaching at the expanding universities, and those studying there, were largely sponsored by the wealth of the Church, and that wealth was derived primarily from tithe income from benefices; if the Church wished to improve the academic standards of parochial clergy by long years of university study, then it frequently had to supply the student with a benefice to support him. It could be seen as an investment aimed at improving the quality of parish priests. Nor could the state have functioned without ecclesiastical civil servants whose revenues from benefices served as their salary; and even if it is contended that this did not compensate for the evils of absenteeism it is nonetheless a reminder that many ecclesiastics operated – and were expected to operate – beyond the bounds of parish and diocese.

The fundamental difficulty in examining pluralism and non-residence is one of quantification. Contemporary sources provide many examples of churchmen who were absent or who held more than one benefice, but give no grounds for an accurate calculation – or even a plausible estimate – of the proportion of the clerical estate that these individuals constituted. Bishops' registers record licences to be absent from cures under various pretexts, and occasional visitation records draw attention to unlicensed non-residence; but this evidence must be used with great care. Visitations were relatively uncommon, and there is no way of knowing how consistently licences to be absent were sought or granted or registered. Papal sources contain similar difficulties of quantification. Dispensations for an individual to hold more than one benefice are not uncommon, although the definition of what constituted pluralism was not fixed, and whether a licence was necessary was partly determined by the nature and status of the benefices in question and by the standing of the individual involved. Information in *non obstante* clauses in petitions to the pope, which often list benefices held or claimed, indicates that many clerks held more than one benefice even though no record survives of any dispensation to do so. In the fourteenth century illegitimate clerks, who usually had to seek papal sanction to obtain and exchange benefices, and whose careers were, therefore, more closely controlled than those of their colleagues, have probably left behind them more traces of pluralism than those born in wedlock. Popes sometimes also licensed non-residence as distinct from pluralism, albeit not on the scale of bishops. The information is copious, but it is very unlikely that the coverage of pluralism and non-residence is consistent over an extended period; this paper does not, therefore, attempt analysis on numerical grounds, but rather offers some general impressions as to the incidence of absenteeism and pluralism and the possible effects they had.

The ecclesiastical authorities from the pope downwards had long seen pluralism as an abuse, but it was hard to bring measures against it to fruition because they adversely affected prominent and wealthy churchmen, the very individuals who were vital agents in any far-reaching reform of contemporary practices but who had the most to lose from such reform. The second half of the thirteenth century provides several scandalous examples of pluralism on a very wide scale.[1] But by the period of the Avignon papacy few clerks held more than one benefice with cure of souls, even though many held several sinecure prebends in cathedrals and collegiate churches; and there is evidence that the licensing of pluralism of incompatible benefices was closely controlled by the papacy and strictly limited. John XXII's constitution *Execrabilis* of 1317 appears to have

[1] A.H. Thompson, 'Pluralism in the Mediaeval Church, with Notes on Pluralists in the Diocese of Lincoln, 1366', intro., *Associated Architectural Societies Reports and Papers*, 33 (1915), 50–9. See this introduction generally for an account of pluralism and the measures against it to 1366.

achieved a high measure of effectiveness, and when the decree *Consueta*, issued by Urban V in 1366, required all pluralists to declare their interests, the returns make it clear that relatively few clerks held more than one benefice with cure such as a parish church, and that most contemporary ecclesiastics had only modest financial resources at their disposal.[2] There were, of course, exceptions, and these have attained a certain level of notoriety. William de Wykeham had thirteen benefices, including prebends in York, Beverley and Southwell; David de Wollore had twelve, including (unusually) three with cure, although his claim to the rich rectory of Bishop Wearmouth was in fact disputed.[3] Their careers in royal service had been amply rewarded, and their status at court meant that they avoided (as did nearly all pluralists) the deprivation of excess benefices envisaged under *Consueta*. But these men were special cases: only twenty-four pluralists who made their declaration in a diocese in Canterbury province in 1366 are recorded with assessed incomes of £100 or more,[4] a small proportion of the total clerical estate.

Throughout the fifteenth century papal dispensations to hold two benefices with cure or otherwise incompatible are frequently encountered in the registers. It is clear, moreover, that these licences were intended to cover parish churches and effectively to set aside both the papacy's own regulations against pluralism and, where appropriate, the thirteenth-century constitutions of the legates Otto and Ottobuono obliging perpetual vicars to reside on their benefices. Most of the clerks concerned had evidently stressed their academic qualifications, noble birth, or record of service to a prelate or secular lord when seeking a dispensation. Some – perhaps most – were doubtless worthy men, and their numbers should not be overestimated. But there is a striking contrast between the number of licences for pluralism of benefices with cure in the fifteenth century and the situation before the Great Schism.

[2] The returns for Canterbury province (excluding St Asaph and Bangor) are in A.C. Wood (ed.), *Registrum Simonis Langham Cantuariensis Archiepiscopi*, Canterbury and York Soc., 53 (1956), pp. 5–109; and R.C. Fowler (ed.), *Registrum Simonis de Sudbiria, Diocesis Londoniensis, A.D. 1362–1375*, with intro. to vol. ii by C. Jenkins, Canterbury and York Soc., 34, 38 (1927–38), ii, pp. 148–82. The corresponding York evidence does not survive.

[3] C.J. Godfrey, 'Pluralists in the Province of Canterbury in 1366', *Journal of Ecclesiastical History*, 11 (1960), 26. For Bishop Wearmouth see A.D.M. Barrell, *The Papacy, Scotland and Northern England, 1342–1378* (Cambridge, 1995), pp. 117–19.

[4] Godfrey, 'Pluralists', 26.

The dispensations had, of course, to be sought and paid for, but clerks apparently assumed that the requisite licence would be forthcoming. In May 1448 Stephen Close was rehabilitated after having held the rectories of Ousby in Cumberland and Banham in Norfolk for well over two years against the terms of *Execrabilis*. Close had not received dispensation, but claimed to have appointed an agent at the Roman curia to obtain a licence and to have mistakenly believed that one had been issued before his representative's death.[5] In due course he received a further dispensation to hold another incompatible benefice in addition to his two churches, over two hundred miles apart.[6] It is clear that a clerk with a suitable academic or other record and with appropriate support could proceed in anticipation of a dispensation for pluralism, and, moreover, apparently suffer no penalties for having acted against *Execrabilis*.

It was rather more usual, however, for an ambitious – or avaricious – cleric to obtain a dispensation in advance. This explains why some men sought a licence before they held any benefices at all. Some, especially those from leading families such as the Nevilles and Percys, sought such dispensations even when well under age, or requested more extensive privileges. That was inevitable, and marks no great departure in principle from the practice of a hundred years earlier. The brothers Thomas and Alexander de Neville had, after all, been allowed in 1347 to hold benefices when only teenagers, and at eighteen, when they held the rectories of Brantingham and Aysgarth respectively, they were each permitted to hold another incompatible benefice.[7] Noble birth was clearly an advantage, albeit one which relatively few could boast.

By no means all beneficiaries of papal favour were, however, from famous families. In December 1451 William Lax, a priest of Durham diocese, was indulted to hold for life either two chantries or one chantry and another

---

[5] W.H. Bliss *et al.* (eds), *Calendar of Entries in the Papal Registers Relating to Great Britain and Ireland: Papal Letters* (London, 1893–), x, pp. 29–30 (hereafter *CPL*).

[6] Ibid., p. 56.

[7] Ibid., iii, pp. 262, 431; D.M. Smith, 'A Reconstruction of the Lost Register of the Vicars-General of Archbishop Thoresby of York', *Borthwick Institute Bulletin*, 3 (1983–4), 29–61, 102–13, no. 114.

benefice, even though this contravened the foundation statutes of the benefices concerned.[8] But in fact inflation had meant that many chantries had become insufficiently endowed: the late fifteenth-century register of Archbishop Rotherham includes several licences to chantry priests to hold other preferments so that they could devote all the chantry revenues to essential repairs, and some chantry chaplains had been pluralists as early as 1366.[9] If few chantry priests suffered the misfortunes alleged by James Iveson, chaplain in Mansfield Woodhouse, who was given leave of absence in October 1482 because of the ruinous state of the buildings and again in February 1484 and June 1488 because of fire,[10] only a minority can have found their stipends better than adequate by the end of the fifteenth century.

Non-residence was the norm among canons of cathedrals and collegiate churches in the late Middle Ages. Some dignities were deemed to involve the cure of souls and required residence, but simple prebends were usually sinecures and were often held by men with interests elsewhere. Such clerks saw such benefices as merely a source of income, and their success in accumulating large collections of them was one of the principal determinants of the extent of their wealth. Absentees did not share in distributions and other revenues earmarked for canons who fulfilled the requirements of residence, but neither were they involved in the expensive hospitality which residence necessitated.[11]

Relatively few canons of York resided in the later Middle Ages. Of thirty-six prebendaries, the number who regularly attended chapter meetings in the fourteenth century was well into single figures,[12] and in the fifteenth century

[8] *CPL*, x, pp. 105–6.

[9] Godfrey, 'Pluralists', 34–5. In 1351 the rector of Winston was dispensed to retain a chantry in York Minster which required residence: *CPL*, iii, p. 457.

[10] E.E. Barker (ed.), *The Register of Thomas Rotherham, Archbishop of York, 1480–1500*, Canterbury and York Soc., 69 (1976), i, pp. 25, 199, 162.

[11] In a petition made in around 1364 the costs of a probationary year at York and some other cathedrals were brought to the pope's attention: W.H. Bliss (ed.), *Calendar of Entries in the Papal Registers Relating to Great Britain and Ireland: Petitions to the Pope* (London, 1896), p. 475 (hereafter *CPP*).

[12] K. Edwards, *The English Secular Cathedrals in the Middle Ages* (Manchester, 1949), pp. 75–6; cf. the records of chapter meetings in the 1340s in York Minster Library, H1/1.

the proportion was probably even smaller.[13] The reasons for this are well known. It was in the interests of the resident canons to discourage others from joining their number, for any increase in the number attending reduced the income of each from common revenues and distributions. When the prebend of Bilton was founded in 1294 it was stipulated that the canon holding it, even if he resided, could take his share of the distributions only after an annual endowment of £20 had been made, and in 1346 the pope exempted William de Ferriby from the obligation to make this considerable payment.[14] The York chapter, at least in its everyday business, was undoubtedly an oligarchy, but probably never one in which birth was a significant factor. Some canons-residentiary were local men; others, especially in the fifteenth century, came with archbishops who had been translated to York.[15] Most were senior clergy who had elected to end their careers as administrators of a great cathedral.

Non-residence among canons had little practical effect on the life of a cathedral. After 1252 all York prebendaries, resident or not, had to supply a vicar-choral to fulfil many of their duties in choir, and the development of the Bedern in the middle of the thirteenth century provided a college for the body of vicars-choral.[16] Collegiate churches in the northern province developed on broadly similar lines, although the system of appointing deputies was less firmly rooted and clearly open to abuse. In the early fifteenth century Bishop Langley of Durham on several occasions warned members of collegiate churches in his diocese either to reside or to provide suitable substitutes; he also took action against the deans of the churches, who were bound to continuous residence.[17] The

[13] R.B. Dobson, 'The Residentiary Canons of York in the Fifteenth Century', *Journal of Ecclesiastical History*, 30 (1979), 153–4.

[14] W. Brown (ed.), *The Register of John le Romeyn, Lord Archbishop of York, 1286–1296*, Surtees Soc., 123, 128 (1913–17), ii, pp. 19–22; *CPL*, iii, p. 190.

[15] Edwards, *English Secular Cathedrals*, pp. 86–7; Dobson, 'Residentiary Canons', 154–5.

[16] Edwards, *English Secular Cathedrals*, pp. 269, 282.

[17] R.L. Storey (ed.), *The Register of Thomas Langley, Bishop of Durham, 1406–1437*, Surtees Soc., 164, 166, 169, 170, 177, 182 (1956–70), i, pp. 121–2; ii, pp. 49–50, 67–8; iii, pp. 109–21; iv, pp. 121–3; v, pp. 101–2, 130.

similarity of successive monitions hints strongly at their ineffectiveness, and it must be concluded that in the Durham collegiate churches little semblance of corporate life now remained.

Absenteeism from parochial benefices was potentially more damaging to the spiritual welfare of the community than absence from colleges and cathedrals, but its extent is hard to assess. The register of William de la Zouche, archbishop of York from 1342 to 1352, records around 370 licences to be absent, an average of over thirty-five a year. When it is considered that clerks in the service of the king appear usually not to have required an episcopal licence to be non-resident,[18] it is easy to come to the conclusion that a significant number of the more able incumbents in York diocese were absentees for considerable periods at university, in the service of a lord, or for other, often unspecified, reasons.

One example will suffice; the church of Winestead in Holderness, which was in lay patronage. The rector Roger Tilyol was licensed to be absent until Michaelmas on 4 February 1341, a concession which was renewed for a further year on 15 November and again for another year on 28 January 1343.[19] His successor, Stephen de Swyne, was instituted in December 1345 and ordained to the subdiaconate on 11 March 1346.[20] He then availed himself of the terms of Boniface VIII's constitution *Cum ex eo* to receive two successive archiepiscopal licences to attend university without further promotion,[21] and

[18] For an example of an episcopal licence to a clerk absent in royal service see R.N. Swanson (ed.), *A Calendar of the Register of Richard Scrope, Archbishop of York, 1398–1405*, Borthwick Texts and Calendars, 8, 11 (1981–5), i, p. 73.

[19] BI, Reg. 5A (Register *sede vacante*), f. 100, 100v; Reg. 10 (Register of Archbishop Zouche), f. 175v.

[20] BI, Reg. 10, f. 182v; Reg. 10A (Ordination Register of Archbishop Zouche), f. 14; cf. f. 13 for his ordination as an acolyte.

[21] BI, Reg. 10, ff. 183, 186v. On *Cum ex eo* see L.E. Boyle, 'The Constitution "Cum ex eo" of Boniface VIII: Education of Parochial Clergy', *Mediaeval Studies*, 24 (1962), 263–302; R.M. Haines, 'The Education of the English Clergy During the Later Middle Ages: Some Observations on the Operation of Pope Boniface VIII's Constitution Cum ex eo (1298)', *Canadian Journal of History*, 4 (1969), 1–22. See also C.J. Godfrey, 'Non-Residence of Parochial Clergy in the Fourteenth Century', *Church Quarterly Review*, 162 (1961), 433–46.

had been a priest for only a few months when the plague claimed him in 1349.[22] A successor in the late 1350s had a similar career. John de Joueby was licensed to be absent from Winestead under *Cum ex eo* in December 1358, and received an extension on 19 September 1360, on which day he was ordained deacon.[23] Death was, however, to claim him too the following year,[24] and his successor, Ralph de Erghom, was also absent from his cure for long periods.[25]

Winestead may have suffered more than most parish churches from the absenteeism of its rectors and from their susceptibility to early death. But the example demonstrates how perfectly lawful, officially sanctioned absenteeism, often with the laudable aim of furthering the education of parochial clergy, could in fact deprive a benefice of its incumbent for years on end. The cure of souls was supposed to be upheld by deputies, even if this is not always specifically stated in the registers, and the number of unbeneficed clergy who were prepared to serve as stipendiary chaplains suggests that it would not have been difficult to find substitutes, especially before the Black Death.[26] But it is nonetheless interesting to observe how seriously education could impinge on the pastoral duties of the theoretical figurehead of the parish in the fourteenth century.

By around 1400 rather fewer absence licences are recorded in York registers. For instance, only fifty-eight are found under Archbishop Scrope, an average of well under nine per annum; and licences to be absent are very rare

[22] BI, Reg. 10A, f. 30v, cf. f. 26v; Reg. 10, f. 199v. He had already obtained another licence to be absent from Michaelmas 1349: BI, Reg. 10, f. 193v.

[23] BI, Reg. 11 (Register of Archbishop Thoresby), ff. 199v, 202, 342v.

[24] Ibid., f. 203v.

[25] Ibid., ff. 218v, 225.

[26] See generally S. Townley, 'Unbeneficed Clergy in the Thirteenth Century: Two English Dioceses', in D.M. Smith (ed.), *Studies in Clergy and Ministry in Medieval England,* Borthwick Studies in History (York, 1991), pp. 38–64. In fifteenth-century Durham, however, there were considerable difficulties in recruiting assistants: R.L. Storey, *Thomas Langley and the Bishopric of Durham, 1406–1437* (London, 1961), p. 181. See also the remarks by A.K. McHardy, 'Some Patterns of Ecclesiastical Patronage in the Later Middle Ages', in *Clergy and Ministry*, p. 36; and by Boyle, 'The Constitution "Cum ex eo"', 276–8.

in the register of Bishop Langley of Durham, whose episcopate spanned over thirty years from 1406. Only five are recorded, a considerable reduction from the forty-one in the somewhat incomplete register of Thomas de Hatfield in the years between 1350 and 1375.[27] Two of those dispensed by Langley, Thomas Newham, rector of Long Newton, in 1411, and Henry Oculshagh, rector of Houghton-le-Spring, in 1427, were given leave of absence to attend university.[28] The canon-regular John Hall, vicar of Hart, was allowed to be non-resident for a year in 1417 to make a pilgrimage to Rome, although, as was usual, he was told to ensure that the church and its chapels were not deprived of services.[29] Both the other licences in Langley's register involved chapels and were for very limited periods.[30] So was there little absenteeism in the early fifteenth century, or was it merely not recorded or even ignored? This cannot be definitively answered, but in 1411 Langley took action against the rector of Boldon, who had farmed out the revenues of his church to go on pilgrimage without seeking the bishop's leave, and against the vicar of Whittingham, who had also absented himself without permission and neglected his cure.[31] This at least suggests that unauthorized absenteeism was still considered unacceptable, and may imply that the decrease in the number of licences cannot be attributed solely to clerks not troubling to acquire them.[32]

Papal licences to hold more than one parochial benefice necessitated the issue also of indults to farm revenues and to enjoy the fruits of churches even during non-residence. For instance, in March 1452 the rectors of Thursby and Rothbury and the vicar of Warkworth were simultaneously permitted to put their benefices to farm while at university, in the service of a prelate or lord,

---

[27] Prior's Kitchen, Durham, Register of Bishop Hatfield. The figures are based on ff. 1–79v only.

[28] *Reg. Langley*, i, p. 144; iii, pp. 59, 87–8. Oculshagh was dead by 6 October 1433: ibid., iv, p. 112.

[29] Ibid., v, p. 101.

[30] Ibid., iv, pp. 181–2; v, p. 1.

[31] Ibid., i, pp. 164, 147.

[32] Against this is the evidence that in 1438, after Langley's death, an enquiry reported that seventeen rectors and vicars in Durham diocese were absent from their benefices: Storey, *Thomas Langley*, p. 186.

or resident on any one of them.[33] Some years earlier the vicar of Kendal had been allowed to take the fruits of the vicarage when residing on another benefice on the grounds of ill-health.[34] Such favours were an inevitable consequence of the increasing frequency with which prominent clerks held more than one parish church simultaneously, but in themselves they were not new. In the fourteenth century episcopal licences to be absent frequently permitted the farming of revenues during absence as well as excusing personal attendance at diocesan synods, and the Avignon papacy too sometimes licensed non-resident clerks to take the fruits of benefices. The actual farming of revenues is poorly documented, however, and its effects on local life are hard to gauge.

The papacy was directly involved in the licensing of non-residence (as opposed to sanctioning pluralism) only rarely, usually if exceptional circumstances rendered the normal procedure inoperative. When in January 1451 Nicholas V dispensed Richard Stephen of York diocese to hold a benefice with cure and be absent for seven years at a university without being promoted beyond the subdiaconate, the clerk in question was under age, and this may explain the papal involvement.[35] The papal licence granted in September 1398 to John Thorp to be absent to study for seven years may have been sought because he held the vicarage of Gringley, and absence by perpetual vicars was rarely sanctioned by bishops.[36] Papal sanction was granted in 1345 to the rector of Brigham so that he could be absent for three further years (beyond the seven he had already had) without first being ordained priest, so as to complete his doctorate in civil law.[37] Even Urban V, who sometimes found that his emphasis on personal residence clashed with his desire for a more highly educated clerical estate, allowed the vicars of

[33] *CPL*, x, pp. 119–20.

[34] Ibid., p. 12.

[35] Ibid., p. 84. In September 1451 he was further dispensed to hold two benefices with cure and exchange them: ibid., p. 102.

[36] *Reg. Scrope*, i, p. 73. Letters of institution to vicars frequently stress the obligation to reside under the constitutions of Otto and Ottobuono. For some examples of vicars being granted leave of absence in the fourteenth century see Barrell, *Papacy*, p. 244.

[37] *CPL*, iii, p. 214.

Clapham and Sutton-on-the-Forest to be absent to study canon law and theology.[38]

Papal involvement was at its most contentious when it was used to the advantage of foreigners or others based at the curia. The number of aliens was closely connected with the number of papal appointments or provisions, because local patronage was rarely used to benefit aliens. Opposition to alien provisors, most notable in the rolls of parliament, was at its most intense in periods of military, economic or political difficulty, such as the 1340s and 1370s, when national consciousness ran strongly against the notion that the pope should endow Frenchmen with the revenues from English benefices. The times of greatest opposition to aliens were not necessarily the periods in which provisions to them were most numerous – the pontificate of John XXII saw many such papal appointments, but relatively little criticism of them – although the feeling against them demonstrates the limits beyond which papal authority could no longer be tolerated.

Not all foreigners were French or Italian. The German Gerlac de Clave successively held the vicarage of Gilling and the churches of St Wilfrid's in York and of Langton; and there is reason to suppose that he lived in England.[39] But most aliens were non-resident, being either based at the papal court or connected with individual pontiffs through kinship or service; many were cardinals, who were effectively exempted from the requirements of constitutions such as *Execrabilis* and so held great collections of benefices. Such benefices were always legally vacant at the curia, and so the pope had the right to fill them almost indefinitely, thereby keeping them away from local nominees. Most were wealthy, which was perhaps inevitable when the incumbent had to pay someone to farm the revenues, even if he did not use those revenues for the upkeep of the benefice. The assessed value of ten benefices in the province of York which were

[38] M–H. Laurent, P. Gasnault, M. Hayez *et al.* (eds), *Urbain V: Lettres Communes* (Ecole française de Rome, Paris and Rome, 1954–86), ii, no. 4994; iii, no. 10561. However, in 1362 the same pope told Hugh de Wymondeswold that it was time to leave university and reside on one of his benefices: *CPP*, p. 386.

[39] BI, Reg. 11, ff. 95, 105, 200. He was ordained subdeacon and deacon in Carlisle diocese in 1356: Cumbria County Record Office, Carlisle, DRC/1/2 (Register of Bishop Welton), pp. 126, 127. For him being German see *CPP*, p. 368.

seized by the crown in 1346 amounted to over £1000, and this is probably a significant underestimate of the true value at the time.[40] The influence of foreigners in the English Church was clearly considerable in financial terms, even if relatively few individuals were involved.

That parliament had a point in objecting to alien provisors is, therefore, apparent; but the number of foreigners in English benefices must not be overstated. Most, moreover, held sinecure prebends rather than parish churches, although rich rectories such as Hemingbrough, Brantingham and Bishop Wearmouth were attractive even to cardinals. Nor was it entirely disadvantageous to have and to cultivate links with members of the Sacred College. The king frequently wrote to cardinals on matters of concern, knowing that they had the ear of the pope, and the fact that for a long period in the fourteenth century successive archdeacons of York were all cardinals may have been not unwelcome to the chapter in that they offered immediate contacts at the Holy See.[41]

The number of aliens declined rapidly after the Great Schism along with the volume of provisions in England generally. A particularly controversial class of absentee was, therefore, removed from the scene. But it is hard to avoid the conclusion that the controls on non-residence and pluralism under the Avignon popes had to some extent broken down by the middle of the fifteenth century. Far more pluralism was authorized, and that implied absenteeism; and even chantries and vicarages were fair game for pluralists. In part, a combination of rising costs and a falling population made it difficult to expect clerks to survive on endowments which had been decreed in a very different economic climate; but the system could clearly be abused, and that is what has given the late medieval Church its bad name. Is the bad name justified? In accordance with an ideal standard of one priest serving one benefice, perhaps; but that is to make a simplistic assessment of a very complex situation. In 1366 Roger de Otery made a spirited and famous defence of pluralism, on the grounds that some clerks could serve several benefices better than others could serve one,[42]

---

[40] Barrell, *Papacy*, p. 140.

[41] Ibid., pp. 94–5.

[42] *Reg. Langham*, p. 44.

and his arrogance must not be allowed to conceal the fact that some ecclesiastics had greater abilities than others. It might be argued that those abilities should have been put to use in parishes rather than in royal or diocesan administration or in universities, but that would be to misunderstand the mentality of the late medieval Church. As an institution with wide, indeed all-embracing, interests in the secular world as well as that of faith, it sanctioned pluralism and non-residence as means whereby those who served it could be rewarded for their efforts, and those who wished to improve their education could do so without undue hardship. It was, and remains, difficult to define the point at which what is expedient becomes morally unjustifiable, because to do so involves a subjective judgement on a practical problem. Historians must be wary of entering so dangerous a minefield.

10

THE CHARACTERISTICS OF THE FIFTEENTH-CENTURY NORTH

A.J. Pollard

In 1969 B.W. Beckingsale published an influential article in which he challenged the notion that the north 'was feudal, that it was Catholic and that it was the home of a violent and backward society'. These characteristics 'were neither so distinctive as to set the north of England apart from the rest of England, nor so marked as to constitute a peculiar regional identity'.[1] Beckingsale's judgement, at least for the Elizabethan England upon which his argument concentrated, has, I believe found general acceptance. Not all have been so convinced about the early Tudor north. Stephen Ellis, for instance, has argued that the extension of central bureaucratic control over the peripheries of the kingdom by the early Tudors was patchy and slow, the growth of law and order retarded, and the Reformation able to make little progress before the 1570s.[2] What then of the fifteenth century, of pre-Tudor England? Was the north before 1485 backward, violent and feudal as well as Catholic?

Before endeavouring to answer this question we need to consider what we mean by the north. While Professor Le Patourel conceded that the north is the nearest we have to a province in England, Professor Dobson has recently suggested that '"the north" is not a meaningful unit for serious historical analysis'.[3] And surely the scepticism is well founded in that generalization about such a large, diverse and ill-defined part of the kingdom of England is

[1] B.W. Beckingsale, 'The Characteristics of the Tudor North', *Northern History*, 4 (1969), 67.

[2] S. Ellis, 'Crown, Community and Government in the English Territories, 1450–1575', *History*, 71 (1986), 191.

[3] J. Le Patourel, 'Is Northern History a Subject?', *Northern History*, 12 (1976), 6–8, 12; R.B. Dobson, 'Politics and the Church in the Fifteenth-Century North', in A.J. Pollard (ed.), *The North in the Age of Richard III* (Stroud, 1996).

unwise, if not impossible. Not only are there significant differences between urban and rural, and lowland and highland, but there is also a fundamental contrast between the far north, the immediate border zones of Cumberland and northern Northumberland, and the counties to the south. This was one of the principal points established by Beckingsale; and it underlies Ellis's discussion of the extension of central government control over the northern borderlands between 1450 and 1475.[4] While it is often remarked that Camden at the end of the sixteenth century noted the peculiar conditions of the border, it is usually forgotten that Piccolimini, who visited Britain in the 1430s, made exactly the same observation in his memoirs in the mid-fifteenth century. The borders, he commented, 'were rude, uncultivated and unvisited by the winter sun'. Yet when he came down to Newcastle he recorded with relief that he had returned to 'a familiar world and a habitable country'.[5] The borders were indeed violent (although not without their own code of law) and 'backward' in the sense that the inhabitants lived a very rough and insecure life, though they were no longer 'feudal' in the sense of being manorialised. No one would now question that the borders have a distinct and different history.[6] This paper is addressed to the rest of the north, the near north as it were.

Yet it is arguable, too, that the history of the central Pennines and lakeland dome is distinct; and that the late-medieval histories of Lancashire to the south of the Ribble and Cheshire share more in common than either do with the

---

[4] Ellis fails to draw a consistent distinction between the borders on which his argument focuses and the north as a whole: Ellis, 'Crown, Community and Government', 190, 193.

[5] Beckingsale, 'Characteristics', 78, 80; A.J. Pollard, *North-Eastern England During the Wars of the Roses* (Oxford, 1992), p. 21.

[6] See A. Goodman, 'The Anglo-Scottish Marches in the Fifteenth Century', in R.A. Mason (ed.), *Scotland and England, 1286–1815* (Edinburgh, 1987); idem, 'Religion and Warfare in the Anglo-Scottish Marches', in Robert Bartlett and Angus MacKay (eds), *Medieval Frontier Societies* (Oxford, 1989); C.J. Neville, 'Border Law in Late-Medieval England', *Journal of Legal History*, 9 (1988); idem, 'Keeping the Peace in the Northern Marches in the Later Middle Ages', *EHR*, (1994); Keith J. Stringer, 'Identities in Thirteenth-Century England: Frontier Society in the Far North', in Claus Bjorn *et al.* (eds), *Social and Political Identities in Western History* (Copenhagen, 1994).

histories of Yorkshire and Durham.[7] The fifteenth-century near north was not one homogeneous province; it was a kaleidoscope of overlapping regions and localities. Indeed, Professor Phythian-Adams has proposed that there were four distinct 'cultural provinces' that constituted England north of the Humber.[8] Despite this, I will propose some generalizations about the fifteenth-century north away from the borders.

First 'backwardness', which has cultural and economic connotations. Backwardness is a problem since it is such a subjective cultural concept. Others are backward in the eyes of we who are advanced. For modern thinkers in the sixteenth century those who had not accepted the new learning, humanism and Protestantism, were backward. And one can see how, particularly in the eyes of those zealous servants of Thomas Cromwell who toured the north in 1535, backwardness was seen on every side. But in the fifteenth century what Layton and his colleagues observed as backwardness was almost up-to-dateness. It has been forcefully argued that the new dynamic, lay-oriented facet of late-medieval spirituality focusing on the concept of the 'mixed life' came out of Yorkshire and that its roots remained there in the fifteenth century. Indeed, it is hardly possible to argue that the vigour displayed in many aspects of Christian life in Lancashire, Yorkshire and Durham displays backwardness.[9] Moreover, if one focuses on the development of education and schooling in the fifteenth century, both Yorkshire and Durham shared in the general expansion of provision, albeit to meet the

[7] For Cumbria, see A.J.L. Winchester, *Landscape and Society in Medieval Cumbria* (Edinburgh, 1987). For the central Pennines, see R.W. Hoyle (ed.), *Early Tudor Craven: Subsidies and Assessments, 1510–1547*, Yorks. Arch. Soc. Record Series, 145 (1987). For Lancashire/Cheshire, see M.J. Bennett, *Community, Class and Careerism: Cheshire and Lancashire Society in the Age of Gawain and the Green Knight* (Cambridge, 1993). For Durham and Yorkshire, see Pollard, *North-Eastern England*.

[8] C. Phythian-Adams, *Societies, Culture and Kinship* (Leicester, 1993), pp. 12–18. See also A.J. Pollard, '"All Maks and Manders": The Local History of the Tees Valley in the Later Middle Ages', *Cleveland History*, 65 (1994), 13–28.

[9] J. Hughes, *Pastors and Visionaries: Religion and Secular Life in Late-Medieval Yorkshire* (Woodbridge, 1988); R.B. Dobson, *'Preserving the Perishable': Contrasting Communities in Medieval England* (Cambridge, 1991); R.N. Swanson, *Catholic England: Faith, Religion and Observance Before the Reformation* (Manchester, 1993); A. Kreider, *English Chantries: the Road to Dissolution* (Cambridge, Mass., 1979); Pollard, *North-Eastern England*, pp. 173–97.

traditional requirement of clerical training.[10] Moreover, in Archbishop George Neville and his circle, the diocese of York even supported one of the fifteenth-century groups that was beginning to show an interest in the new learning.[11] If one looks at its religious culture from a perspective other than Protestant and without foreknowledge of the Reformation, one might even be forgiven for thinking that the near north was in fact at the forefront of advanced ideas.

Well-placed humanists in the early sixteenth century roundly condemned the old chivalric culture of the English nobility. Yet in the second half of the fifteenth century the most vocal criticism of the upper classes, as expressed by such as William Worcestre and William Caxton, was that they were not chivalric enough. In view of the well-documented involvement of a significant number of northerners in the king's wars against both Scotland and France it seems likely that such men might have been exempt.[12] On the other hand, there is little evidence to show that the northern nobility was quick to catch on to the newly fashionable learned chivalry exemplified by the likes of Earl Rivers, the Haute Circle and the Calais group in the later decades of the century. But one suspects that the distinction here is not to be drawn between down-to-earth north and sophisticated south, or Yorkshire and Kent, but between court and country. How well received, one wonders, was learned chivalry in say Devon, or Herefordshire?[13] If the north was slow to pick up

[10] J.A.H. Moran, *The Growth of English Schooling, 1340–1530* (Princeton, NJ, 1985); J.J. Vickerstaff, *A Great Revolutionary Deluge? Education and the Reformation in County Durham,* Teesside Paper in North Eastern History, 2 (1992), pp. 6–22.

[11] R.G. Davies, 'The Church and the Wars of the Roses', in A.J. Pollard (ed.), *The Wars of the Roses* (Basingstoke, 1995), pp. 138–9; G.I. Keir, 'The Ecclesiastical Career of George Neville, 1432–1476' (unpublished B.Litt. thesis, University of Oxford, 1970).

[12] A.B. Ferguson, *The Indian Summer of English Chivalry* (Durham, NC, 1960), pp. 144–53; Pollard, *North-Eastern England,* pp. 207–16; Neil Jamieson, 'The Recruitment of Northerners for Service in English Arms in France, 1415–50', in D.J. Clayton, *et al.* (eds), *Trade, Devotion and Governance: Papers in Later Medieval History* (Stroud, 1994), pp. 102–15.

[13] G. Kipling, *The Triumph of Honour* (Leiden, 1977), pp. 11–30; P.W. Fleming, 'The Hautes and their "Circle": Culture and the English Gentry in the Fifteenth Century', in D. Williams (ed.), *Fifteenth-Century England* (Woodbridge, 1987), pp. 85–102; A.F. Sutton and L. Visser-Fuchs, 'Choosing a Book in Late-Fifteenth-Century England and Burgundy', in C. Barron and N. Saul (eds), *England and the Low Countries in the Later Middle Ages* (Stroud, 1995), p. 82.

humanist influences this was not because it was backward, but because it was provincial.

The northern counties were not economically backward. The economic history of the fifteenth-century north has been much misunderstood. The poverty which struck contemporary observers in the early sixteenth century was not structural or absolute. I have argued elsewhere that the north-east suffered a severe and lasting economic recession in the fifteenth century which left it both absolutely and, as far as contemporary perceptions were concerned, comparatively depressed as south-eastern and south-western economies came out of recession earlier and more quickly. The causes of this decline were multiple; agrarian crisis and rural depopulation led to a reduction in arable production; shortage of circulating coinage curtailed investment and reduced prices; commercial rivalry from London and the Hanse undermined the prosperity of east-coast towns and ports, especially York, and much of its cloth manufacturing; and the bottom fell out of the lead and coal markets. Even so one sector, pastoral farming in the uplands, was buoyant and working people in all walks of life seem to have shared in the rise in the standards of living that characterized England as a whole during the century, especially in its second half. The lowland north suffered a secular economic decline in the fifteenth century. But the prosperity of York and its hinterland at the end of the fourteenth century indicates that the late-medieval north was not structurally an economically backward region.[14]

Was the north, away from the borders, exceptionally violent and lawless? On this question the jury can only return a verdict of not proven. Understanding the effectiveness of law enforcement and the level of violence throughout fifteenth-century England poses intractable evidential and conceptual problems. We have more surviving legal evidence than for earlier centuries, but that evidence is largely of alleged violent crime; violence it has been demonstrated, that was often alleged fictitiously or perpetrated ritualistically so as to ensure a speedier course of

---

[14] A.J. Pollard, 'The North-Eastern Economy and the Agrarian Crisis of 1438–40', *Northern History*, 25 (1989), 88–105; idem, *North-Eastern England*, pp. 30–80, 399–400; R.H. Britnell, 'The Economic Context', in *The Wars of the Roses*, pp. 41–64; J.I. Kermode, 'Merchants, Overseas Trade and Urban Decline', *Northern History*, 23 (1987).

law. Moreover, the use of violence in or out of the law during the fifteenth century was inherent and taken for granted.[15] The records surviving for the northern counties are fewer than elsewhere. What they show is nothing exceptional. The records of the commission of the peace in Durham do not reveal in 1471–3 that the bishopric was riven by violent crime.[16] The King's Bench records for Cumberland, Durham, Lancashire, Northumberland, Westmorland and Yorkshire for 1461–1509 reveal that the level of reported alleged crime that reached the central court was lower for the borders than Yorkshire and lower in the reign of Edward IV than for Henry VII. This could say more about the efficiency of the administration of justice than the level of actual crime; but it plainly gives no reason to support the proposition that the north was more lawless before 1485 than after. There was, however, as in other parts of England, a high level of gentry involvement in violent crime referred to King's Bench.[17] On the other hand many avoided going to law altogether and like their counterparts in more southerly counties resorted to arbitration and informal processes of reconciliation.[18] Fifteenth-century northerners valued social peace as highly as anyone. Moreover, there is nothing to suggest that the level of disorder was any greater than in the marches of Wales and the English counties bordering Wales. Indeed, the most shocking fifteenth-century crime, the murder of Sir Nicholas Radford in1455, took place in Devon; the most notorious gangster of the age, Sir Thomas Malory of Newbold Revel, plagued the Midlands; and the best documented violent lawlessness took place in East Anglia.[19]

Yet, as we are constantly reminded, the fifteenth-century north is renowned for its political disorder and violence; the feud between its leading magnate

---

[15] P.C. Maddern, *Violence and Social Order: East Anglia, 1422–1442* (Oxford, 1992), pp. 1–110; E. Powell, 'Law and Justice', in R. Horrox (ed.), *Fifteenth-Century Attitudes: Perceptions of Society in Late Medieval England* (Cambridge, 1994), pp. 29–41.

[16] Pollard, *North-Eastern England*, pp. 167–9; C.M. Fraser (ed.), *Durham Quarter Session Rolls, 1475–1625*, Surtees Soc., 199 (1991), pp. 39–65.

[17] R.C.E. Hayes, 'Ancient Indictments for the North of England, 1461–1509', in *Age of Richard III.*

[18] See Pollard, *North-Eastern England*, pp. 113–19.

[19] M. Cherry, 'The Struggle for Power in Mid-Fifteenth-Century Devon', in R.A. Griffiths (ed.), *Patronage, the Crown and the Provinces* (Gloucester, 1981), pp. 123–44; P.J.C. Field, *The Life and Times of Sir Thomas Malory* (Brewer, 1993), pp. 96–125.

families, the Nevilles and the Percys; and the ease with which they defied the crown. The north knew no prince but a Percy, or a Neville, or a Dacre, or whoever you care to name. Here we come to its feudalism. Seignorial lordship within the extensive liberties of the north was still significant. Wards and fines were still paid, honourial courts still sat, the sheriffs writ did not run. Mesne lordship retained a social as well as a financial and legal meaning which it had apparently lost further south. To this limited extent it is true to say that the north was still feudal. Moreover, as the heads of old feudal honours the magnates, especially the Nevilles and Percys, tended to be as great a focus of local loyalty as the crown. These two enjoyed the backing of extensive affinities which existed over several generations. Their good lordship created stabilizing social bonds within the districts they dominated. Their leading retainers also dominated royal office holding. And they provided, through their control of the wardenships of the marches, the necessary reserves of military strength in depth to defend the border in times of war. Furthermore, because the crown was territorially weak in parts of the region and its central administration geographically distant, the northern magnates enjoyed greater *de facto* independence than any of their peers elsewhere in England. This, one might say, was the bastard-feudalism of the north.[20]

Nonetheless one must be careful not to exaggerate this 'late-feudal' characteristic of the north. In particular, it would be wrong to see the circumstances that prevailed between, say, 1437 and 1483 as typical. Far from it: there were particular political circumstances that made this half-century highly exceptional. In theory the crown should have been more powerful in the north after 1399 than it had been before; and indeed for a quarter of a century it was. The exercise of royal control over the crown's greater subjects depended on the mystique of monarchy and ingrained respect for and obedience to royal authority, on the skilled handling of personal relationships by the king, and on the effective deployment of the local power. In respect of the last, it might be said that the greater the local resources of the crown in lands and offices, the greater the opportunity it had to enforce its rule through its own personal

[20] Pollard, *North-Eastern England*, pp. 400–2.

servants. Before 1399 the royal presence in the north was weak. The crown held Carlisle, but only Bamburgh and Newcastle in Northumberland, little in Yorkshire beyond York Castle and Scarborough and nothing in Lancashire. Its greatest asset was the bishopric of Durham, which included the far north of Northumberland (Norham and Holy Island) as well as the land between Tyne and Tees. Throughout the fourteenth century, kings made sure that they appointed their trusted and able agents to this strategically vital see. Constitutionally the greatest feudal liberty in the kingdom it might have been, but politically it was in practice an arm of the crown.[21]

The Lancastrian usurpation extended the direct royal presence in the north, not only in Lancashire itself, but also in Yorkshire where four great honours were reunited with the crown. After 1405 the north was not a problem for Henry IV or Henry V. The great Lancastrian affinity, whose leading member was Ralph Neville, earl of Westmorland, exercised the royal will in Lancashire, Yorkshire, Westmorland and Cumberland; Bishop Langley did so in Durham. Yet again it is the unfortunate Henry VI who can be seen to be largely at fault in allowing this control to slip from royal hands and into those of the grasping Nevilles, especially Richard, earl of Salisbury. Not only did Henry VI allow Salisbury to annex the greater part of the duchy of Lancaster in Yorkshire, but he also in 1437 committed the extraordinary blunder of handing him, through the person of his brother Robert, the bishopric of Durham.[22] That the crown lost control of the north in the fifteenth century had less to do with its feudal character than with the political folly of a particular king.[23] And what Henry VI allowed to happen, Edward IV was unable, or disinclined to undo. It was left to Richard III to begin the process of restoring royal control, taken further by the early Tudors, by the old and tried methods of deploying the royal affinity in

[21] R.B. Dobson, 'The Church of Durham and the Scottish Borders, 1378–88', in A. Tuck and A. Goodman (eds), *War and Border Societies in the Middle Ages* (London, 1992), pp. 129–31.

[22] See A.J. Pollard, 'The Crown and the County Palatine of Durham, 1437–1494', in *Age of Richard III*.

[23] Musgrove's image of the golden age of the north under Richard of Gloucester takes no account of the failure of Edward IV to assert the potential power of the crown there: *The North of England: A History from Roman Times to the Present* (Oxford, 1990), pp. 155–82.

strength, now supported by a larger crown estate, and using the bishopric of Durham once again as an extension of the central administration.[24]

To describe even the near north in the fifteenth century as backward, violent and feudal does little to provide the basis for meaningful historical analysis. Yet the notion that there was, and still is, a distinctive difference between the north and the south in our history is still very marked. Recently it has been given new life by Dr Jewell.[25] It becomes apparent as one reads Jewell's book that relatively little is known about a distinctive northern consciousness, although there is a wealth of material, going back many centuries, demonstrating a southern consciousness of an alien north. We know what that is. The north was unstable, barbaric and threatening, backward and violent; by the mid-sixteenth century it was feudal and Catholic as well. This is not telling us about the north as it ever was, but of how the southern English conceptualized northernness.

This frightening north was a cultural construct, a state of mind. The north of England was always a vague location for those who lived in and around London and the court. Chaucer's two Cambridge students in the Reeve's Tale were northerners, who spoke with northern accents, swore by St Cuthbert and were born in 'Strother', 'far in the north, I cannot tell you where'.[26] Chaucer seems to have been familiar with northerners, but for his audience there was no need to be specific about somewhere so distant. In literary convention the north was somewhere largely unknown, a long way away when one travelled with one's back to the sun. Of course, one's sense of what was north and what was south depended much upon where one stood. As far as the authorities of the University of Oxford were concerned, who for disciplinary reasons divided their students into northern and southern nations, the north began once one crossed the River Nene. And for them, both English and Scottish students were as alike

---

[24] Pollard, *North-Eastern England*, pp. 355–61, 383–92, 403–4. For a different interpretation, see Helen M. Jewell, *The North–South Divide: The Origins of Northern Consciousness in England* (Manchester, 1994), pp. 5, 57.

[25] See note 24.

[26] G. Chaucer, *The Canterbury Tales*, translated by Nevill Coghill (Harmondsworth, 1958), pp. 125–35.

northern.[27] From Northumberland it looked different. In 1429 disruption of the
peace was equated with disruption of the peace of the north, which was to be
restored by the banishment of John Manners to the south. And so he was
ordered to live no nearer than York.[28]

The lack of consensus about where the boundary between north and south
lay did not prevent the formation of a powerful stereotype about northernness.
The characteristics conventionally attributed to the northerner by the
southerner, hard, cruel, violent, have their roots deep in Christian-Judaic
traditions. There is biblical authority that 'Out of the north an evil shall break
forth upon all inhabitants of the land'; a prophesy which seemed to be fulfilled
by the Viking descents on Northumbria.[29] It was assimilated into the
conventional medieval stereotype, expressed in the fourteenth century in
Trevisa's translation of Higden as, 'the men of the south be easier and more
mild; the men of the north be more unstable, more cruel and more uneasy'.[30] It
is repeated, in the famous statement of the Crowland continuator in 1486 that
all evil spreads from the north and taken up by Polydore Vergil and Hall in the
sixteenth century.[31] Significantly too, a Northumbrian, John Hardyng, held
exactly the same attitude towards those who lived to the north of him, the Scots:
of whom he declared 'scripture saith of the north all evil is showed'.[32] On to this
long tradition were grafted in the sixteenth century the prejudices of the
Protestant humanists who took command of the government of the kingdom
and the education of its subjects.

Even in the fifteenth century the portrayal of the 'north' as savage and unruly
was far more of a literary convention than a reliable contemporary description
of the character of the province. It was given credence by what was known of
the borderers and their life-style. Indeed, one could go as far as to say that

[27] J. Catto, *A History of the University of Oxford: I. The Early Schools* (Oxford, 1984), pp. 64, 186; A.B.
Cobban, *The Medieval English Universities* (Oxford, 1988), pp. 103–6.

[28] Dobson, 'Politics and the Church'.

[29] Jeremiah, I: 14.

[30] C. Babington (ed.), *Polychronicon Ranulphi Higden Monachi Cestrensis* (London, 1869), ii, pp. 166–7.

[31] N. Pronay and J. Cox (eds), *Crowland Chronicle Continuations, 1459–1486* (Richard III and Yorkist
History Trust, 1986), p. 191.

[32] H. Ellis (ed.), *The Chronicle of John Hardyng* (London, 1812), p. 420.

reports of the borders and the borderers were extended into a sweeping exaggeration of the north as a whole. But fear of the highland thieves was not restricted to the conventional south. Their occasional forays into Tyneside gave everyone south of the borders sleepless nights.[33] And the fear of the savage and unruly folk of the north was inflamed by propaganda and fed by rumour in the great hysteria of 1461 and again after 1485.[34]

Yet this 'literary locale' was also a place of adventure and freedom, a place where these same violent and unruly men resisted corrupt authority and dispensed true justice.[35] It is no coincidence that the great ballad sequences created in the later Middle Ages and set down in the fifteenth century celebrate the north as an imagined setting for escape from and defiance of government. Whether it is Robin Hood in Barnsdale, or Adam Bell in Inglewood, or the feats of Hotspur and Douglas in the Cheviots, northern forests provide the context for stories celebrating the violent but cleansing lives of bandits, outlaws, cattle rustlers and chivalric heroes who 'did their own thing'.[36] Here, for southern audiences in particular, was a world safely distant and not to be experienced first-hand, but sufficiently founded in reliable report, to create an illusion of reality. For the savage north in fifteenth-century England read the Wild West in nineteenth-century America.

Fifteenth-century ballad literature provides no more reliable evidence of the 'real' north in the fifteenth century than does the ballad of Jesse James provide reliable evidence of the 'real' American west.[37] But the experienced world and the ballad world undeniably coexisted; one the actuality of the life of those who lived in the northern counties; the other a construct of the north that satisfied

[33] H.E. Craster, *A History of Northumberland: VIII. The Parish of Tynemouth* (Newcastle upon Tyne, 1907), p. 291; R.A. Griffiths, *The Reign of Henry VI* (London, 1981), p. 578.

[34] Pollard, *North-Eastern England*, pp. 25–7.

[35] C.F. Richmond, 'An Outlaw and Some Peasants: The Possible Significance of Robin Hood', *Nottingham Medieval Studies*, 37 (1993), 91. See also S. Knight, *Robin Hood: A Complete Study of the English Outlaw* (Oxford, 1994), pp. 44–81 for the latest discussion of the early ballads.

[36] Summerson, *Carlisle*, ii, pp. 432–4; J. Reed, *The Border Ballads* (Stocksfield, 1991), pp. 124–35; idem, 'The Ballad and the Source', in *War and Border Societies*, pp. 94–123.

[37] R.B. Dobson and J. Taylor, *Rymes of Robin Hood* (Oxford, 1976), pp. 11, 278–80.

certain fantasies of those who lived elsewhere. The coexistence is illustrated by
the confession of an approver before the court of King's Bench in 1471. Alan
Grenesyde, identifying himself as either a hosier or hosteler, resident variously
in Middlesex, Holborn, Westminster, or Surrey informed the coroner John West
that on 25 March 1463 he had with William Bowster, late of Newcastle, pedlar,
robbed an unknown man at Chesterdene in the bishopric of Durham of £300
and two horses; that on 9 September 1466, with John Rogers of Benwell in
Northumberland, franklin, he had lain in ambush in the forest of Barnsdale at
Wentbridge in Yorkshire and robbed William Jackson, a jeweller, of £20 in cash
and goods to the value of £60; and that two years later, on 1 August 1468, with
William Welles of Wheteslade in Northumberland he had on the royal highway
outside Romford on the way to London robbed a monk of Bury St Edmunds of
£100 and later on the same day relieved a merchant of Lynn of £600.[38]

This short but profitable career of highway robbery is doubly instructive.
First, one may note the uncanny way in which it reflects the fictional exploits of
Robin Hood, at that very time being set down in writing and being performed
in plays before gentry families like the Pastons. The exploits of Robin Hood,
even though in ballad they were performed in a safely distant, perpetually
spring-time northern forest, were nevertheless in life all-too close encounters,
met on the open road not far from London. Secondly, this contemporary Robin
Hood was a Londoner, a Buster Edwards of his day, who by his own confession
ranged from Durham to Essex, while his accomplices were on every occasion
Tynesiders. This was not crime committed by northerners on southerners, but
in each case a partnership of a northerner and southerner robbing both
northerners and southerners indiscriminately, north and south. Does it not
suggest, notwithstanding the concurrent construct of a north–south divide in
fifteenth-century England, that there is a different scenario? If Cockneys and
Geordies could commit crime in partnership roaming up and down the Great
North Road, they surely were capable of amicably collaborating in all manner
of other transactions, legitimate as well as illegitimate.[39]

[38] PRO, K.B. 9/992, m. 95. I am grateful to Rosemary Hayes for supplying a transcript of this
record.

[39] Pollard, *North-Eastern England*, pp. 22–7, for other examples of day-to-day business between
northerners and southerners.

There is therefore another characteristic of the fifteenth-century north: the idea of the 'north' itself as a contemporary myth. The imagined north of the fifteenth century was portrayed in fiction, propaganda and history as backward, violent and feudal; characteristics which were approved in fiction but condemned in propaganda, and were accepted unquestioningly by historians until more modern times. While the near north of the fifteenth century, with all its different worlds and particular religious, economic, social and political histories, was in fact no more backward, violent or feudal than the rest of England, contemporary perceptions of northernness endowed it with these characteristics. The north had northernness thrust upon it. In this respect the fifteenth-century north was the invention of the fifteenth century. That, perhaps, is its most important characteristic of all.

11

NEW BROOMS IN EARLY TUDOR CHESTER?

Jenny Kermode

In 1539–40, during the second mayoralty of Henry Gee, Chester city council began the regular recording of its ordinances in an Assembly Minute Book.[1] Chester had not been without records before this; after all one requirement for an active entrepot was the provision of financial services supported by a reliable court of record and Chester had its Pentice, Portmoot and Crownmoot courts, but the Assembly Book provides a more focused and regular account of the decisions of the city's governing body.[2] The impression conveyed by the first eighty or so folios of the book is of an assertive administration, restating its claim to be a long-established and independent constitutional body. The book conveys a powerful impression of the arrival of a new management. It includes records covering all manner of civic business, some pre-dating the commencement of the book, others in roughly chronological order. This remarkable series of assembly orders addressed among others, the conduct and dress of women, begging, children's education, and the influence of country gentlemen in civic matters.[3] However, the dating of the Assembly Book poses certain difficulties. It has been suggested that it was not copied in its present form before 1567–8 and that the prefatory material of eighty or so folios, may have been added by the copyist or perhaps even

[1] I am grateful to Nick Alldridge, Claire Cross, Janet Hollinshead, Colin Phillips, Tony Pollard, Mike Power and Alan Thacker for suggestions and comments.

[2] Chester's government is discussed by Kevin Wilson, 'Political Organization in the Sixteenth-Century Town', Unit 6 of *English Urban History 1500–1780* (Open University, 1977); A.M. Kennett, *Archives and Records of the City of Chester. A Guide to the Collections in the Chester City Record Office* (Council of the City of Chester, 1985); *VCH Chester* (forthcoming).

[3] Chester C[ity] R[ecord] O[ffice], AB 1, ff. 58–62, 69v–72v.

compiled by him.[4] We cannot be certain if entries were copied in from loose sheets, or from an earlier memorandum book, or if they were inserted during some later editing.[5]

The language of the first Assembly Book is strikingly different in tone from many other towns' records, in that it is suffused with the rhetoric of moral reform. It might be excessive to see Chester at this time as an example of an emerging self-conscious, godly commonwealth of developed Protestant thinking, or even as the sort of town where, 'there was a protestant constituency, the nucleus of an audience' (for radical preachers). Although Protestant reformers have been identified in several Kentish towns in the 1520s and '30s,[6] the evidence for Chester is less clear-cut and reflects more of the fluid ambiguities of the contemporary debate, before ideologies began to coalesce in Edward VI's reign. Social ethics and moral reform were central issues for Catholic, humanist and early Protestant thinkers and ascribing particular reforming ideas to any single group obscures their common ground. For instance, the 'work ethic' is generally associated with Protestant ideology but late-medieval social ethics also equated idleness with loose living. A telling example is the justification given by Sir John Percevale for the founding of his grammar school in Macclesfield in 1503: 'many Children for lak of such techyny and draught, in conying fall to Idleness And so consequently live disolately all their daies'.[7]

---

[4] L.M. Clopper, *Records of Early English Drama: Chester* (Toronto, 1979), p. xii; D. Mills, 'Chester Ceremonial: Re-creation and Recreation in the English "Medieval" Town', *Urban History Yearbook 1991*, 4–5.

[5] For example, there are on folio 43 two inserted entries in a later hand dated 1569; on folio 50 the explicit statement 'Here after ensuyth dyuers notable thinges to be had in memorie and xpedyant compendyously writen and lately set furthe by the right worshipfull William Bexwyk mayre [1542] . . . most dylygently by hym shereshed to be used and frequented within this citie.'

[6] P. Collinson, *The Birthpangs of Protestant England: Religious and Cultural Change in the Sixteenth and Seventeenth Centuries* (London, 1988), pp. 37, 55; P. Clark, 'Reformation and Radicalism in Kentish Towns c. 1500–1553', in W.J. Mommsen (ed.), *The Urban Classes, the Nobility and the Reformation. Studies on the Social History of the Reformation in England and Germany* (Stuttgart, 1979), pp. 107–27.

[7] Quoted in C. Richmond, 'The English Gentry and Religion, c. 1500', in C. Harper-Bill (ed.), *Religious Belief and Ecclesiastical Careers in Late Medieval England* (Woodbridge, 1991), p. 126. I am grateful to Tony Pollard for this reference.

Although direct evidence of personal religious attitudes in Chester is sparse, the reforming ideology of the council, or at least of some of its members, is visible in its records. It was during the mayoralties of Henry Gee that the most thorough reforms appear to have been introduced. According to the retrospectively enrolled entries in the Assembly Book, Gee's first mayoralty in 1533–4 was marked by a determined effort to invest the city's government with a proper sense of dignity and order, and his energetic commitment to improve the quality of government and moral tone of the city had a profound and long-lasting impact. Of course, the extent to which Gee reflected only his own views or those of a wider consensus is problematic. If the Assembly Book was first compiled in 1567–8, eighteen or so years after his death, it is possible that Gee was given a retrospective prominence to bolster the reforming case in disputes over the mystery plays. Gee's son-in-law, Henry Hardware, was described by a local chronicler as 'a godly, over-zealous man', and as mayor in 1559–60 and 1575–6, was intervening in the production of the plays.[8]

Perhaps we can take Gee to personify a growing element in the Chester oligarchy, a group whose composition was changing in response to a major transformation of the city's economic fortunes. The port was enjoying boom conditions, extending the range of its trading partners, drawing increasing Cestrian investment into overseas trade and attracting growing numbers of migrants.[9] As the capital of the palatinate and of the new diocese from 1541 Chester had a regular influx of county gentry and bureaucrats.[10] The social topography included houses of senior gentry families

[8] The plays had become closely associated with the mayoralty. Christopher Goodman, the local Puritan divine, was arguing for their suppression in 1572: D. Mills, 'The Chester Mystery Plays: Truth and Tradition', in D. Dunn (ed.), *Courts, Counties and the Capital* (forthcoming, 1996); Clopper, *English Drama*, pp. 104–5, 109–10, 184, 197–9, 234–8; Collinson, *Protestant Birthpangs*, p. 101.

[9] N.J. Alldridge, 'The Mechanics of Decline: Immigration and Economy in Early Modern Chester', in M. Reed (ed.), *English Towns in Decline 1350–1800*, Centre for Urban History (Leicester, 1986); J.I. Kermode, 'The Trade of Chester, 1480–1550,' in R.H. Britnell and J. Hatcher (eds), *Progress and Problems in Medieval England* (Cambridge, 1996) pp. 286–307.

[10] D.J. Clayton, *The Administration of the County Palatine of Chester, 1442–85*, Chetham Soc. 3rd ser., 35 (1990), pp. 132–7, 230–1, 226, 241–60; T. Thornton, 'Political Society in Early Tudor Cheshire 1480–1560' (unpublished D.Phil. thesis, University of Oxford, 1994), pp. 30–3, 118–288; *VCH Cheshire*, ii, pp. 35–8.

such as the Breretons, Savages and Stanleys,[11] and the interweaving of mercantile and gentry connections gave the city's elite a hybrid quality.

As in other late-medieval towns, membership of the ruling circle and the pattern of office-holding reflected economic rather than numerical superiority. In Chester we can chart the emergence of a dominant group active in overseas trade. Some came from old families, others were new to the city. Whatever their formal occupational identity, increasingly office holders and common councillors invested in Chester's expanding continental trade.[12] The circulation of office was fairly limited and does not suggest an expanding oligarchy of ambitious newcomers. Alongside overseas traders, members of old landed county families such as the Alderseys, Davenports, and Duttons held civic office. The Aldersey family, seated at Aldersey and Spurstowe in East Cheshire, provided five office holders between 1500 and 1550.

Just as there was no hard and fast separation between trade and county interests within the council, so there was not always a sharp separation of business interests among the traders. Townsfolk owning rural property were quite common, but in Chester, the nature and size of rural estates reflected an active interest in agriculture. Several overseas merchants had sizeable country estates and farms, and others were members of established gentry families. It is difficult to tell which way investment flowed between trade and real estate, but some property was probably inherited rather than newly acquired. Ralph and William Aldersey both owned farms, as did Ralph Bostock. The Alderseys invested in overseas trade, importing wine and iron and exporting hides.[13] Henry Hardware left arable land and water mills, houses in the city, and twenty-two tons of Spanish iron in his cellar: Richard Massy, cattle, corn and farming implements, as well as current ventures in three different ships.[14]

---

[11] Chester CRO, AB 1, ff. 37v–40, 53–8.

[12] K.P. Wilson, 'The Port of Chester in the Later Middle Ages' (unpublished Ph.D. thesis, University of Liverpool, 1965), p. 162; Chester CRO, MB 8, ff. 10–11; 12, ff. 73v, 76; 13, ff. 221–4; 14, f. 3.

[13] Chesh. R[ecord] O[ffice], WS 5/1; *Cheshire Sheaf*, 11 (1914), pp. 1–2; idem, 17 (1920), p. 30. See also Chesh. RO, WS6/3, 4, 7; 8/1, 3; W. Fergusson Irvine (ed.), *Lancashire and Cheshire Wills*, Rec. Soc. of Lancs. and Chesh., 30 (1896), pp. 189–90.

[14] G.J. Piccope (ed.), *Lancashire and Cheshire Wills and Inventories, III*, Chetham Soc., 54 (1861), pp. 26–30; Chesh. RO, WS6/7.

Henry Gee personified many of these characteristics. He was an *arriviste* merchant, probably a migrant to the city from Manchester, who achieved remarkably rapid civic promotion; becoming a freeman in 1526, sheriff the following year, and mayor in 1533. His main trading investment between 1527–31 was in Spanish iron averaging eight voyages a year.[15] In 1545, he left cattle and corn, a farm and mill in Little Molesworth and his recently acquired interest in Manley manor.[16] Ralph Aldersey, on the other hand, came from an established gentry family and exemplifies the closely interwoven county and city relationships characteristic of the city at this time. He died in 1551, the merchant son of Richard Aldersey of Picton,[17] and father of William, mayor of Chester in 1614. Ralph's cousins included the Spurstow and Aldersey Alderseys and William Hockenhull, gentleman of Preston. His sons-in-law included Roger Glegg of the influential Wirral family, and William Dod, a Chester shipowner. Three Chester merchants: Dod, Fulk Aldersey and Thomas Bellyn witnessed Hockenhull's will in 1567, Bellyn having witnessed Ralph Aldersey's in 1553. Ralph was also a tenant of the powerful local magnate, Sir William Brereton.[18]

Another example of an influential city–county network was extended through the marriages of the daughters of Fulk Dutton, a draper and three times mayor of Chester. Elizabeth married John Legh, stepson of Sir William Savage of Macclesfield; Grace, a successful Chester merchant William Davenport; and Anne's second husband was Edward Hassell, son of the recorder of Liverpool. Fulk Dutton left money to his cousin Thomas Egerton and made a group of influential county men overseers of his will; Sir Philip Egerton, and William Gerrard esquire, recorder of Chester and chief clerk to the Council in the Welsh Marches.[19] Perhaps

---

[15] K.P. Wilson (ed.), *Chester Customs Accounts 1301–1566*, Rec. Soc. of Lancs. and Chesh., 111 (1969), pp. 48–55, 64.

[16] Chesh. RO, EDA 2/1, ff. 188–9; *Lancs. and Chesh. Wills, III*, p. 159.

[17] G. Ormerod, *The History of the County Palatine and City of Chester*, revised by T. Helsby (2nd edn., London, 1882), iii, pp. 739–40; Wilson, 'Port of Chester', pp. 163–4.

[18] *39th Dep. Keepers Rep.*, p. 3; Chesh. RO, WS 5/1.

[19] Chesh. RO, WS8/1; Ormerod, *History of the County Palatine*, i, p. 87; ii, p. 202; iii, p. 374; G.J. Piccope (ed.), *Lancashire and Cheshire Wills and Inventories, II*, Chetham Soc., 51 (1860), pp. 93, 214.

it was this sort of intermingling that gave rise to Gee's accusations of country interference in civic elections.

The impression this evidence provides is of a ruling group neither wholly entrepreneurial nor fiercely gentry in complexion. Rather it embraced incomers as well as men from established county families, some investing in trade, others also retaining agricultural property and rural associations, drawing in new blood through marriage and business.

It was this group which agreed to the regulations enrolled in the Assembly Book and ascribed to Gee's mayoralties (1533–4, 1539–40), articulating a number of priorities which were unmistakably reforming if not Protestant. Attention was given to godly behaviour, good citizenship and personal conduct, and an emphasis on the common weal and responsible government. We cannot be sure, of course, but it is likely that Gee's personal ideology lay behind this reforming legislation and the phrasing of one particular order for 1539 is wonderfully transparent. 'For as moche as the wretched life of ociositie or idleness is the rote of all vices and engendreth slouth, pouertie, myserie, and other inconuenienties as voluptuosite and all other vayne thinges sleynge the bodye, wasting good dedes, and letting vertue and goodness, to prosede whereunto youth and tender age by course of nature dothe enclyne and obeye unles some grace otherwyse be sent from aboue or els the vse and exercise of busynes in learning good and vertuus leuing. Therefore and in advoydinge of the same wreched lyfe of ociosite and to set fourth the good and vertuus of working, learning, and doing goodnes, it is ordred by the right worshipful Henry Gee, mayre, that . . .' No children of six and over were to be idle on a work day but should attend school or learn a 'virtuous' craft.[20]

Some local regulations were responses to national legislation, but Gee's concerns were more ambitious and intrusive. From 1539 no women aged between fourteen and forty were allowed to serve ale because it 'creates

---

[20] Chester CRO, AB 1, f. 62; R.H. Morris, *Chester in the Plantagenet and Tudor Reigns* (Chester, 1894), pp. 337–42. In Exeter the council promoted a 'godly education' for apprentices in 1559: W.T. MacCaffrey, *Exeter, 1540–1640. The Growth of an English County Town* (2nd edn, Cambridge, Mass., 1975), pp. 92–3.

slanderous rumours about Chester', and women were forbidden to wear caps or hats, except when riding or walking in the fields, or for health reasons. One justification was that the cost of such fripperies was 'ageynest the comon welthe of this citie'.[21] Women attracted disproportionate attention from Gee. Regulations passed in 1539–40 curtailed parties accompanying childbirth and the churching of women, to avoid 'superfluous costs'. Other regulations were more prosaic: controlling prices, markets and legitimate beggars.[22]

Some of the targets of Gee's reforms could be found earlier in other towns. Although there is no evidence that Chester's finances were particularly weak, the sale of common lands was banned in 1539 to protect the city's rent income.[23] Other regulations required that the whole council be consulted about expenditure, that only honest men should be allowed in the city's exchequer and then only when accompanied by a sheriff.[24] Another familiar theme was the need to attract able men into government while preventing corrupt patronage and prevent 'gentlemen's servants of the county being preferred to the offices and rooms [of the city]'.[25]

This was a tenacious problem, recurring after Gee's time in office. An order of 1546 spoke of 'sinsistre labour for the appointement of an unmete person' and the need for those so labouring to 'preferre their dieuties to the king and the common wealth of their Citie before theire owne fantasies'.[26] By 1549–50, there was some difficulty in attracting 'suitable' candidates for office, and it was claimed that men 'of lasse habylytie, substaunce, and not so apte nor mete to be electid and chosyn' had indeed been chosen. Heavy fines for evading election to office were introduced, and a clear statement of civic responsibility, was directed

---

[21] Chester CRO, AB 1, ff. 70, 72v. Chester's ale-wives already enjoyed notoriety for their role in 'The Harrowing of Hell' pageant in the Chester Mystery Plays and continued to attract criticism from Chester's pulpits later in the century: Mills, 'Truth and Tradition'.

[22] Chester CRO, AB 1, ff. 6–1, 64v–5, 70v–9, 85v, 87, 91; Morris, *Chester*, pp. 335–6, 397, 399–400.

[23] From the few extant treasurers' rolls for this period, the city appears to have been in surplus. Chester CRO, TAR 1, 7–8; S. Reynolds, *An Introduction to the History of English Medieval Towns* (Oxford, 1977), pp. 176, 178 for other towns.

[24] Chester CRO, AB 1, ff. 68v, 70, 74v.

[25] Ibid., ff. 58–9, 69v–70, 79v.

[26] Ibid, ff. 78, 85; *Acts of the Privy Council*, i, p. 448.

at 'summe persons which have coum and enquyesyd to grete aboundauntes of ryches by ther abode in the same cyte and by reason that they were partakers of this libertiez and fraunchez vnto the said cytye belongyng'. It was the duty of government 'to keep the laws of god' as well as of the king.[27] The message was clear: good government and responsible citizenship required men to contribute and not to exploit the advantages of their freedom for selfish profit.

Once elected, men were expected to conduct themselves in a manner which attested to their fitness for civic office. Ceremonial display reinforced civic authority,[28] and the status of rulers was consolidated by their public behaviour. In 1549 members of the common council were reminded to wear their tippets, and the aldermen their scarlet robes on eight popular holy days 'for the worship of their office'.[29]

Picking out the regulations from one man's terms of office perhaps affords him undue credit. Doubtless some of these reforms were underway before Gee's term as mayor in 1533 and later assemblies endorsed some by repeating and refining them. But Gee's name continued to be associated with good government long after his time in office, and during the reigns and changing religious ideologies of three monarchs. In 1556–7, during Mary's reign and the mayoralty of a mercer, John Webster, the assembly referred to the 'good ordynaunces' of Henry Gee's time and repeated those controlling the sale of corn. A regulation, probably issued that year, would certainly have enjoyed Gee's approval: 'Whereas heretofore of late tyme yt hathe been vsed that diuerse of the worshipfull of this cytie haue caused breckfastes to be made in ther houses vpon Christenmasdaie in the mornyng before dyvyne seruice endyd, by reasone wherof manye dysorderid persons haue vsed them selues rayther all the days after idellie in vyse and wantonnes then yeuen them selues holy to contemplacion and prayre the same sacryt holye and prynsepaule feaste

---

[27] Chester CRO, AB 1, ff. 80, 83: quotation at f. 80r. Coupling God and the king in this way was common among evangelicals: M. Dowling, 'The Gospel and the Court: Reformation under Henry VIII', in M. Dowling and P. Lake (eds), *Protestantism and the National Church in Sixteenth-Century England* (London, 1987), p. 44.

[28] Mills, 'Chester Ceremonial', 4–5; idem, 'Truth and Tradition'.

[29] Chester CRO, AB 1, ff. 74v, 79v–81, 83, 85–6, 92.

according to ther most bounden dutye vnto God the Sone, redemer of the
worlds, who as that daye came into this worlde and was borne of our blessed
Virgyn Marye for the redemption of all mankynd, and to the intent the same
feste maye be better and more hollier kept according to thorder of God and his
Holy Churche, Master mayre, by the advyse of his worshipful brethern
thalderman of this cytie, haue thought good that those breckefastes . . . shall not
be vsed and kept herafter. yeuen them selues holy to contemplacion and
prayre.'[30] The council had been discouraging such festivities for at least a
decade,[31] and although the association of drinking and gaming with disruptive
behaviour inevitably gave local councils the colour of 'Puritan' attitudes as they
reiterated orders controlling the sale and consumption of alcohol,[32] the
language of this order is an unambiguous expression of the piety and religious
beliefs of Chester's government.

Where did such attitudes come from and what other evidence is there of
reforming sympathies in Chester at this time? This was a period of intense
debate among contemporary theologians: humanists, evangelicals and Catholic
reformers used a similar language of social reform. Some of the issues addressed
in Chester echoed Sir Thomas More's *Utopia*[33] and Christopher St German's
1531 parliamentary bill proposing social reform.[34] The extent to which any of
these arguments percolated downwards and enjoyed wider discussion, is
contentious. There were Lutherans in Lancashire in the 1520s and an itinerant
preacher, expressing ideas similar to More's, in Lancashire and Cheshire in the

---

[30] Chester CRO, AB 1, ff. 87–8; Morris, *Chester*, pp. 336–7. Other regulations were against
unlawful gaming and mumming.

[31] See, for example, Chester CRO, MB 15, f. 23v (1546).

[32] Morris, *Chester*, pp. 426–8. The picture was complicated in Chester where merchant oligarchs,
including Hugh and Robert Aldersey, William Davison, William Goodman and David Middleton,
were said to own taverns in 1533: *LP*, vi, no. 202.

[33] More inveighed against gaming and gambling, forestallers and engrossers, displays of luxury
and excesses in dress. His remedies included learning skills, a literary education and the
requirement that everyone should work, though for no more than six hours each day: J. O'Hagan
(ed.), *Utopia with The Dialogue of Comfort by Sir Thomas More* (London, 1910), pp. 25–6, 56–7, 59,
69–70, 112.

[34] A. Fox and J. Guy (eds), *Reassessing the Henrician Age* (Oxford, 1986), p. 17; J. Guy, *Christopher St.
German on Chancery and Statute*, Selden Soc., Supplementary Ser., 6 (1985), pp. 127–35.

1530s.[35] Texts were distributed widely though, and might have been available in the regions, although *Utopia* was not published in English until 1551. The library of at least one Cheshire gentleman included a copy of the New Testament, a Lollard text, and Erasmus's *Enchiridion* in 1557.[36]

Across the country the response of individual towns to religious changes was mixed.[37] Divisions were common and in Chester the succession of liturgical requirements which marked the course of Protestant reform and Catholic restitution had a mixed passage in the city's churches, with St Oswald's jettisoning the appurtenances of Catholic worship in 1538 but Holy Trinity retaining them until 1549. More obviously conservative were the earliest bishops of the new Chester diocese and the strong continuity within the personnel of the abbey and new cathedral of St Werburgh. Three local men (including a Chester merchant, John Hall), had been imprisoned in 1536 for their support of the Pilgrimage of Grace.[38] During Mary's reign, few heretics were uncovered in Cheshire and the single Cheshire martyr, George Marsh, came from near Manchester. His execution at Chester was an administrative convenience.[39]

Religious affiliation is difficult to identify within the ruling group; scarcely any of their wills survive. Those of Henry Gee and his son-in-law, Henry Hardware, express clear statements of Protestant faith.[40] In 1545 Gee commended his soul to 'Christ Jesue my maker and redeemer . . . in whos blessed passion is all my

---

[35] C. Haigh, *Reformation and Resistance in Tudor Lancashire* (Cambridge, 1975), pp. 82, 111.

[36] W.E.A. Axon, 'The Library of Richard Brereton of Ley, 1557', *Trans. of the Lancs. and Cheshire Antiq. Soc.*, 11 (1893), 110–11. I owe this reference to Colin Phillips.

[37] D.M. Palliser, 'Popular Reactions to the Reformation During the Years of Uncertainty 1530–70', in C. Haigh (ed.), *The English Reformation Revised* (Cambridge, 1987), pp. 94–113, esp. 105–8; R. Hutton, 'The Local Impact of the Tudor Reformations', in ibid., pp. 114–38.

[38] Ormerod, *History of the County Palatine*, i, p. 522. In Holy Trinity the Prayer Book services were being read quickly, to sound like the Latin mass, according to one observer in 1562: C. Haigh, *English Reformations. Religion, Politics and Society under the Tudors* (Oxford, 1993), p. 248; *VCH Chester* (forthcoming).

[39] Haigh, *Reformation and Resistance*, pp. 43, 183–5.

[40] The phrasing of each of these wills is so distinctive within the local 'pattern' that we are probably justified in accepting them as expressing individual sentiments. For a discussion of the problems of interpretation, see J.D. Alsop, 'Religious Preambles in Early Modern English Wills as Formulae', *Journal of Ecclesiastical History*, 40 (1989), 19–27.

whole trust', and in 1582, Hardware hoped 'eternallie as one of Gods elect to lyve and raigne in heaven'. Alderman William Davison left money for a mass vestment in 1543.[41] However, of the remaining dozen or so wills extant for the period 1520–60, most preambles were generally non-comittal or ambivalent.[42] There is other evidence which suggests Protestant sympathies within the ruling group.[43] The famous Nonconformist, Christopher Goodman, was a member of the Chester Goodman family. He went up to Brasenose College c. 1536, became an associate of John Knox, and spent time in Geneva and Scotland before returning to England in 1565. Another Brasenose fellow, John Leche, was probably a relation of the Chester drapers, and Matthew Smyth of King's Hall and Brasenose, became a city property owner in 1546–7.[44]

Prominent Cestrians[45] were appointed commissioners to survey monastic lands, chosen by Sir Piers Dutton and Sir William Brereton, cousin to the executed intimate of the evangelical queen, Anne Boleyn.[46] The alacrity shown by several merchant oligarchs in attempting to take advantage of the depressed property market before the Chester houses were dissolved, suggests a degree of pragmatism if not of Protestant sentiment.[47] Anticipating the surrender, wealthy Cestrians, including several merchant aldermen, paid for exceptionally long

[41] Chesh. RO, EDA 2/1, f. 188 (Gee); *Lancs. and Chesh. Wills, III*, p. 25 (Hardware); BL, Harl. MS 2079, f. 50 (Davison).

[42] Thomas Aldersey's will of 1557 commended his soul to 'my savior Jesu christ and by ye merytes of his passion in the shedyng of his blode I trust thereby to be saved' and then left money for a daily mass for one year: Chesh. RO, EDA 2/1, f. 163. See also William Orphew's will of 1548, Chester CRO, MR 112, f. 4v and Haigh, *Reformation and Resistance*, p. 194.

[43] According to R.C. Richardson there was a slight balance in favour of reform among Cheshire magistrates in the 1560s: *Puritanism in North-West England* (Manchester, 1972), p. 172.

[44] A.B. Emden, *Biographical Register of the University of Oxford, 1501–1540* (Oxford, 1974), pp. 241–2; *7th Dep. Keepers Rep.*, App. 2, p. 297; Chester CRO, MR 112, ff. 6, 9.

[45] Dutton had been mayor in 1512 and 1513. The co-opted local men included Hugh Aldersey, mayor in 1528 and 1541, Richard Sneyd, sheriff in 1541, William Goodman, mayor in 1532, 1536 and 1550 and William Glaseor, mayor in 1551: J. Beck, *Tudor Cheshire* (Chester, 1969), p. 98.

[46] E.W. Ives, 'Court and County Palatine in the Reign of Henry VIII: The Career of William Brereton of Malpas', *Trans. of the Historic Soc. of Lancs. and Cheshire*, 123 (1971), 31–3; Ormerod, *History of the County Palatine*, ii, pp. 686–7; iii, p. 89.

[47] In York, the initial purchasers were country gentry: D.M. Palliser, *The Reformation in York*, Borthwick Paper, 40 (York, 1971), pp. 14–15. In Exeter, the city council rather than individuals was eager to purchase monastic lands: MacCaffrey, *Exeter*, pp. 183–5.

leases of sixty, seventy, and a hundred years on abbey and friary property.[48] Many of the lessees' rights were ignored after the surrender and Ralph Wryne, the city recorder, broke into a pasture of the Franciscans he claimed was legally his.[49] Two aldermen, Thomas Smyth and Ralph Rogers refused to vacate part of the Carmelite friary, compelling the purchaser John Cokkes to take them to court. These were scarcely the actions of Catholic reactionaries.[50]

If the reforming ideas evidenced in the Assembly Book emanated from evangelical circles, how and when did they reach Chester? One possible channel was the increasing trade in textiles and yarn between Chester and the Manchester and south-east Lancashire textile region.[51] Traders from this area accounted for the second largest group of outsiders pursuing cases through the Chester courts between 1500 and 1550. Such men were effective vehicles for the spread of Lutheran and then Calvinist ideas,[52] and Manchester did become famous later on as a stronghold of Puritanism where radicalism was well established in the collegiate church by the 1570s. It is difficult to establish how early these tendencies began to emerge. George Marsh was preaching in Chester in 1552, and he and John Bradford were examples of that generation of Manchester scholars returning from university in the 1540s and '50s. They may have had predecessors. Henry Pendleton, for example, was an active preacher before Bradford.[53]

---

[48] *VCH Cheshire*, iii, pp. 141, 175–6, 188. Henry Gee was among the group of citizens who formally witnessed the surrenders: J.H.E. Bennett, 'The Black Friars of Chester', *J[ournal of] C[hester and] N[orth] W[ales] A[rchaeological] S[ociety]*, n. s., 39 (1952), 51.

[49] J.H.E. Bennett, 'The Grey Friars of Chester', *JCNWAS*, n. s., 24 (1921), 39–43; R. Stewart-Brown (ed.), *Lancashire and Cheshire Cases in the Court of Star Chamber, Part i*, Rec. Soc. of Lancs. and Chesh., 71 (1916), pp. 102, 114.

[50] Several aldermen and common councillors continued to lease former friary and abbey properties: J.H.E. Bennett, 'The White Friars of Chester', *JCNWAS*, n. s., 31 (1935), 30–1; idem 'The Grey Friars', 42–3.

[51] Kermode, 'Trade of Chester'; N. Lowe, *The Lancashire Textile Industry in the Sixteenth Century*, Chetham Soc., 3rd ser., 20 (1972), pp. 1–5.

[52] D.M. Palliser, 'Popular Reactions to the Reformation During the Years of Uncertainty 1530–70', in *Reformation Revised*, pp. 95–6.

[53] Haigh, *Reformation and Resistance*, pp. 166, 168–9; Richardson, *Puritanism in North-West England*, pp. 8–15.

Chester merchants were trading up country in partnership with Mancunians and as is often the way, business association led to closer connections. Henry Gee owned property in Manchester where the Gee family was prominent in public affairs and close friends with identifiable radicals. A John Gee was active in trade and served as a juror in the court leet in 1552, in the company of Edward Janny and Richard Shalcrosse.[54] Shalcrosse was Henry Gee's son-in-law and business partner, and executor to Henry's son Edmund. He was also the executor and next-door-neighbour of Edward Janny, Henry Gee's brother or brother-in-law and one of his executors. Janny appeared in the Chester Pentice Court in his capacity as executor for another Manchester draper.[55] He was a Protestant of Calvinist persuasion, judging by his will of 1553 in which he trusted in 'the merytes of Christs passion yt to be on of the nomber that shalbe elect and chosen into everlastynge glorye'. He held the advowson and vicarage of Bowden in Cheshire, where he endowed a free school.[56]

The Gee family may have already embraced Protestant beliefs and two members became radical preachers early in the seventeenth century.[57] Another Chester merchant, Thomas Aldersey, was drawn into Manchester circles through his daughter's marriage to a Mancunian. The Alderseys were an ancient county family, some of whom may have been early radicals. A second Thomas Aldersey certainly was by 1594, when although settled in London, he bought the tithes of Bunbury in Cheshire to endow a preachership and curacy there.[58] If families as characteristic of Chester's councillors as Aldersey and Gee

---

[54] H. Fishwick (ed.), *Pleadings and Depositions in the Duchy Court of Lancaster, in the Time of Edward VI, Philip and Mary*, Rec. Soc. of Lancs. and Chesh., 40 (1899), p. 9; J. Harland (ed.), *Court Leet Records of the Manor of Manchester in the Sixteenth Century*, Chetham Soc., 63 (1864), pp. 65, 83, 146, 153.

[55] Chesh. RO, EAD 2/1, ff. 188–9; Chester CRO, SR 554, mm. 1v, 6.

[56] G.J. Piccope, *Lancashire and Cheshire Wills*, I, Chetham Soc., 33 (1857), pp. 157–62; F.R. Raines, *Francis Gastrell, Notitia Cestriensis*, I, Chetham Soc., 8 (1845), p. 314 note 11.

[57] Edward Gee published *A Treatise of Prayer and of Divine Providence* in 1653: Richardson, *Puritanism in North-West England*, pp. 63, 187; G.J. French (ed.), *Bibliographical Notices of the Church Libraries at Turton and Gorton*, Chetham Soc., 38 (1855), pp. 178–9.

[58] Richardson, *Puritanism in North-West England*, p. 128. Several Alderseys and Gees attended Brasenose College from the late sixteenth to early seventeenth centuries: *Register of Brasenose College, 1509–1909*, Oxford Historical Soc., 55 (Oxford, 1910), pp. 217, 258.

were enjoyed and developed close relations with Manchester, then it is likely that other local men trading with Manchester merchants were also exposed to whatever reforming and radical ideas were current there. Moreover, the evidence of Gee's personal beliefs and of some of his associates suggests that their ideology was becoming firmly established before the late 1540s, however uncertain and divided their contemporaries were.

Was Henry Gee, 'the most influential citizen in his generation',[59] a reforming Protestant whose vision of government chimed with that of his fellow rulers, or was he adopted by one faction in Chester which invoked his name to lend authority to later reforms? It is difficult to be certain. Gee and his reputation were products of a period of profound religious and economic change, when challenges to authority provoked intrusive regulation and the fashioning of a strongly corporate ethos. Behind the rhetoric of government, the council had a clear view of its civic responsibilities and of the duties of Chester citizens articulated within a strong Christian ethic.[60] This was explicit in the language of thrift and respect for the common weal which permeated most of the assembly orders during this period. Thus, the orders to regulate the trade in barley and malt in 1536 inveigh against 'sondry couetuose and greyde persons, not hauing regarde nother to ther conshyence ne to the common and publik welthe . . . at ther oune pleasurez and prycez, to ther oune singler profutez . . . which uncaritable and unlawfull meanez' caused prices to rise, while those of 1556–7, a year of locally high prices, were accompanied by admonishments against 'dyuers gredye persons [manipulating the market] for ther owne lucre and profyt'.[61]

Inevitably, perhaps, for a government dominated by mercantile interests, 'lucre and profyt' proved to be too strong a temptation and individual aldermen

[59] Chester CRO, David M. Palliser, 'A Revised List of Chester Freemen 1392–1538', unpublished typescript, p. 3.

[60] Ceremonies to establish the corporate view of community were common in late fifteenth- and early sixteenth-century towns. One of Chester's civic displays, the Midsummer Show and Watch, was probably first staged in 1497: Morris, *Chester*, pp. 323–5; Mills, 'Chester Ceremonial'.

[61] Chester CRO, AB 1, ff. 65, 87; Sidney Jones Library, Liverpool University, MS 23.5, f. 298 (Archdeacon Roger's MS).

ran their own taverns while agreeing regulations to control the sale of drink. The Gee family once again provides the example, this time of a civic dignitary whose commercial instincts overwhelmed good citizenship. In 1546, Henry Gee's son Edmund was accused of committing the most heinous offence of the day: of importing Spanish wine through Chester's rival port of Liverpool in contravention of the council's own orders. Notwithstanding his betrayal of Chester's common weal, he was elected to serve as mayor in 1550, but died of the sweating sickness while in office.[62]

---

[62] H. Fishwick (ed.), *Pleadings in the Duchy Court of Lancaster, in the Time of Henry VIII,* Rec. Soc. of Lancs. and Chesh., 35 (1897), pp. 135–7; Roger's MS f. 292.

12

THE DISSOLUTION OF THE MONASTERIES AND THE YORKSHIRE CHURCH IN THE SIXTEENTH CENTURY

Claire Cross

In the early sixteenth century Yorkshire possessed a greater number of religious houses than any comparable English county and in consequence the abolition of monasticism by Henry VIII presented the region with a major problem in absorbing the former monks, canons, friars and nuns. How the dilemma was ultimately solved forms the burden of this paper. Before, however, an attempt can be made to assess the short and longer term effects of this revolutionary change, it is necessary to survey the process of the Dissolution in the county.

By the early Tudor period Yorkshire had accumulated a total of no fewer than seventy-eight abbeys, priories, hospitals, friaries and nunneries, some admittedly very small. The Benedictines could lay claim to five of the most ancient and wealthy houses, followed by the Cistercians with their eight great abbeys. The county also contained eleven Augustinian priories, four Gilbertine monasteries, two Charterhouses and three Premonstratensian priories in addition to single houses of Cluniac and Grandimontine monks. Since the early thirteenth century the Dominican, Franciscan and Carmelite friars had each maintained five convents in the most prominent towns, the Austin friars three and the Trinitarian friars of Knaresborough one. In York in 1529 the large hospital of St Leonard was functioning as much as a monastery as a hospice for the sick, as was a much smaller hospital in Ripon. Finally came the religious houses for women, twenty-three in all, mostly small and poor. The Cluniac nuns and the Augustinian canonesses had one priory each, the Benedictines nine and the Cistercians twelve. With over a thousand monks, canons, friars and nuns, these foundations accommodated approximately one ninth of all the religious in England.[1]

Between February 1536 and January 1540 the state suppressed every one of these seventy-eight religious houses. The Act permitting the dissolution of monasteries with revenues of under £200 a year completed its passage through parliament in the spring of 1536. From the middle of May until the end of August 1536 royal commissioners dissolved nineteen Yorkshire houses, ten for men, Sawley, Holy Trinity, York, Healaugh, Marton, Haltemprice, North Ferriby, Drax, Easby, Warter and Coverham; and nine for women, Sinningthwaite, Moxby, Keldholme, Nun Monkton, Nunburnholme, Rosedale, Ellerton, Arden and Clementhorpe. With so many government agents active within the county in the summer of 1536 and all apparently hostile to monasticism it is scarcely surprising that a number of the surviving Yorkshire religious gave explicit or covert support to the Pilgrimage of Grace when it erupted at Beverley in the ensuing October.[2]

Robert Ashton, a Trinitarian friar from Knaresborough, who was in the town at this critical moment called upon the commons of the East Riding to follow the example of the Lincolnshire rebels. The Observant Franciscan, Bonaventure, recently imposed upon the Beverley Franciscans, 'rejoiced much [at] their rising'. Dr John Pickering, prior of the York Dominicans, bade the 'faithful people of the Boreal region . . . boldly go forward in their peregrination'. The heads of other Yorkshire friaries also sympathized with the pilgrims. The prior of the York Dominicans, John Aske, helped entertain Robert Aske and his host when they entered York on 16 October 1536, while John Boroby, the prior of the Scarborough Carmelites, made his collection of subversive prophecies available to local clergy.[3] Some Augustinian and Gilbertine canons also participated in the pilgrimage. The prior of Bridlington, William Wood, dispatched men, money and horses to the rebels. At Malton the prior, William Todde, told Sir Francis Bigod that 'the church should abide woe

---

[1] G.W.O. Woodward, *The Dissolution of the Monasteries* (London, 1966), p. 139.

[2] S.M. Jack, 'Dissolution Dates for the Monasteries Dissolved Under the Act of 1536', *BIHR*, 43 (1970), 179.

[3] *LP*, xi, no. 1047; xii, pt i, nos. 201 (p. 90), 392 (pp. 182–4, 189), 854, 1021; pt ii, nos. 918, 1212 (p. 427); M.H. and R. Dodds, *The Pilgrimage of Grace* (Cambridge, 1915), i, p. 281.

for three years and then reflourish as well as ever'. Bigod planned his second rising at Watton where the canons were alleged to have said 'it would never be well as long as the king was supreme head of the church'.[4]

Apprehension that the government intended to eradicate monasticism was not confined to East Riding religious. In January 1537 some Jervaulx monks called upon the men of Masham to revolt, fearing that 'if Norfolk came into the country, their abbey would be put down and they would go a begging'. The deposed abbot of Fountains, William Perte alias Thirsk, helped politicize the Jervaulx monks. Edward Kirkby or Cowper, the quondam abbot of Rievaulx, similarly made overtures to the insurgents in an attempt to regain his office. Dr James Cockerell, the erstwhile prior of Guisborough, publicly commended Bigod's book attacking the royal supremacy.[5]

Other Yorkshire religious took advantage of the unrest to get their houses restored. With the help of local people on 12 October 1536 Sawley monks evicted the new owner, Sir Arthur Darcy, and resumed monastic life under their former abbot, Thomas Bolton. The monks of Holy Trinity Priory returned to their monastic practice when the pilgrims entered York and the rebels may have reinstated the Clementhorpe nuns. It also seems that at Warter the canons made an attempt to re-enter their house.[6]

A minimum of fourteen Yorkshire monks and friars were condemned to death for opposing the royal supremacy during the Pilgrimage of Grace, ten certainly died and others only saved their lives by fleeing the country. The attainder of Adam Sedbar and William Wood brought disaster not only upon themselves but also upon their communities, Jervaulx and Bridlington both being forfeited to the crown in the early months of 1537.[7]

A year elapsed between the seizure of Jervaulx in May 1537 and the suppression of the rest of the religious houses in Yorkshire. Despite the loss of

[4] *LP*, xii, pt i, nos. 201 (pp. 85–7), 534, 1019, 1023, 1087 (p. 499).

[5] Ibid., vii, nos. 724, 1654; ix, no. 1152; xi, no. 1295; xii, pt i, nos. 1012, 1035, 1087 (pp. 499–500), 1207 (8), 1269; pt ii, nos. 212 (p. 428).

[6] Ibid., xi, nos 783, 784, 879, grant 519 (1); xii, pt i, nos. 410, 416 (2), 536; R.B. Dobson and S. Donaghey, *The History of Clementhorpe Nunnery* (London, 1984), pp. 26–7.

[7] *LP*, xii, pt i, nos. 1172, 1192.

many of the smaller priories and nunneries in 1536, fifty-seven out of the
original seventy-eight had still to be dissolved. Unlike the period before the
Pilgrimage of Grace, when royal officials systematically closed a selection of the
lesser houses, the government now proceeded by means of 'voluntary'
surrenders. The Cistercian abbey of Roche capitulated in June 1538, followed
by a further twenty-eight houses in the autumn, winter and spring of 1538–9.
For the first time the friaries, of little economic importance but a potential
source of political opposition, attracted the state's attention. Starting with the
two Doncaster convents, the Tickhill friary, the Pontefract friary, and the four
York convents in November, royal officials went on to suppress the Trinitarian
friars of Knaresborough on 1 December, the Northallerton Carmelites on 20
December and the Yarm Dominicans just after Christmas, before tackling the
Richmond convent in January and dealing lastly with the two Beverley houses
in February and the two Hull convents and the three Scarborough convents in
early March.[8]

In addition to the confiscation of some of the lesser priories, Monk Bretton,
Ellerton, and Holy Trinity and St Andrew's, York, in November and December,
this period also witnessed the fall of Kirkham, Newburgh and Bolton as well as
of some of the greatest of the Cistercian abbeys, including Fountains, Byland
and Rievaulx.[9] The fifteen surviving Yorkshire nunneries escaped the
government's notice until August 1539 when Yedingham, Wilberfoss,
Wykeham, Handale, Basedale, Thicket and Esholt went down in quick
succession to be followed by Swine, Nunkeeling and Marrick in September,
Hampole, Kirklees and Arthington in November and Nun Appleton and the
double house of Watton before the end of the year.[10]

The last of the monks to be ejected belonged either to some of the most
influential foundations or to orders which maintained only a single house in the
county. The Grandimontines, a small and insignificant community, were
expelled from Grosmont in August 1539. Pontefract Priory, dissolved on

[8] J.W. Clay (ed.), *Yorkshire Monasteries. Suppression Papers*, Yorks. Arch. Soc. Record Series, 48
(1912), p. 179.

[9] Ibid., pp. 179–81.

[10] Ibid., p. 180.

23 November, was the only Cluniac house in Yorkshire. The Gilbertine priory at Watton together with its sister house at Malton, both surrendered in December, represented the last two houses of their order. The two Charterhouses at Hull and Mount Grace, preserved until then because of their reputation for sanctity, continued until December. The final two Cistercian houses, Kirkstall and Meaux, were suppressed in late November and early December when the substantial Augustinian priories of Nostell and Guisborough also fell. The large and wealthy Benedictine houses of St Mary's, York, Selby and Whitby survived until 29 November, 6 December and 14 December 1539 respectively, but by the beginning of January 1540 with the closure of Egglestone, a Premonstratensian foundation, monasticism in Yorkshire was at an end.[11]

The dissolution of the Yorkshire houses resulted in the expulsion between 1536 and 1540 of 609 monks and canons, 230 nuns and sisters and approximately 200 friars. Even though some former monks and friars moved away from the county and some of the more elderly soon died, the incorporation of an initial eight hundred dispossessed male religious into the secular Church presented a formidable challenge. While the great majority of these Yorkshire religious tended to be reactionary or conformist at best, a minority whole heartedly supported radical reform, and these were drawn exclusively from the thirty-three or so Yorkshire religious, fifteen monks and eighteen friars, who had attended Oxford and Cambridge between 1500 and 1540.[12]

Four friars with Yorkshire connections surfaced as reformers of national and even international standing. Miles Coverdale, the first scholar in the sixteenth century to translate the entire Bible into English, was ordained subdeacon and deacon from the York Augustinian convent in the winter of 1523/4 before he went south to Cambridge and devoted himself to a career of evangelical preaching which led to his promotion as bishop of Exeter in the Edwardian Church. In about 1530 another equally radical Carmelite friar, and Cambridge Doctor of Divinity, John Bale, took charge of his order's house in Doncaster where he publicly attacked the worship of saints and the doctrine of purgatory.

[11] Ibid., pp. 179–81.

[12] A.B. Emden, *Biographical Register of the University of Oxford, 1501–1540* (Oxford, 1974), p. xxi.

Like Coverdale, Bale was also elevated to the Edwardian episcopate. The crown permitted another Carmelite prior, and Oxford Bachelor of Theology, Simon Clerkson, to use the revenues of the vicarage of Rotherham, to which he had been appointed after the surrender of his York house, to finance his itinerant preaching. Gilbert Berkley, an Oxford Bachelor of Divinity, and a member of the York Franciscan friary in 1538, demonstrated his commitment to Protestantism as Clerkson had done by taking advantage of the licence to marry in Edward's reign. He served for over twenty years as bishop of Bath and Wells in the Elizabethan Church.[13]

In contrast with these one time friars, two former canons concentrated their efforts more specifically upon the region of their birth. Robert Ferrar, ordained in quick succession acolyte, deacon and subdeacon from Nostell Priory in 1524, graduated Bachelor of Divinity after twelve years' study at Oxford in 1533. Converted to Lutheranism at the university by Thomas Garret he eventually came to the notice of Thomas Cromwell who in 1538 procured his election as prior of Nostell. Realising that the dissolution of his house could not be long averted, in September 1538 he pleaded with the crown in vain to transform it into a seminary for the training of preachers. Advanced to the bishopric of St David's in the reign of Edward VI he was deprived for marriage within months of Mary's accession and burnt for his faith at Carmarthen in 1555.[14]

Of all this little band of radical former Yorkshire religious Robert Holgate, a Gilbertine, did the most to advance Protestantism in the north in the mid-century. At Cambridge, where he associated with the reformers who met in the 1520s at the White Horse Inn, he proceeded Bachelor of Divinity in 1524 and Doctor of Divinity thirteen years later. By 1534 he had been elected Master of the Gilbertine Order and in 1536, on Cromwell's intervention, prior of Watton. In 1537 the crown nominated him both bishop of Llandaff and president of the Council in the North, and two years later at the government's behest he

[13] BI, Abp. Reg. 27, ff. 196r, 200v, 201v; Abp. Reg. 28, ff. 85v, 91r–v; *LP*, ix, no. 230; xiii, pt i, no. 144, p. 53; xvi, no. 1308 (38); Emden, *Oxford, 1501–1540*, p. 123; *Dictionary of National Biography* (London, 1885–1901), iii, pp. 41–2; iv, pp. 359–60; xii, pp. 364–72.

[14] BI, Abp. Reg. 27, ff. 203r, 204r; Emden, *Oxford, 1501–1540*, pp. 202–3; *LP*, xiii, pt i, no. 1518; pt ii, nos. 285, 1265.

superintended the surrender of all the Yorkshire Gilbertine priories. In 1545 he succeeded Edward Lee as archbishop of York and during Edward's reign actively encouraged Protestantism in the province, endowing grammar schools at York, Malton and Hemsworth. Like many of his clerical contemporaries as an outward sign of his theological alignment he married in the Edwardian period and on this account was deprived of his see early in 1554.[15]

Holgate's conversion to Catholicism some months before his death in retirement in November 1555, an undoubted victory for the conservative cause, could not alter the fact that as archbishop he had actively promulgated Protestantism. His failure to gain a mass following for the new religion in the diocese may have been partly due to the indifference, if not outright antipathy, of the majority of his fellow former religious. With the possible exception of the friars, the dissolution of the Yorkshire monasteries does not seem to have resulted in a large exodus of the religious from the county. Indeed, the relationship with the laity of members of those orders which habitually served a cure of souls may have continued virtually unchanged. This was particularly the case with the Augustinian and Gilbertine canons who between them had a major presence in Yorkshire. Christopher Brodbelt, made acolyte, subdeacon, deacon and priest in 1519, received the priory's vicarage of Broughton in November 1534 and was still serving there in 1555 when officials in the consistory court warned him to abstain from the company of Agnes, wife of Richard Smyth. At Kirkham in the East Riding James Parkinson was acting as curate of the village church before the Dissolution and seems to have continued in the same capacity after the surrender of his house. Similarly in the North Riding John Clarkson, ordained priest as a canon of Guisborough in 1531, stayed on in the town until his death in 1556.[16]

---

[15] A.G. Dickens, *Robert Holgate, Archbishop of York and President of the King's Council in the North*, Borthwick Paper, 8 (York, 1955).

[16] N.K.M. Gurney and C. Clay (eds), *Fasti Parochiales, vol. IV; Deanery of Craven*, Yorks. Arch. Soc. Record Series, 133 (1971), pp. 28, 110; BI, Abp. Reg. 27, f. 55; Sede Vac. Reg. 5A, f. 670v; Abp. Reg. 28, f. 10r; Cons. AB 20, ff. 403v, 404r; Cons. AB 22, f. 179v; CP G 601. Prob. Reg. 15, pt i, ff. 242v–43r.

The Gilbertines furnish analogous examples. Richard Dobson, canon of Malton, presented to his community's living of Brompton in September 1531, was still there in 1546. Roger Dowe, a former canon of Ellerton, became curate of the village church and was witnessing wills at Ellerton between 1548 and 1552 while William Ryngwode, canon of Malton, remained as curate in Malton for more than twenty years after the Dissolution.[17]

As well as the religious who went on officiating in the livings which had once belonged to their communities, others established households in the neighbourhood of their former monasteries. The last prior of Monk Bretton, William Browne, acquired a house in Worsborough where he lived with his sub-prior, Thomas Frobisher and two other of his former monks, Thomas Wilkinson and Richard Hinchcliff. In semi-retirement these four priests systematically set about acquiring a hundred and fifty books previously part of their monastic library. When he made his will in 1557 Browne mentioned nine of his former monks by name before proceeding to instruct his executors to restore his property, vestments and books to 'the late dissolved monastery of Monk Bretton' if it were ever again 'inhabited with religious persons'.[18]

Some York Benedictines acted in a similar way. After the suppression of St Mary's Abbey, the sub-prior, William Clint, alias Staveley, B.D., settled in the Micklegate area of York. At his death in 1550 he left his tippet to a former monk of St Mary's, Thomas Baynes, who had obtained the living of St Mary, Castlegate. A third St Mary's monk, John Thompson, served as curate first of the very poor York rectory of St Wilfrid, previously appropriated to the abbey, and then of the adjacent parish of St Michael le Belfrey.[19] Members of the other York Benedictine house of Holy Trinity, Micklegate, maintained a similar presence in the city. William Gryme stayed on as curate of the secularized priory church where his former prior, Richard Speght alias Hudson, also ministered until his death in 1545.

[17] BI, Abp. Reg. 28, f. 22v; Prob. Reg. 11, f. 690v; Prob. Reg. 13, pt i, f. 342v, 405r; pt ii, ff. 384r, 739r, 741r, 890r; Prob. Reg. 14, f. 267v; Prob. Reg. 17, pt i, f. 356v; pt ii, f. 460v.

[18] J.W. Walker (ed.), *Chartularies of the Priory of Monk Bretton*, Yorks. Arch. Soc. Record Series, 66 (1924), p. 5; BI, Prob. Reg. 15, pt iii, ff. 151r–2r.

[19] BI, Prob. Reg. 13, f. 683r; D.M. Palliser, *The Reformation in York*, Borthwick Paper, 40 (York, 1971), p. 13.

A fellow Triniter, Richard Stubbs, held St Katherine's chantry in St John's, Ousebridge, in combination with that of St Christopher in York Minster.[20]

Chantries in fact seem to have been the first refuge of many dispossessed religious. In York the erstwhile Austin prior, John Aske, almost certainly acquired Northumberland's chantry at St Mary's altar in the Minster. Peter Glenton served both St Stephen's chantry in the Minster and another in St Helen's, Stonegate, while a third member of this convent, William Watson, held a chantry dedicated to All Hallows in the Minster together with Sir Ralph Bulmer's chantry in St Michael le Belfrey. Ralph Clayton, a former York Franciscan, obtained a chantry in St Mary's, Castlegate and between 1538 and 1542 his former colleague, John Wickham, assisted at obits in St Michael's, Spurriergate. Until his death in 1541 the past prior of the York Dominican priory, Brian Godson, had a chantry in St Mary's, Bishophill, Junior, and another former Dominican, John Wilson, may have been a chantry priest in Holy Trinity, King's Court. John White, a former York Carmelite, secured a chantry in St Crux. Edward Sandall, previously a Kirkstall monk, was appointed to the chantry of St Agnes on Foss Bridge and, lastly, Thomas Grayson, a former canon of Newburgh, procured St Lawrence's chantry in the Minster.[21]

The situation in York had parallels elsewhere in the county. After the Dissolution the former Cistercian, Thomas Jackson, moved from Rievaulx to minister to Pockley chantry in the adjacent town of Helmsley. Three monks of another Cistercian house, Meaux, also became chantry priests, Robert Robinson in Beverley Minster, John Lote in Wansford church which had been appropriated to his abbey while William Thompson served Yokefleet chantry in Howdenshire. Robert Appleby a chantry priest in Holy Trinity, Hull, in 1548, may well have been a former canon of Warter and another Warter canon, William Modye, seems to have held a chantry in Pocklington church.[22]

[20] Palliser, *Reformation in York*, p. 13; W. Page (ed.), *The Certificates of the Commissioners Appointed to Survey the Chantries, Guilds, Hospitals etc. in the County of York. Part II*, Surtees Soc., 92 (1895), pp. 448–9, 459; BI, Prob. Reg. 13, f. 51r–v; Prob. Reg. 15, f. 64v–5r.

[21] *Certificates of the Commissioners II*, pp. 436, 440, 451, 453, 454, 466, 468, 470; BI, PRY/MS3.

[22] W. Page (ed.), *The Certificates of the Commissioners Appointed to Survey the Chantries, Guilds, Hospitals etc. in the County of York. Part I*, Surtees Soc., 91 (1894), pp. 89, 127; *Certificates of the Commissioners II*, pp. 459, 521, 534; BI, Cav. Bk. 1, f. 19v.

The Act for the dissolution of the chantries provided financial compensation for all dispossessed priests with the result that some former friars, and monks who had sought dispensations to hold benefices when the lesser monasteries were suppressed, now received pensions for the first time. A particularly fortunate former religious like Thomas Grayson even found himself in possession of two. Pensions, however, might not always be paid punctually, as many clerical pensioners discovered in the difficult economic climate of Edward VI's reign. Only a benefice could bring lasting security.[23]

With the fall in the number of men offering themselves for ordination in the late Henrician and Edwardian periods the surviving former religious stood an increasingly good chance of gaining a permanent living. By Mary's accession the number of such clergy in Yorkshire had dropped by almost two-thirds from 610 former monks with pensions in 1540 to 230 in 1556. This seems largely to have been caused by clerics dying over the previous fifteen years, though priests whose pensions were extinguished when they acquired a crown living of equivalent or greater value, would also have contributed to the decline.[24]

Many former Yorkshire religious obtained benefices in the middle years of the sixteenth century. Taking the survivors of Meaux Abbey as a fairly typical example, William Robinson, having acted as a curate in the East Riding at Thorngumbald, Lockington and Roos on different occasions between 1552 and 1560, in 1559 secured the rectory of Harswell. At least five of his colleagues appear to have attained comparable financial security.[25]

Conservatism seems to have been the hallmark of the former Yorkshire religious promoted to benefices at this time. Edward Sandall, once a Kirkstall Cistercian, appeared before the High Commission in 1568 on a charge of misliking the religion then in force. Thomas Lather, the cellarer of Watton who

---

[23] *Certificates of the Commissioners II*, p. 436; PRO, E 101/76/24.

[24] The figure is calculated from PRO, E 164/31.

[25] BI, Abp. Reg. 28, f. 20v; Abp. Reg. 29, f. 27r; Inst. AB 1, f. 51v; Chancery wills 1558; V 1567/8 CB 1, f. 194v–5r; A.G. Dickens, *The Marian Reaction in the Diocese of York; Part I, the Clergy*, Borthwick Paper, 11 (York, 1957), p. 27; *Calendar of Patent Rolls, Philip and Mary* (London, 1938), iii, p. 365; G.A J. Hodgett (ed.), *The State of the Ex-Religious . . . in the Diocese of Lincoln*, Lincoln Record Soc., 53 (1959), p. 134.

had supported the rebels during the Pilgrimage of Grace, died in 1567 as rector of St Saviour's in York, still suspected of being 'backward' in religion. The erstwhile canon of Newburgh, Thomas Grayson, having lost his chantry in the Minster in 1548, went on to serve in plurality the York livings of St Martin's, Coney Street, and St Lawrence's with the rural parish of Stillingfleet until his death in 1578. In 1568 he was called before the High Commission for hiding vestments and papist books from Stillingfleet in his parish church in York, and when he made his will in 1578 he left a remembrance to Margaret Clitherow's mother, Mistress Maye.[26]

Priests such as Lather, Sandall and Grayson provide some links between late-medieval monasticism and post-Reformation Catholic recusancy. Initially in the reign of Henry VIII virtually all the Yorkshire religious had recognized the royal supremacy, though the king's commissioners had encountered resistance in particular at Mount Grace where three monks at first refused to conform. A solitary Jervaulx Cistercian, George Lazenby, with close contacts with the Carthusians of Mount Grace, and two London Carthusians, John Rochester and James Walworth, sent north to the Hull Charterhouse in the vain hope of gaining their conformity, had placed their loyalty to the pope above their allegiance to the king, and suffered death for their beliefs. On Mary's accession of all the surviving monks in Yorkshire only the Carthusians attempted to return to the religious life, with three former Hull Carthusians and five Mount Grace Carthusians joining the refounded Charterhouse of Sheen. Other former religious who remained in their parishes looked forward to a time when monasticism would return to the county and a number of Benedictines, Cistercians and Augustinians, like Prior Browne, in their wills expressed the not unrealistic hope that their houses might once again be restored.[27]

The re-establishment of Protestantism on Elizabeth's accession marked a watershed in Yorkshire Catholic history. Once again the Carthusians led the

---

[26] J.C.H. Aveling, *Catholic Recusancy in the City of York, 1558–1791*, Catholic Record Soc., 61 (1970), pp. 324, 325, 326; BI, Abp. Reg. 30, ff. 30r, 45r–v; D/C Prob. Reg. 5, f. 92r.

[27] *LP*, vi, no. 932; viii, nos. 1038, 1069; ix, no. 37; D. Knowles, *Religious Orders in England* (Cambridge, 1961), iii, pp. 238–9; C.B. Rowntree, 'Studies in Carthusian History in Late Medieval England' (unpublished D. Phil. thesis, University of York, 1981), pp. 192, 510, 521, 532, 533, 536,

way. Three survivors from the Hull Charterhouse went into exile to persevere in
the religious life with William Remington dying in the Perth Charterhouse in
1560, John Bennet going even further afield to the Charterhouse of Roermond
and Thomas Syndeton moving with the Sheen community to Bruges. Mount
Grace provided an equally impressive witness. Whereas three former Mount
Grace Carthusians had died at Sheen in the Marian period, two others, John
Saunderson and Leonard Hall, lived long enough to accompany their brethren
to the Continent. There they were joined by Roger Thomson, a novice at
Mount Grace in 1538, who had gone on to become vicar of Ampleforth.
Deprived of his living in 1559 for refusing to recognize the royal supremacy he
also made his way to the Low Countries where he rose to be first vicar and then
prior of Sheen Anglorum.[28]

Mary's death also proved to be a turning point for former members of other
orders. The last prior of Guisborough, Robert Pursglove alias Silvester, had
conformed and been appointed suffragan bishop of Hull after the Dissolution,
in the reigns of Henry VIII, Edward VI and Mary in addition to his not
inconsiderable pension of 250 marks accumulating preferments which included
the rectory of Tideswell, the mastership of Jesus College, Rotherham, and
prebends in York and Southwell Minsters. In 1559, however, he sacrificed
everything on his rejection of the royal supremacy, and retired to his family
home at Tideswell where he lived 'stiff in papistry' for a further twenty years.[29]

Besides Thomas Lather, John Grayson and Edward Sandall who, though
conforming, all had connections with York recusancy in the Elizabethan period,
John Bolton, a recusant priest imprisoned for many years in the Hull Block
houses for his faith may possibly be identified with the former Warter canon of
the same name. One or two former nuns also helped to maintain continuity
between pre-Reformation Catholicism and the later recusant tradition. Isabel
Whitehedde, twenty-seven years old when Arthington Nunnery was dissolved in
1539, subsequently found refuge at Arthington Hall. For refusing to disclose the
whereabouts of two seminary priests in 1586 she was committed close prisoner

---

[28] Rowntree, 'Studies', pp. 180, 491, 510, 529, 532, 536, 537; H. Aveling, *Northern Catholics; The
Catholic Recusants of the North Riding of Yorkshire, 1558–1790* (London, 1966), p. 24.

[29] Aveling, *Northern Catholics*, pp. 37–42; idem, *Catholic Recusancy*, pp. 298–9.

to York Castle, where she died the following year. The founder of the Institute of the Blessed Virgin Mary, Mary Ward, heard 'histories of religious' such as these from 'an old Catholic woman', Margaret Garett, when a young girl in her grandmother's Yorkshire household at the turn of the sixteenth century.[30]

In 1582, nearly fifty years after the Dissolution of the Monasteries, twenty former monks or canons were receiving their pensions in Yorkshire. Apparently the longest survivor, Thomas Mooke, a one time monk of Kirkstall, who had gone on to serve as a chantry priest at Thorpe near Newark, died at Farnedon in 1586 leaving to his brothers and sisters and their families the arrears on his Kirkstall and Thorpe pensions. An erstwhile nun of Hampole, Isabel Coxon, was still being paid her pension in 1601. A small minority of these former Yorkshire religious consciously renounced monasticism to become committed Protestants, suffering martyrdom or exile for their beliefs under both Henry VIII and Mary, but from either choice or necessity they almost all eventually left the region. The continuing presence of the very much more numerous traditionalist former monks, canons and friars, first mostly as chantry or stipendiary priests, then increasingly as beneficed clergy, must have been at least partly responsible for the lethargy, amounting in places to antagonism, with which the new religion was received in so many parts of the county. The most lasting consequence of the Dissolution of the Monasteries, therefore, seems to have been the conservatism of much of the Church in Yorkshire in the second half of the sixteenth century.[31]

---

[30] H. Aveling, *Post Reformation Catholicism in East Yorkshire 1558–1790*, East Yorks. Local Hist. Series, 11 (1960), p. 11; Aveling, *Northern Catholics*, p. 45; J. Morris (ed.), *Troubles of Our Catholic Forefathers* (London, 1877), p. 328; M.C.E. Chambers, *The Life of Mary Ward, 1585–1645*, ed. H.J. Coleridge (London, 1882), i, pp. 45–8.

[31] BI, Prob. Reg. 23, pt i, f. 386r–v; PRO, LR 6/122/10, m. 12.

13

VICTIMS, VIRAGOS AND VAMPS: WOMEN OF THE SIXTEENTH-CENTURY ANGLO-SCOTTISH FRONTIER

Maureen M. Meikle

He slew my knight, to me sae dear;
He slew my knight, and poin'd his gear;
My servants all for life did flee,
And left me in extremitie.

I sew'd his sheet, making my mane;
I watch'd the corpse, myself alane;
I watch'd his body night and day;
No living creature came that way.

I took his body on my back,
And whiles I gaed, and whiles I sat;
I dig'd a grave, and laid him in,
And happ'd him with the sod sae green.[1]

These stanzas from Sir Walter Scott's 'Lament of the Border Widow' portray one of the best-known female casualties of the Anglo-Scottish frontier, namely Margery, widow of Cockburn of Henderland. In 1529 Cockburn was hung in Edinburgh for his reiving activities, though the poem suggests that he was executed at his own gate. Scott was using his accustomed poetic licence to

---

[1] T. F. Henderson (ed.), *Sir Walter Scott's Minstrelsy of the Scottish Border* (Edinburgh, 1902), iii, pp. 112–13.

improve the story, yet the circumstance of a lady left on her own to bury her husband is plausible. A woman paying the penalty for her husband's disgrace is thus a victim of border history. No one dared help a rebel's kin for fear of retribution against themselves and in the poem even the household servants disappeared.

The frontier added complexity to the lives of women living along either side of it during the sixteenth century. Patriarchy, chauvinism and lack of legal rights were enough to bear without the threat of personal violence and loss of property from border raiding. There were many more victims than viragos or vamps, though border violence was not gender specific. Trouble was mostly instigated by men rather than women, who normally had to confine their battles to the domestic or private spheres of early modern life. There were definitely no Calamity Janes on this frontier. Sixteenth-century records invariably tell us more about women of the elite and the pre-Reformation monasteries. There are occasional glimpses of the world of ordinary women but their lack of literacy leaves them almost hidden from history. Scottish women usually kept their own name after marriage while English wives took the surname of their husband. Scottish heiresses were known as lady of their estate, the female equivalent of laird. This does not indicate independence among Scotswomen; it merely emphasizes the importance of kinship in Scottish society. All border prioresses and wives of knights could take the title 'dame'.

The definition 'victim' would not have sat squarely on some female shoulders if a journalist in the *Carlisle Journal* of May 1844 is to be believed. When reporting a fire at Naworth Castle he witnessed women carrying valuables to safety in advance of the flames and noted their 'courage, activity and resolution, which were ancient characteristics of the sex on the border, – qualities which centuries before had been so often displayed on the same spot, amidst the din of war and turmoil of midnight surprise'.[2] Did these women simply pick up the pieces after a raid and start afresh? Hungry children would certainly have brought their mothers back to reality as they were 'commonlie in the mother's care' in the borders, as elsewhere.

---

[2] The *Carlisle Journal*, May 25th, 1844, reprinted in *Historical Notices of Naworth Castle* (Carlisle, undated), pp. 3–4.

Among the border women who were most at risk of becoming victims in the sixteenth century were widows, especially the elderly. Widow Smyth of Lanercost decided to pay blackmail demanded by the Grahams, though none of her neighbours did and probably derided her for doing so. The Grahams duly raided the village in 1596 and 'inquired where the widow who paid blackmail dwelt, and harried all the rest, except her'.[3] Her neighbours could retaliate, but there was no one to protect her in a world where women did not fight back in public. She obviously wanted to protect what little property she had and therefore decided to avoid becoming another victim of border violence. An example of an elderly widow who became a victim is provided by Dame Elizabeth Ker, Lady Scott of Buccleuch, who at the age of eighty was unable to escape from the tower of Catslak after it was set on fire by her own kinsmen, the Kers of Cessford, in 1548. It is unclear if they knew she was in the tower at the time, but the Kers cared little for any property of the Scotts, with whom they were at deadly feud. Lady Buccleuch had outlived her usefulness to the Kers as she had been widowed for forty-four years. Her death was mourned by many including her son the 'Old Laird of Buccleuch', who was himself murdered four years later as part of the same feud. The longevity of the female sex could cause all sorts of inheritance difficulties. How they survived property tussles with their sons or even their grandsons depended on how strong and respected these women were. Dame Jean Hepburn, for example, was prepared to feud with her impatient nephew Sir George Home of Wedderburn in 1580.[4]

If being an elderly widow did not protect against violence, then neither did being pregnant. In the 1580s Dickie Armstrong of Dryhope was cited for burning John Noble and his pregnant wife in their home. Armstrong went on to ransack the home of Margaret Forster of Bewcastle and he stole eighteen of her cattle as well. The nefarious Elliots tended to spare the lives of women during

---

[3] *Calendar of Letters and Papers Relating to the Affairs of the Borders of England and Scotland* (London, 1894–6), ii, nos. 276, 287 (hereafter *CBP*).

[4] Scottish Record Office, GD40/15/2/2; GD224/529/1/108 (hereafter SRO); *Registers of the Privy Council of Scotland* (Edinburgh, 1877–84), iii, pp. 290–1 (hereafter *RPC*); J. Balfour-Paul (ed.), *The Scot's Peerage* (Edinburgh, 1904–14), ii, p. 228; W. Fraser, *The Scotts of Buccleuch* (Edinburgh, 1878), ii, p.187.

English raids though they killed their husbands and stole their property all the same. They perhaps hoped that a widow would be more likely to pay blackmail than their late husbands.[5] The sixteenth-century lists of border wrongdoings only record misdemeanours against the property of women if they were widows. Heiresses and widows were the only women able to hold property in their own right. A noticeable absence from the lists are citations for rape. It is hardly credible that border reivers went about their looting and pillaging without indulging in sexual transgressions. Is this perhaps another reason why the Elliots spared women and the Armstrongs killed pregnant wives? Rape would have been dealt with by domestic courts rather than border laws, but it could still have appeared on the lists as a demand for monetary recompense. However, the likelihood of a border woman admitting this was slight, as unmarried and married women had few legal rights to pursue such cases. Their husbands or fathers may have been reluctant to admit that rape had occurred.

Disputes concerning women's property were not necessarily cross-border. On both sides of the frontier women had to fend off interlopers, even from among their own kin. Marriage contracts were often the root cause of trouble and there are numerous cases concerning lands held by widows in liferent. Married women could only transact property deals with the consent of their husbands, but they would have defended their wives' property as their own. Ann Cranstoun, wife of Andrew Ker of Cessford resigned lands in Selkirk 'not moved by force or fallen in error . . . of her own free will.' However, Alison Douglas, widow of Home of Wedderburn had to call in the sheriff of Selkirk to see if her son had leased lands at Blackhaugh without her consent.[6] In wills wives were frequently named executor to their husband's estates. This displeased James Brounfield of Pittlesheugh, who had to be ordered not to trouble his mother as executor in 1576. The settlement of an estate could be a convenient mechanism for a son and heir to attempt to oust his mother or stepmother from her assigned third. The grounds for doing this could be an emotional blackmail that the other siblings had to be paid their portions. These financial arrangements could,

[5] *CBP*, i, nos. 101, 668, 678; ii, nos. 366, 815, 1383.

[6] T. Maley and W. Elliot (eds), *Selkirk Protocol Books 1511–47*, The Stair Soc. and the Walter Mason Trust (Edinburgh, 1993), pp. 11, 173–5.

nevertheless, be amicable like that of Alexander Home of Manderston and his mother Barbara. She resigned her liferent in return for an annuity in 1555.[7] However, there would probably have been more hostile situations when women refused to hand over property that was theirs in law.

During 1594 Isobel Home, widow of Home of Huttonhall, did not resign her third until her son offered 2,577 marks and the inside goods. There was still enough profit in this to pay the dowries of all her daughters. She must have excluded her fishing rights on the River Tweed as these were the subject of a border dispute in 1602, which Isobel pursued with vigour. Her tenants were English and had been caught fishing in the closed season, so 'Mistris Hume' invoked ancient legislation that said the Tweed could be fished when Berwick was in English hands to win her case.[8] Another indefatigable border widow Dame Isobel Ker of Cessford was a major money-lender to kinsmen and others in the 1570s and '80s, owing to the size of her husband's estates. Dame Isabel Gray of Chillingham's inventory of 1581 recorded the substantial sum of £871 owed to her. Unfortunately, the interest rates they charged have not been recorded.[9]

At the other end of the female age spectrum were young border heiresses who could be fought over as fiercely as the terce of a widow. Differences between Scots and English law did not prevent poor treatment of local heiresses. In England the increasing use of male-only entail was subverting the common law rights of women, while in Scotland kidnapping and enforced marriages were not unknown.[10] The case of Anne and Elizabeth Dacre was a *cause célèbre* in the 1560s with their uncle Leonard Dacre claiming the estates in entail against their husbands the Lords Arundel and William Howard. They appeared to be pawns of the duke of Norfolk who had held their wardship and determined that no Dacre relative was going to scupper his plans to ensnare their lucrative estates.

---

[7] SRO, CC8/8/5, f. 80; GD 158/203; GD 267/27/76.

[8] SRO, CC8/8/26, f. 181; RD1/48, ff. 200–201; *CBP*, ii, no. 1484.

[9] Durham Probate Registry: Register of Wills 1582 (hereafter DPRW); SRO, CC8/8/16, ff. 96r–98r; William Greenwall (ed.), *Wills and Inventories from the Registry at Durham Part 2*, Surtees Soc., 38 (1860), pp. 49–54.

[10] A.L. Erickson, *Women and Property in Early Modern England* (London, 1993); E. Spring, *Law, Land and Family* (Chapel Hill, NC, 1993).

During the Northern Rebellion Leonard Dacre lost no time in seizing his nieces' estates in a futile attempt to reinstate the Dacres in the north-west. In the long term the avaricious Howards won.[11] In Northumberland the daughters of Sir Thomas Gray of Horton were denied their common-law rights of patrimony and co-inheritance when their father made a late deed of entail. To keep his estates within the Gray family he opted to bequeath them to Ralph Gray of Chillingham, the second son of his eldest daughter. The other five daughters and their husbands were incensed and made their feelings known publicly, to little avail.[12] Another Northumbrian case concerned Elizabeth Heron of Ford, whose marriage to a non-kinsman created a long-lasting bloodfeud. Although her Heron kinsmen tried to forge a deed of entail to force their claim, the Court of Chancery rejected it. Here common law prevailed, yet opposition to her children inheriting Ford divided the county for decades.[13]

The rights of female inheritance in the Scottish borders were being threatened by tailzie (*anglicé* entail), but not to the same extent as in England. It was still possible for a woman to inherit an estate and title under Scots law. Isabel Murray of Bowhill, Selkirkshire, was sole heir to her father and was not persuaded to marry by her kinsmen which was unusual in early modern times. She may have lost a potential husband at the battle of Flodden, or been unable to find a suitable spouse because of the high death toll this battle inflicted on Scottish landed society. Whether she was a genuinely independent woman is open to question as she sold her estate in 1529 to her uncle Michael Scott of Aikwood 'of her own free will . . . being of mature age . . . for her own convenience'.[14] Helen Grahamslaw of Newton witnessed her eight brothers being murdered by the Turnbulls during their bloodfeud. When her father died she was declared heir, though the estate was really part of her dowry to Robert Ker of Newton. Her father arranged this match to prevent

[11] G. Ormsby (ed.), *Selections from the Household Book of Lord William Howard of Naworth*, Surtees Soc., 68 (1877), pp. xi–xii, 365–409.

[12] PRO, C3/71/11.

[13] M. Meikle, 'Northumberland Divided: Anatomy of a Sixteenth-Century Bloodfeud', *Archaeologia Aeliana*, 5th ser., 20 (1992), 79–89.

[14] *Selkirk Protocol Books*, pp. 65–6.

the Turnbulls abducting her, though they continued to annoy Helen by stealing her sheep.[15]

Janet Newton, lady of Dalcove, was ward of James Ker of Mersington when she opted to elope rather than accept his marriage selection. There was nothing illegal about this if a financial penalty was paid to her guardian. Ker opted to be as mean as possible and demanded £2,000 (Scots) in 1533 knowing that Janet would have to mortgage the bulk of her estates to fulfil payment. It took until 1547 for Janet and her husband Adam Ker of Shaw to recover these lands, but trouble was never very far away. Janet was forfeited, restored and though she later remarried, her son Thomas became a ward of another Ker of Mersington.[16] Janet's plight was ironically linked to that of the Rutherford heiresses by marriage.

Katherine and Helen Rutherford of that Ilk in Roxburghshire were the subject of a deed of entail. Unlike the English examples, their claim was granted in 1503 against their Rutherford kinsmen, though Katherine was excluded for running away with James Stewart of Traquair and 'committand hir person to him in fornication'. Though they subsequently married, it was within the forbidden degrees and the estates were given to Helen. As lady of Rutherford, Helen was as strong-willed as her sister and rejected husbands proffered by her kinsmen. She married four lairds including Ker of Mersington, but all without issue. This made Helen the feudal superior of Janet Newton of Dalcove, provoking squabbles over rent and fishing rights on the Tweed. Being woman to woman this landlord–tenant dispute was different. Helen's death in 1557 opened up the Rutherford claims again, but as Katherine's marriage had been legitimated in 1506 the Stewarts of Traquair won and made a lasting settlement with the Rutherfords in 1560. The latter reluctantly accepted the situation, yet probably cursed the original entail for not being male only.[17] In the Merse

---

[15] SRO, GD40/1/379/4; RD1/24/1, ff. 182–3; R. Pitcairn (ed.), *Ancient Criminal Trials in Scotland*, Bannatyne Club (Edinburgh, 1833), ii, p. 419.

[16] SRO, GD239/2/1/8; RD1/6, f. 222; *Selkirk Protocol Books*, pp. 22, 118–19; M. Meikle, 'Lairds and Gentlemen: Landed Society in the Eastern Anglo-Scottish Borders c. 1540–1603' (unpublished Ph.D. thesis, University of Edinburgh, 1989), pp. 518–19.

[17] National Library of Scotland, ACC 7676/A/II; A/IV; K.R. Davis, *The Rutherfords in Britain* (Stroud, 1987), pp. 21–6.

heiresses were similarly guarded by their male kin, but this did not always prevent them from marrying elsewhere. The Homes had been known to kidnap heiresses to serve their own interests, yet when the earl of Morton as regent of Scotland in the 1570s married two local heiresses to outsiders they were incensed. They had hoped to persuade these women to marry their kinsmen.[18]

It would be wrong to argue that border men were always aggressive towards their women as there are many examples of kindness and concern for wives and daughters. When facing forfeiture for taking part in the Northern Rebellion, Tristram Fenwick of Brinkburn worried about his wife, though he was pardoned in 1571.[19] In Scotland William Cairncross of Colmslie wanted to ensure that his Hamilton nieces at St John's Chapel were paid their portions. He ordered their uncle and tutor, James Hamilton, to marry his widowed sister and pay the bairn's parts from the estate instead of keeping the money to himself. These bairn's parts were often used for dowries, male education or apprenticeships. Daughters usually took priority over younger sons as they could not hope for an independent career. Therefore Nicol Brounfield of Whitehouse gave 500 marks to his sister Barbara and 300 marks to Alison, whereas his brothers Robert and James were given only inside goods. This was amicable, yet divisions had caused a feud within the Cairncross family in 1560, so William may have been trying to avoid this trouble for his nieces.[20] David Home of Blackadder West sold his estate to his cousin John Home of Blackadder East, with the proviso that he pay a £3,000 (Scots) dowry to each of his daughters. This reunited an estate that had been divided in 1518 when the heiresses of Robert Blackadder of that Ilk were forcibly married to Homes along with their widowed mother.[21] David Home, ironically, wanted his daughters to avoid the same fate his ancestors had imposed on the Blackadder women.

Reports of marital discord in the borders are rare, but some evidence of it can be gleaned by reading between the lines of surviving documents. The story

---

[18] SRO, CC8/8/7, ff. 245–6; *RPC*, iii, pp. 227, 387.

[19] *Calendar of the Patent Rolls Preserved in the Public Record Office 1569–72*, p. 292 (hereafter *CPR*); A. Luders *et al.* (eds), *Statutes of the Realm* (London, 1810–28), 13 Eliz. c. 16. I; R. Sadler, *The State Papers and Letters of Sir Ralph Sadler*, ed. A. Clifford (Edinburgh, 1809), ii, p. 118.

[20] SRO, RD1/4, f. 172; RD1/45, f. 153; RD1/47, f. 44.

[21] Ibid., GD362/36/7/2; *Scots Peerage*, iii, p. 281.

of the woman who served up a pair of spurs before her reiver husband, to indicate that the larder was empty, is apocryphal. More concrete is the will of Thomas Ilderton of Ilderton, who named his wife Isabel as his executor yet left her very far down his list of bequests. He clearly valued horses and hounds above her as the thoroughbreds were left to his elite friends. Isabel got the sheep, 'a black nage, a browne mere and a white meare, to doo hir busines withal'. She received a liferent of the house in Newcastle, but he was careful to mention the 'two wenches of the Newcastell' who 'kepes my house'. They received 'a fetherbedde, with sheetes and blankettes', and were probably providing sexual favours for their unhappily married master.[22]

Mistresses of the gentry tended to be either venerated or ignored vamps. In 1565 the widower Sir Robert Ellerker of Hulne owed 2s. 6d. 'to a woman that company's with me'.[23] Cuthbert Ogle, the illiterate pre-Reformation priest of Stanehope and Ford who was progenitor of the Ogles of Eglingham, co-habited with Isabel Musgrave. She may have been a daughter of Sir Robert Musgrave and gave Cuthbert four sons though she was listed as a 'servant' in his will. Isabel received a liferent from Cuthbert that was more substantial than anything a servant could hope to inherit.[24] Isabel Sheppard, onetime mistress of Sir John Forster, married him in his old age. She is credited as saving his life at Bamburgh Castle when Scots intruders were 'espyed coming up the staires' and 'his lady gott the chamber doore put to and bolted'. It was fortuitous that he had been generous to Isabel before they married.[25] In Scotland Sir John Ker of Hirsel indulged in some wife swapping. He abandoned his wife Juliana Home of Wedderburn for Margaret Whitelaw of the Ilk, who was equally compliant as she left her husband Sir Alexander Hamilton of Innerwick in 1588. They subsequently gained divorces and married, but the Church of Scotland disallowed this as they were excommunicated for double adultery at the time. Juliana's kinsmen harried Ker for repayment of her dowry as she was destitute

[22] DPRW, v, f. 68.

[23] DPRW 1560–9; J.C. Hodgson (ed.), *Wills and Inventories . . . Part 3*, Surtees Soc., 112 (1906), p. 33.

[24] PRO, ADM 75/71; *LP*, xx, pt ii, no. 1010; E. Bateson *et al.*, *A History of Northumberland* (Newcastle upon Tyne and London, 1893–1940), ix, pp. 395–6.

[25] M. Meikle, 'A Godly Rogue: The Career of Sir John Forster, an Elizabethan Border Warden', *Northern History*, 28 (1992), 126–63.

and could not remarry until their divorce was sanctioned by the Church. She was thus a victim while her unfaithful husband remained with his lover. In 1603 Juliana remarried James Pringle of Whytbank, but it had taken thirteen years for the Kirk's wrath to abate.[26]

Across the border in 1601 Thomas Carr of Ford was allegedly making chauvinistic remarks about Elizabeth I. He felt that men were having a tough time for 'were she gon, then men might be sett by [esteemed], but as long as she lived, men would not be cared for'.[27] Perhaps he was just in a moaning mood, for these remarks were made in his mother-in-law's house. If anything it was women who were not being cared for, as his neighbour Henry Collingwood of Etal had jilted Eleanor Muschamp of Barmoor the preceding year and the children of Alice Conyers were trying to evict her from Lemmington because she had remarried. Alice was trying to borrow money from gentry friends to pay her recusancy fines at this time so her compounded troubles rather belittle the irritations of Thomas Carr.[28] Nonetheless, Lord Home must have been taken aback when his wife walked out in 1595 taking the 'platte and beste stuffe at Dunglass . . . with her to fife to her lyving there'. Being an elite woman with property from a previous marriage made this possible, but they were reconciled. When Home left Scotland on a diplomatic mission in 1602 Lady Home was riding the bounds of Innerwick on behalf of her absent husband.[29] Wives deputising for absent husbands are fairly commonplace among the elite border women when warfare or political exile intervened such as Isabel Ker, lady of Linton in 1547 or Lady Isobel Home for Sir James Home of Eccles in 1602.[30]

---

[26] SRO, CC8/8/31, ff. 8–9; GD267/31/6; National Register of Archives for Scotland, 859/6/4 (hereafter NRAS); *Historical Manuscripts Commission, Salisbury MS* (London, 1892), iv, p. 31 (hereafter *HMC, Salisbury*); *RPC*, iv, pp. 380, 407; v, p. 81; D. Calderwood, *History of the Kirk of Scotland* (Edinburgh, 1842–9), vi, p. 205; D. Home of Godscroft, *De Familia Humia Wedderburnensi Liber* (Edinburgh, 1839), pp. 107–10; *Trials*, i, pt 2, pp. 282, 293.

[27] *CBP*, ii, 1434.

[28] PRO, C142/201/96; E377/1 & 10; Chillingham Castle Documents, no. 6; *HMC, Salisbury*, xi, p. 585; xii, p. 94.

[29] SRO, GD 267/27/76; *Calendar of the State Papers Relating to Scotland and Mary Queen of Scots* (Edinburgh, 1898–1969), xii, no. 38.

[30] SRO, RH15/19/12; the Walter Mason Trust, Protocol book of Ninian Brydin, no. 9.

They proved to be just as efficient as their husbands at managing estates, though some went further than this and took on the diplomatic intrigues of their husbands.

Dame Janet Scott, the long-suffering second wife of Sir Thomas Ker of Ferniehirst, played a far greater role than she has been given credit for. As the daughter of William Scott of Buccleuch, she was forced to marry Ker in an attempt to pacify their bloodfeud. They married just before the Northern Rebellion began and this thrust Janet into politics as Ferniehirst Castle was used as a refuge for fleeing rebels. Her home was subsequently razed by an English army, though it was rebuilt. She initially converted to Catholicism to please her husband, yet her conviction thereafter was genuine.[31] Ker had two sons and three daughters from his first wife Janet Kirkcaldy. Janet Scott provided him with three more sons and a daughter including the infamous earl of Somerset who created havoc in the court of James VI and I.

Ker had long been sympathetic to the cause of Mary, Queen of Scots and Janet shared these views. For this they were forced into exile in France during 1579–81, and from 1583–4 Ker left Janet in charge of his family and estates. Janet signed writs on his behalf and even sent coded letters to Mary. She was evidently acting on her own initiative in a letter of 22 October 1583, or 4 November according to the French calendar as Janet duly noted. The letter contained diplomatic news and hoped that Mary would intercede with James VI on her husband's behalf. Janet had 'looked every day theis 250 daies for my husband's coming home but yet have noe word from him'. She thanked Mary for 'a ringe in token of your Majesties good wil' and said she would 'keepe it with gods grace till I shall see your majestie'. Janet went further by promising that her good son would someday 'doe your majestie acceptable service if he were kept some where at schooles in France as I intend to have him with your Majesties help'.[32] In another letter of 25 November Janet noted Scottish court politics and reported that 'the church of Scotland are . . . as evill affected' as ever. She added that 'I must beseech humblie your majesty to write again to the

[31] SRO, GD40/15/2/3; RD1/11, f. 75; Calderwood, *History of the Kirk of Scotland*, ii, p. 562; iv, p. 662.

[32] BL, Cotton MS Caligula C.VII, f. 338; SRO, GD402/9/66.

King of Spayne and such others as your majestie thinkes mete to write unto for
the continuance of his pensions.' Ker was short of cash because of his
continuing exile and Janet wrote 'I beleeve nowe seeing that the winter season
cometh that my husband shall not come into Scotland before the Spring time.'[33]

Ker's finances became Janet's sole responsibility when a letter arrived from
Paris in January 1583 giving her full power of attorney during his 'will and
absence', much to the annoyance of her eldest step-son Andrew. He quarrelled
with his stepmother on several occasions and insisted that she surrender power
if Ker died.[34] This aggravation added to Janet's financial worries for during
their shared exile Ker had borrowed money for her use in France and now that
he was back there on his own the bills were mounting up. The debts were not
confined to Scotland as Janet received a reminder for £30 due to Sir Cuthbert
Collingwood of Eslington in Northumberland. Collingwood sympathized and
'wold not acharged or called of your husband or you for so small a matter', but
he too needed money and proceeded to threaten legal action against her. Ker's
debts were still unresolved at his death in 1585, when Janet as his widow and
Andrew Ker of Ferniehirst as eldest son began fighting over property. Ker
widows were accustomed to this as Janet's mother-in-law had fought with her
son Thomas, Janet's husband, in the 1560s.[35]

Janet was not a virago, as her husband had entrusted her with power of
attorney, though the borders did have viragos in the form of prioresses. They
were often from powerful local families such as Pringle of that Ilk at Coldstream
or Home of Polwarth at North Berwick. Fights between candidates for the
position of prioress were not unknown as Christian MacDougal and Janet
Hunter battled over Eccles Priory during 1530 and 1531. One was the pope's
candidate and the other that of King James V as creeping secularization in pre-
Reformation Scottish monasteries caused confusion.[36] Janet Pringle, prioress of

---

[33] BL, Cotton MS Caligula C.VII, f. 341.

[34] SRO, GD40/2/9/64 & 67; GD40/2/10/61; GD40/3/2/9.

[35] Ibid., GD40/2/9/71; RD1/20/1/1, f. 60; *RPC*, i, pp. 305, 394, 457; G. Donaldson (ed.),
Registrum Secreti Sigilli Regum Scotorum, (Edinburgh, 1908–82), vii, no. 2231; viii, no. 380 (hereafter
RSS).

[36] NRAS, 3215/2/5; 3215/3/15; 3215/6/2; *Scots Peerage*, iv, p. 298; *Selkirk Protocol Book*, pp. 80,
83, 87–8.

Coldstream, was both virago and vamp. The priory was on a strategic site close to the frontier and had been intriguing with England since the battle of Flodden, if not before.[37] Janet took up the mantle of her predecessor, Isabel Pringle, around 1537. She sent Scottish news south and provided shelter for English spies providing her 'name be kept secret'. Her whole family was involved in espionage at this time and Sir William Eure noted that if the king of Scots found out 'it would be a great hindrance to obtaining further information'. Janet's English overtures were in vain as the priory burned alongside all the other houses destroyed by the earl of Hertford in 1545. Janet had to seek refuge in Berwick with a widow 'of scant good name'. She tried to win reparations from her English contacts, yet shrewdly was also in contact with the Scottish government about the same matter.[38] Though the captain of Berwick and the Scot-loving John Selby favoured their reinstatement the nuns were unsuccessful. The priory remained in ruins and the nuns had to live elsewhere. Janet chose to remain in Scotland unlike her traitorous kinsman Sandy Pringle, who married a Northumbrian and became a denizen of England. Janet continued to take the profits of the monastery and defended them against aggressors. At some point in the 1550s she married her kinsman James Pringle of Langmuir.[39] Dame Elizabeth Lamb, prioress of St Bothan's, had assured to England in the mid-1540s to protect herself and the priory's tenants and servants. Although she was forfeited for this, Elizabeth never engaged in spying activities and was thus more loyal than Janet Pringle.[40]

Women of the sixteenth-century borders therefore varied from victims of raids to gentlemen's mistresses, spymaster prioresses or masters of estates during their husband's absences. Their everyday lives would not have been different to any other woman's lot in the sixteenth century, had it not been for the proximity of the international frontier.

---

[37] *LP*, xi, pt i, nos. 1672, 2116; iv, nos. 762, 1047; viii, no. 633(3); C. Rogers (ed.), *Chartulary of the Cistercian Abbey of Coldstream* (London, 1879).

[38] *LP*, xii, no. 422; xiv, nos. 684, 723; xviii, pt i, no. 58.

[39] SRO, CS6/27, f. 130; *CPR, 1548–9*, p. 81; *Calendar of State Papers Domestic Addenda 1547–65*,) (London, 1856–72), p. 430; J.M. Thomson (ed.), *Regestrum Magni Sigilli Regum Scotorum*, (Edinburgh, 1882–1914), iv, no. 298.

[40] Bodleian Library, MS Top, Yorks. C. 45, f. 68v; *RSS*, iii, nos 1732, 1836.

14

WENTWORTH AS PRESIDENT OF THE COUNCIL OF THE NORTH, 1628–41[*]

Fiona Pogson

Thomas Wentworth, earl of Strafford was the last effective lord president of the Council of the North.[1] Although his presidency lasted for over twelve years, Wentworth spent seven years in Dublin as lord deputy of Ireland during which time he governed the north of England through a vice-president in York. However, modern studies devote little attention to Wentworth's presidency during his absentee government from 1633 to 1639, even though investigation of the Strafford Papers indicates that he did not surrender his responsibility for the government of the north.[2] F.W. Brooks's comment that the Strafford Papers 'do not throw as much light as it was hoped they might on Wentworth's activities as President' is accurate in the sense that they do not fill the gap left by the disappearance of the council's records.[3] But they do disclose something of his attitude towards the government of the north, and of his relationship with his vice-president, Sir Edward Osborne. In particular, they show that even in Dublin, Wentworth remained an active lord president and that his association with the Council of the North was more than nominal.

Wentworth struggled for over a decade to gain preferment at court in keeping with his wealth and county status. In 1628 he was raised to the peerage and his new status was confirmed by his appointment as lord president of the Council of the North in December.[4] The council had been designed to provide effective

[*] I would like to thank Liverpool Hope University College for financial assistance toward the reasearch costs for this paper.

[1] Thomas, Lord Savile of Pontefract was lord president from April to August 1641: F. Drake, *Eboracum* (London, 1736), p. 370.

[2] R. Reid, *The King's Council in the North* (London, 1921), pp. 427–30.

[3] F.W. Brooks, *The Council of the North* (London, 1966), bibliographical notes.

[4] T.D. Hardy, *Syllabus of the Documents Relating to England and Other Kingdoms Contained in the Collection Known as 'Rymer's Feodera'* (London, 1873), ii, p. 875; James Howell, *Epistolae Ho-Elianae: The Familiar Letters of James Howell*, ed. J. Jacobs (London, 1892), i, p. 269.

administration of the northern counties in the wake of the Pilgrimage of Grace; it had jurisdiction over England north of the Humber, except Lancashire. By 1628, however, it had little effective authority outside Yorkshire. The council also functioned as a court of law handling both civil and criminal matters, allowing northerners easier access to the law, but also attracting resentment from common lawyers.[5] Wentworth's immediate predecessors, Lord Sheffield and Lord Scrope, had both damaged the council's reputation and the activities of Vice-President John, Lord Savile, and the council's secretary Sir Arthur Ingram were not helpful.[6] In Charles I's view, Wentworth was an ideal choice as president: his undoubted energy could be put to good use in the north and the king preferred to keep such an independent-minded character away from court.

Wentworth's vision of the council's role became clear in December 1628, in his first speech to the council in York. It must have been evident to his audience that their new president aimed to repair the damaged reputation of the council and to defend it from attempts to remove it or curtail its powers. As part of this vision Wentworth warned the king's attorney in the north, his cousin George Radcliffe, that his position gave him responsibility for maintaining justice and removing oppression and that if necessary he was to use a heavy hand to effect this.[7] But the new president's vision stretched further than the court itself. Throughout the 1630s Wentworth promoted the Council of the North as an efficient, local body which handled a variety of administrative business.[8] In his speech he exhorted both the deputy lieutenants and the justices of the peace of Yorkshire to look to their responsibilities and the justices were informed that they owed an account of their proceedings to the council.[9] In October 1632 Ferdinando Fairfax informed his father Thomas, Lord Fairfax, of a conversation he had with the lord president regarding a sentence given by the justices against

[5] M.J. Tillbrook, 'Aspects of the Government and Society of County Durham, 1558–1642' (unpublished Ph.D. thesis, University of Liverpool, 1981), pp. 153–4,166.

[6] Reid, *King's Council*, pp. 371–403; A.F. Upton, *Sir Arthur Ingram* (Oxford, 1961), pp. 161–71; PRO, C115 M35/8401.

[7] Bodleian Library, Tanner MS 72, f. 300, Restoration copy of Wentworth's speech.

[8] Sheffield City Library, Wentworth Woodhouse Muniments, Strafford Papers 6/238; 11a/269 (hereafter SCL). I would like to thank Olive, countess Fitzwilliam's Wentworth Settlement Trustees and the Director of Libraries.

[9] Bodl., Tanner MS 72, f. 300.

Francis Steele, high constable for the wapentake of Claro. Wentworth criticized the details of the sentence and advised Fairfax and his colleagues in future to allow the council to 'support' the work of the justices in important cases. Fairfax recognised that Wentworth was trying to establish the council's right to concern itself with the justices' work and while he allowed that there might be occasions when its assistance would be valuable, he would not accept its automatic right to intervene.[10] If Wentworth's attempt to oversee the work of the justices elicited a firm response from Fairfax, Bishop Howson of Durham was furious about his intervention in a dispute within the cathedral chapter.[11]

Wentworth was also prepared to intervene in the affairs of corporate towns. The presence of the council on the outskirts of York was a mixed blessing for the corporation. Disputes had occurred between the corporation and the council during previous reigns over taxation and matters of precedence.[12] If the lord president failed to prove himself a friend to the city, then the council was regarded as an unwelcome agent of the central government prying into the activities of the magistrates. But the presence of the council conferred certain benefits on the city. The lord president or his deputy could be a valuable asset to the city if he was prepared to further its interests. The Corporation House Books of York record a number of instances in which Wentworth was prepared to use his influence to the city's advantage or in which his instructions to the lord mayor and aldermen assisted their business. In November 1632 the lord mayor informed Wentworth that there were several citizens who had refused to pay an assessment levied for the repair of roads in York. He expected assistance from the lord president and he was not disappointed.[13] Wentworth sent the lord mayor lengthy and detailed instructions during the outbreak of plague in the summer of 1631, requiring him to report daily to the council on how these were being implemented.[14] After Wentworth's departure to Ireland the council under

---

[10] G.W. Johnson (ed.), *The Fairfax Correspondence* (London, 1848), i, pp. 245–7; J.T. Cliffe, *The Yorkshire Gentry* (London, 1969), p. 299.

[11] G. Ornsby (ed.), *The Correspondence of John Cosin*, Surtees Soc., 52 (1869), p. 208.

[12] B. Wilson, 'The Corporation of York, 1580–1660' (unpublished M. Phil. thesis, University of York, 1967), pp. 225–35.

[13] York City Archives, Corporation House Books 35, f. 185v (hereafter YCA).

[14] YCA, CHB 35, ff. 115v–117.

Vice-President Osborne appears to have continued in a similar vein, requiring that the corporation submit a report to it in the summer of 1634 on the problem of vagrancy.[15] Throughout the decade York appears to have requested Wentworth's assistance in its disputes with neighbouring authorities.[16] If any of the magistrates resented the council's intervention in the city's affairs, and in particular Wentworth's rather abrasive manner, there is no evidence until 1640. A dispute between William Allanson, lord mayor in 1633, and Osborne over the right to sit in the most prestigious pew in St Michael le Belfrey did cause lasting ill-feeling between the two individuals, but this did not prevent the corporation and common council in early 1640 deciding to ask Wentworth to accept the vacant position of high steward of the city.[17] While this decision reflected his high standing at court, it also demonstrates his reputation with the majority of the corporation, as the job of the high steward was to press the city's point of view on matters which concerned it at the Privy Council. But this decision was not unanimous, and by the autumn of that year it had become clear that Wentworth was no longer a wise choice.[18]

Opposition to Wentworth's presidency was evident in York in 1640, but more dramatic opposition to his government emanated years earlier from the northern peerage and gentry. In 1631 Henry Bellasis, son of Lord Fauconberg, insulted Wentworth by keeping his hat on as the lord president was leaving the council chamber. When called to the Privy Council to answer for his conduct, Bellasis was willing to make a submission to the place of the lord president, but not to his person.[19] A more serious incident involved Fauconberg himself, who accused the lord president of injustice and then refused to obey the king's order that he appear before the council at York.[20] Another incident concerned Sir Thomas Gower who had allegedly slandered the king's attorney in court and then moved to London. On being arrested by the council's sergeant-at-arms he

[15] Wilson, 'The Corporation of York', p. 163.
[16] Wilson, 'The Corporation of York', pp. 104, 197.
[17] SCL, Str. P. 13/233.
[18] YCA, CHB 36, ff. 36v, 39v, 40.
[19] PRO, PC 2/40, pp. 448–50; SCL, Str. P. 21/67.
[20] PRO, PC 2/40, pp. 383–4.

challenged the council's authority to do this outside its jurisdiction. In late 1632 Attorney General Noy supported the council's use of precedents to justify Gower's arrest, but this episode taught Wentworth that the council's present Commission and Instructions were inadequate to deal with such cases.

Wentworth's position as receiver of knighthood fines in Yorkshire led to a clash with another determined foe.[21] Sir David Foulis was suspected of having embezzled £5,000 when he had been cofferer to Prince Charles, and in what appears to have been a desperate attempt to shift attention from himself he began spreading rumours that Wentworth had not paid in all the profits from this commission into the exchequer. Wentworth eventually sued Foulis for slander in Star Chamber. His attempts to delay his departure to Ireland suggest that he hoped to attend the case and witness Foulis's downfall, but after annoying Charles by intervening in the king's prosecution of Bishop Bridgeman of Chester, Wentworth departed for Dublin before the case was heard. Before he left, however, he persuaded Charles to issue a revised Commission and Instructions. Sir John Melton's appointment as secretary in March 1633 meant that a new commission was required and Wentworth used this opportunity to restore certain powers to the council which it probably possessed during the reign of Elizabeth, particularly concerning the right to make arrests outside its own jurisdiction and the legal status of depositions taken before the council.[22] Scarcely had these new instructions been issued, than they were challenged. At the Durham assizes in 1633 Baron Davenport refused to accept such depositions, rejecting the council's argument that its instructions empowered it to take them and declaring that the instructions meant nothing to him.[23] From the limited evidence available, J.S. Cockburn has argued that the relationship between assize judges on the northern circuit and the council in the sixteenth century had been generally harmonious and that the occasional disputes which arose were over the question of precedence, rather than jurisdiction.[24] Davenport's stance, therefore, was in the lord president's eyes a dangerous

[21] See PRO, E401/2449, 2450, 2454, 1923 all unfol.

[22] Reid, *King's Council*, pp. 423-5.

[23] SCL, Str. P. 3/23.

[24] J.S. Cockburn, 'The Northern Assize Circuit', *Northern History*, 3 (1968), 123-5.

departure and he was not prepared to ignore it. Wentworth was made aware of this incident in general terms by Osborne, but he jumped to the conclusion that the judge involved was Vernon, who had already crossed him in his work as receiver-general of recusant revenues.[25] In October 1633 Wentworth made lengthy complaints about Vernon's conduct which resulted in Davenport's removal from the northern circuit.[26]

Wentworth's powers as lord president were strengthened by his role in the northern commission for compounding with recusants. He was appointed receiver-general in July 1629 and there was in fact a close connection between this body and the Council of the North. The 1629 commission's quorum of four men were all active members of the council, and both the council and the commission conducted business in the king's manor in York. The commission had control over a larger geographical area than the council, however, dealing with recusants living north of the Trent.[27] The commissions, both north and south, were new bodies set up in 1627 to allow the crown to tap recusant wealth more effectively. But in order to encourage recusants to enter into a composition with the crown, it was essential that they be assured of freedom from the attention of other local and central bodies. The commission's work therefore brought it into conflict with other authorities who regarded it as a threat to both their legal power and their financial profits. Opposition came from assize judges and northern ecclesiastics, especially Bishop Morton of Durham, whose insistence on prosecuting recusants in his diocese for clandestine marriages and baptisms threatened to damage the commission's profits.[28] Morton's activities in 1633 appear to have been encouraged by Vernon's assize charge at York. Vernon had ordered the justices of the peace to enforce the recusancy statutes rigorously, citing Lord Keeper Coventry's directions.[29] In a letter to the chancellor of the exchequer, Francis, Lord

---

[25] SCL, Str. P. 13/31.

[26] Tillbrook, 'Durham', pp. 148n.,156–7; Cockburn, 'The Northern Assize Circuit', 125; and see idem, *A History of English Assizes 1558–1714* (London, 1972), p. 42, where Vernon's name has been replaced by Davenport.

[27] C. Talbot (ed.), *Miscellanea*, Catholic Record Soc., 53 (1961), pp. 295–303.

[28] SCL, Str. P. 6/3; 6/8; 3/98.

[29] Lambeth Palace, MS 943, p. 221.

Cottington, Wentworth attacked Vernon's conduct, claiming that he had damaged the commission's work. He also criticized the activities of exchequer officials who made no distinction between compounders and non-compounders when issuing warrants binding recusants to good behaviour. He accused them of self-interest, instead of aiding the commission in its service.[30] Reid argued that Wentworth was 'probably right in ascribing this course, not to zeal for Protestantism, but to a desire to stop the compounding which, in filling the king's coffers, emptied the pockets of the exchequer officials'.[31] However, the northern commission also brought Wentworth financial advantages. J.P. Cooper has shown that despite Wentworth's insistence to Lord Treasurer Weston that he always immediately surrendered the king's revenue to the exchequer, Wentworth commonly borrowed it to purchase land.[32] But he was determined to defend his control of this work. In 1634 Sir Arthur Ingram attempted to interfere with the farming of recusancy monies: he planned to increase the profits from the farm from which he would take £2,000 owed him by the crown. His interference led to a breach between the two men which was never mended and caused Wentworth to write several angry letters to Weston, arguably Charles's most powerful minister, contrasting his willingness to allow Ingram the repayment of 'a filthy debt' with his reluctance to allow Wentworth to claim legitimate expenses incurred in the recusancy work. But above all Wentworth was furious that Ingram had in effect threatened his honour and reputation by claiming that he could perform a more impressive service for the king than the lord president himself.[33] In 1637 Wentworth was faced with a more delicate situation when he was informed by his principal ally, Archbishop Laud, that he had been granted the profits of fines in the High Commission courts of both provinces by the king to provide additional income for the repair fund for St Paul's Cathedral. Laud claimed that the actual recusancy compositions would not be affected, but that he intended to fine recusants for

[30] SCL, Str. P. 3/22–3; 3/64–6.

[31] Reid, *King's Council*, p. 426.

[32] J.P. Cooper, 'The Fortune of Thomas Wentworth, Earl of Strafford', *Economic History Review*, 11 (1958), 233–4.

[33] SCL, Str. P. 3/86–9; 14/119; 3/112.

clandestine marriages, among other offences.[34] In reply, Wentworth informed Laud that there was a private resolution in the north that minor misdemeanours should not result in prosecution, lest this lead annoyed recusants to refuse to compound.[35] More startling than these disagreements, however, was Wentworth's attempt to wreck the king's prosecution of Bishop Bridgeman of Chester, a key figure in the work of the northern recusancy commission. Bridgeman's handling of the Lancashire recusants caused Wentworth to try and influence the Privy Council in his favour in 1633, while both Charles and Laud were in Scotland. Securing a settled revenue from recusancy compositions enabled him to make a regular contribution to royal revenue which enhanced his reputation as an efficient administrator of the northern counties. His success in this field was one of the reasons why he was chosen to run the government of Ireland.

On Wentworth's appointment as lord deputy of Ireland, court gossip assumed that he would be replaced as lord president and the earl of Newcastle was named as the likely man.[36] But Wentworth thought otherwise. In a letter written in October 1631 by a family friend, Sir Edward Stanhope, is a list of conditions which Wentworth had apparently told Stanhope he hoped would be met before he went to Ireland. Only one of these conditions was met immediately by the king, but it was the most important: that he would retain both the presidency of the Council of the North and the lieutenancy of Yorkshire.[37] It meant that Wentworth's influence appeared to be growing. To have been stripped of the presidency and sent into Ireland would have suggested that he was being demoted and he was probably confident that his choice of deputy would serve the north well. Sir Edward Osborne was Lord Fauconberg's son-in-law and Wentworth might have hoped that his appointment would end that family's animosity towards the council. Osborne was consistently loyal towards Wentworth, dutifully sending him regular and detailed letters. Although instructions from the Privy Council were then usually

---

[34] SCL, Str. P. 7/79v–80.
[35] SCL, Str. P. 7/83v.
[36] PRO, SP 16/204/72.
[37] SCL, Str. P. 21/79; 21/81.

addressed to the vice-president and the council, Osborne still expected Wentworth to give him instructions. He does not appear to have gone ahead with any substantial business without consulting his superior. Indeed, he was occasionally hampered by Wentworth's failure to leave him basic information regarding recusancy and lieutenancy business.[38] The vice-president's reports show that Wentworth was kept informed of the council's administrative work and that of the recusancy commission.[39] Osborne also discussed affairs relating to the city of York, such as the debate concerning its new charter in 1637.[40] But their correspondence was not simply a series of business reports of varying importance: Osborne also acted as one of several channels by which political news from court reached the isolated lord president.[41] Their relationship was that of patron and client and while the vice-president kept Wentworth informed of court matters following his occasional visits to London, he expected his patron to further his career.[42] Their correspondence indicates that they had a smooth working relationship. But Osborne did not have Wentworth's status or his intimidating personality, and Wentworth found himself struggling to uphold Osborne's authority.

A constant theme running through Osborne's letters to Wentworth was his inability to make council members accept his authority and show due respect to his position.[43] Wentworth had hardly been in Ireland more than a few weeks before Osborne requested his assistance in handling one of the judges of the court at York, Sir William Ellis. Osborne feared the consequences of Ellis's conduct in a case concerning the king which the council was handling.[44] Ellis caused trouble in the work of the recusancy commission, provoking Osborne to describe him as 'soe over legall and full of scruples, . . . as I wish we were rid of him, his power beinge such with the rest of the Counsell as I feare I shall scarce

[38] SCL, Str. P. 13/43; 15/98.

[39] SCL, Str. P. 13/56; 16/69; 17/224; 10a/361; 10a/363.

[40] SCL, Str. P. 17/39.

[41] SCL, Str. P. 13/88; 14/30; 15/58.

[42] See Osborne's unsuccessful bid in November 1633 to serve as sheriff of Yorkshire and his request for Wentworth's support: SCL, Str. P. 13/83; 13/88.

[43] SCL, Str. P. 13/198; 13/233.

[44] SCL, Str. P. 13/31; BL, Add. MS 64,906, ff. 132–133v.

be able to doe the kinge the service I desier'.[45] In an attempt to pull the rest of
the council behind him, Osborne asked Wentworth to remind councillors of
their duty towards the king.[46] Weeks later in November 1633, Osborne again
asked Wentworth to assist him with a strict letter, this time concerning the
recent poor showing at the mustering of the horse bands of Yorkshire.[47] The
vice-president's inability to command the same level of respect and obedience
that was generally given to his superior, even within the Council of the North
itself, became a major problem from 1638 onwards when the council was
expected to play a part in the administration of the king's policy towards
Scotland.

The king's failure to settle religious and political turmoil in Scotland in
1637–8 led to the likelihood of armed conflict and the prospect that the
northern counties, particularly Yorkshire, would be called upon to play a major
role in the king's military preparations.[48] From the summer of 1638 Osborne's
work began to include the implementation of Privy Council orders concerning
the developing crisis.[49] Wentworth consistently supported Osborne during this
difficult period, when the Yorkshire gentry, some of whom were councillors,
were reluctant to cooperate fully with the king's military plans. Both Wentworth
and Osborne acknowledged that Yorkshire had received unfairly high demands
for troops, and the deputy lieutenants, including Osborne, were concerned that
plans to march the trained bands to the border would endanger the safety of the
county.[50] But Wentworth expected the deputy lieutenants to comply with the
crown's demands and, in his absence, to accept Osborne's authority and he was
forced to rebuke his own nephew, Sir William Savile, for disobedience. Savile
objected to Osborne's order that horse troops should be mustered and trained
at York, stating publicly in council that he would muster and train his troop in

[45] SCL, Str. P. 13/43; 13/56.

[46] SCL, Str. P. 13/31; 13/88; 14/8.

[47] SCL, Str. P. 13/88.

[48] M.C. Fissel, *The Bishops' Wars: Charles I's Campaigns Against Scotland 1638–1640* (Cambridge, 1994), p. 4.

[49] PRO, PC2/50, pp. 126–7; 2/52, p. 554.

[50] PRO, SP16/409/53; BL, Add. MS 64,918, ff. 29–30; SCL, Str. P. 11a/212.

the West Riding. Fearing that Savile's attitude would encourage others to be equally uncooperative, Osborne asked Wentworth to order Savile to appear in York.[51] The crux of the problem was that control over the trained bands in Yorkshire lay not with Wentworth in his capacity as lord president, but in his office of lord lieutenant of the county. Since 1580 it had been customary for the two offices to be held by the same man. But Osborne was merely one of several deputy lieutenants and had little authority over his colleagues. One solution to this problem was to invest him with greater power and in early 1639 he was appointed Wentworth's deputy-lieutenant general.[52] The deputy lieutenants of Yorkshire were subsequently informed that Osborne enjoyed Wentworth's complete power regarding lieutenancy matters.[53] Another solution would have been for the king to recall Wentworth from Ireland and allow him to take personal control of the north, which was his wish. He was concerned that rumours of difficulties in Yorkshire would harm his reputation and he remained convinced that the Yorkshire gentry would respond well to his presence among them. But Charles refused to recall him until the failure of other ministers to solve the Scottish problem left him with little choice.[54]

Even after Wentworth's return to England in September 1639, he was unable to devote his energies solely to council and lieutenancy business. He spent the bulk of the next twelve months in London and Dublin, attending parliaments in Ireland and England and advising Charles on military policy. Osborne's enhanced status failed to rouse the rest of the deputy lieutenants into action. In March 1640 they sent a letter to the Privy Council, which Osborne refused to sign, complaining that in a recent demand that the county levy 200 men to be sent to Berwick, the council had not guaranteed the repayment of coat and conduct money. While insisting that this was simply an unfortunate omission, the council criticized the deputy lieutenants for their lack of action in the meantime.[55] Their inaction provoked the anger of the lord president who

[51] SCL, Str. P. 10a/198.
[52] SCL, Str. P. 10a/249.
[53] SCL, Str. P. 10a/250; 11a/154, 157, 158–9, 182–3; 10a/285, 289.
[54] SCL, Str. P. 11a/185.
[55] PRO, PC 2/51, p. 405.

threatened those who were dilatory that he would give them 'something to remember it by hereafter'.[56] But Wentworth exaggerated the extent of his influence with the Yorkshire gentry. At the York assizes in July 1640, when he was in London incapacitated by serious illness, the gentry delivered a calculated snub to him by complaining to the king about Wentworth's demand that they billet troops from the south. When he was once again in the north he was at least able to coerce the Yorkshire gentry into displaying some show of willingness to serve the crown, which his deputy appeared unable to do. Even after the disaster of the second Bishops' War in the summer of 1640, which led to the Scottish occupation of Northumberland and Durham, he was still able to exact a promise of support for the county's forces from the majority of the gentry gathered in York.[57]

However, this success merely fooled both Wentworth and the king into believing that the lord president enjoyed continuing loyalty and respect in Yorkshire. A more accurate picture of the gentry's attitude to the government can be gathered from the growing opposition to the king's financial demands. The king had demanded the payment of ship money, a means of paying for a fleet, from every English and Welsh county since 1635. During Wentworth's visit to England in the summer and autumn of 1636, he was commanded by the king to recommend the 'justice and necessity' of ship money, both publicly and privately in the north. He claimed to have resolved the rating dispute between the city of York and the county and was confident that the rates for the northern counties would be paid. Initially the counties under the council's jurisdiction maintained a good record of payment, encouraging Wentworth to suggest that the king might consider sending out the writs for the following year's charge to the northern counties first, if he felt that the south needed to be shown an example.[58] A year later, however, Wentworth was less optimistic that the payment of ship money would fulfil the king's expectations and from 1638 onwards the north proved to be no more compliant than the rest of the kingdom.[59]

[56] SCL, Str. P. 11a/280.

[57] PRO, SP16/467/54; 16/467/60.

[58] SCL, Str. P. 3/263.

[59] SCL, Str. P. 7/54; 10a/324; PRO, SP 16/398/18; 16/452/53; M.D. Gordon, 'The Collection of Ship-Money in the Reign of Charles I', *TRHS*, 3rd ser., 4 (1910), 156–62.

By 1640 the collection of ship money in most counties had ceased.[60] Opposition to it was often couched in complaints of inconsistencies between and within counties and the Council of the North appears to have heard cases of this type. But Wentworth believed that Sir Marmaduke Langdale's attempt as sheriff of Yorkshire in March 1640 to have the county's assessment reduced was a demonstration of outright opposition to the rate. Wentworth asked the secretary of state to send directions from the Privy Council to Osborne authorizing him to call Langdale before the council and command him to levy the rate. Wentworth advised that Osborne be given the power to order sheriffs of the other northern counties to appear before the council.[61] The loss of the council's records makes it impossible to know the details of its ship money work, but clearly Wentworth envisaged that it should be empowered by the Privy Council to handle complaints of unequal assessments. While he recognized that the rate might be unfairly high in relation to other counties, he was not prepared to countenance an unwillingness in the counties under his charge, particularly Yorkshire, to support the king financially.

During the autumn of 1640, following the Scottish invasion, it became clear that Wentworth's power and influence were waning. In September he was unable to secure the return to parliament of his supporters either as knights of the shire or as burgesses for York, despite his presence in the city.[62] Among those who were elected to represent the northern counties and boroughs were a number of his enemies who played a part in his destruction. He was executed in May 1641 and the council itself ceased to exist a few months later. Wentworth's determination to make the northern counties play a significant role in the Bishops' Wars had brought him into conflict with the senior gentry of the region who resented his overbearing ways and seized their opportunity to assist in his downfall. His belief that the north had a duty to defend the rest of the country against a Scottish invasion was not shared by men who took the view that the real enemy to their liberty was Charles I's system of government. As the last, active president of the Council of the North Wentworth had reminded the

---

[60] *The Memoirs of Sir Hugh Cholmley* (privately printed, 1787), pp. 60–1.

[61] SCL, Str. P. 11a/269.

[62] PRO, SP 16/469/77(2).

northern elite of its potential power. During the 1630s Wentworth certainly tried to use the council to support the collection of ship money and to impose the crown's military policies. If those military policies had succeeded the council might have had a much longer existence, but in the autumn of 1640 the king had little choice but to summon a parliament which was determined to secure the redress of its grievances, two of which were Thomas Wentworth, earl of Strafford, and the Council of the North.[63]

---

[63] Reid, *King's Council*, pp. 436–49.

15

RECUSANTS, DISSENTERS AND NORTH-WEST POLITICS BETWEEN THE RESTORATION AND THE GLORIOUS REVOLUTION

Michael Mullett

This paper deals with the prospects for Catholic political activity, potentially in alliance with Protestant Nonconformists, in Lancashire and the rest of north-west England during the period from 1660 to 1688. A central dilemma for English Catholics was their divided loyalty to the papacy and the English crown. While most Catholics were patriotic, the loyalty of some of them was compromised by the papal bull of excommunication of Elizabeth, recurrent difficulties over finding an acceptable oath of allegiance to the crown, and their own persistent hopes for a reversal of the Reformation and the re-Catholicization of the country. The penal laws operated on the assumption that all Catholics were actual or potential traitors, and their savagery had the effect of making a reality of that assumption as far as significant elements in the English Catholic community were concerned. In those parts of Lancashire, especially in the south and west of the county, with large recusant populations, where it remained for some time easy to believe that the Reformation was no solid achievement but a passing heretical fancy, Catholic truculence encouraged unstructured or structured violence by elites and plebeians alike, generating fears of the 'popery' that haunted the early modern English Protestant imagination. That there was an ongoing 'popish plot' against the lives, religion, properties and laws of English people seemed to some north-westerners a credible conclusion, not least in the light of an upsurge of Catholic activism during the civil wars. Such beliefs were likely to vitiate schemes for Catholics to be admitted to civilian political activity in the region, a

prospect that was tested by James II in 1687–8 with his scheme to bring
Catholics and Anglicans together in regional government.[1]

The period surveyed in this paper is one of exceptional interest and
importance in the history of English local government and politics, especially
from the point of view of relations betwen the centre and the counties and
boroughs, and also in terms of the increasing assumption of power by
Westminster and Whitehall over units of local administration. Time out of
mind, the crown in England had exercised some supervision over the localities,
appointing sheriffs, lords lieutenant and justices of the peace in the shires and
issuing and re-issuing the charters under which corporate boroughs exercised
their authority. The military and fiscal requirements of the civil wars intensified
central control, while the dominance of ideological partisanship aligned the
localities with national political allegiances over against the cherished
harmonious integrity of the self-sufficient county community. As far as borough
government was concerned, Oliver Cromwell was an active centralizer.

The partisan nature of local politics and government in the period 1642–60
created a need in and after 1660 to purge personnel so as to take account of the
altered circumstances of the Restoration. The purge occurred in the corporate
towns, particularly in the parliamentary boroughs. These boroughs returned the
overwhelming majority of members of parliament by one form of franchise or
another. The systematic elimination from positions of power and influence of
parliamentarians, republicans, Cromwellians and religious Puritans, chiefly
Presbyterians, Independents and Baptists, was set in motion shortly after the
king's return. The traditional method of control through the recall and re-issue
of charters was a relatively clumsy one, but in 1661 a new Act of Parliament,
the Corporations Act, was passed, shifting the emphasis of the regulation of
urban government from the royal prerogative through charters to parliament
through statute.[2]

[1] Arnold Pritchard, *Catholic Loyalism in Elizabethan England* (London, 1979); Alexandra Walsham,
Church Papists, Catholicism, Conformity and Confessional Polemic in Early Modern England (London, 1993);
John Miller, *Popery and Politics in England 1660–1688* (London, 1973).

[2] J.P. Kenyon (ed.), *The Stuart Constitution: Documents and Commentary* (Cambridge, 1966),
pp. 376–8.

In its turn, parliament devolved its newly acquired statutory powers over the boroughs to panels of commissioners in the counties, each one entrusted with the task of eliminating unreliables from the boroughs in its shire, using political and religious criteria. These included oaths of loyalty and subscriptions to Anglican orthodoxy with sacramental tests, so as to root out subversives, real or imagined. The commissions were composed of Anglican-Cavalier county gentry, which led to a dramatic shift of authority from the towns to the county squirearchies, a class by tradition typically resentful of urban autonomy.

Tests and purges continued to characterize English local government in the post-Restoration period, and all the more so as religio-political discourse became polarized in the late 1670s with the Popish Plot and the campaign to exclude the Catholic heir presumptive, James, duke of York, from the succession. With a royalist recovery evident from 1679, the county magistracies and the Dissenter-linked Whig elements within them were the targets of a concentrated offensive from the centre to ensure that all magistrates were reliable Anglican loyalists, or Tories.[3] In the politics of these years, when the voting behaviour, affiliations and opinions of every man in office were subject to intense scrutiny, religious tests remained a primary method of assessing political conformity, using Anglican orthodoxy as the definition of a loyalist. In the Tory Reaction that marked the closing years of Charles II's reign, and the triumphant accession of his Catholic brother in 1685, an emphatic reassertion of royal authority took place. A well-orchestrated administrative drive saw the widespread recall and re-issue of corporation charters, seventy-six in just nine months of 1685, involving the royal appointment of lists of Tory corporation personnel, and reserving powers to the crown in future to dismiss and appoint new corporation members.[4]

The final year of James II's reign witnessed an extraordinary *volte-face* in central policy towards the localities, especially the chartered boroughs, as the

---

[3] Lionel K.J. Glassey, *Politics and the Appointment of the Justices of the Peace, 1675–1720* (Oxford, 1979).

[4] John Miller, 'The Potential for Absolutism in Later Stuart England', *History*, 69 (1984), 197–207; idem, 'The Crown and the Borough Charters in the Reign of Charles II', *EHR*, 100 (1985), 53–84.

king, using prerogative powers enshrined in the new charters of the Tory
Reaction, set about demolishing the Anglican monopoly over English public life
that had been so firmly established during those years. Setting out to build and
lead a coalition of non-Anglican minorities disadvantaged by all the religious
penal laws passed since the reign of Elizabeth, James promoted Nonconformists
and Catholics to office. James's ambitious policies brought him down in 1688,
and although the Toleration Act of the following year gave Protestant
Nonconformists some religious toleration, it did not allow them to obtain
positions within the government of those urban communities in which they
were becoming concentrated. Meanwhile, the Catholics reverted to their pariah
status, with new legal disqualifications added on to existing ones, while the
majority Church resumed its hegemony over public life.

How did these developments affect north-west England, and, in particular,
how did the relative strength of Catholicism in Lancashire affect the politics of
religious allegiance in the region? The answer may be that within the north-
west, Lancashire's seemingly ineradicable and strongly militant Catholicism
confirmed a popular belief in the active malignancy of 'popery' and so
polarized politics sharply. In 1681, in the elections for the third in the series of
Whig-dominated parliaments pressing for the duke of York's exclusion from the
succession, 95 per cent of voters in the areas of Cheshire adjacent to Lancashire
supported unswervingly anti-Catholic Whig candidates.[5]

It seems clear that such voting patterns reflected fears in overwhelmingly
Protestant Cheshire of strident Catholicism over the county border. Lancashire
Catholics had a long tradition of militancy and defiance, which was based on
their numercial strength, at least within certain areas of the county. Indeed,
local Catholic dominance created a conviction among some recusants that in
some sense the Reformation had not happened in their localities; that they, the
Catholics, occupied by right the high ground in their communities and even
that church premises remained rightfully theirs, or what Professor Bossy calls
'some consciousness of a claim to constituting the genuine parochial or
congregational community'. Indeed, in some parts of the county Protestant

---

[5] P.J. Challinor, 'Restoration and Exclusion in the County of Cheshire', *Bulletin of the John Rylands University Library of Manchester*, 64 (1981–2), 383–5.

numbers were so 'slender that [Protestants] dare not deny the Romans whatsoever they are pleased to call a neighbourly civility'.[6]

A tradition of more structured Catholic militancy in the north-west can be traced back to plebeian rebellion in defence of the monasteries during the Pilgrimage of Grace of 1536–7. Thirty years after the suppression of that rising, the Ecclesiastical Commission heard of a Lancashire 'confederacy [which] is so great that it will grow to a commotion or rebellion'. Subsequently, at the time of Pope Pius V's bull of deposition of Elizabeth in 1570, there were rumours of a Lancashire Catholic rising timed to coincide with a threatened Spanish invasion. In the years after 1590 there were riots in Wigan, Prescot, Altcar and Garstang to repel enforcers of the recusancy laws. These riots established traditions of resistance in local Catholic political culture that survived well into the seventeenth century. Even in regions such as the northern hundred of Lonsdale, where Catholics were not particularly numerous, they tended to take an obstreperous stance, strongly influenced by gentry self-assertiveness. In 1625 at Quernmore Park near Lancaster, the Catholic gentleman Sir Thomas Gerard warned Protestants of the consequences they were to expect from a Catholic restoration. Singling out two Protestant notables of the shire, Gerard stated that 'he hoped they [the Catholics] should have a day, and that the first throats to be cut in Lancashire should be Sir Ralph Ashton and Thomas Standish of Duxbury'.[7]

If reports of such truculence were likely to feed fears of militant popery in the wider region, the same reaction was to be expected as a result of the armed royalism of the recusants in the civil wars, fuelling fears of armed Catholicism. One estimate indicates that 57 per cent of the Lancashire gentry in the royal service were Catholics, 44 per cent of the earl of Derby's royalist officers were recusants, and 'the proportion of catholics in Derby's army [nicknamed 'the Catholic army'] was certainly greater than their proportion in the county as a

[6] John Bossy, *The English Catholic Community 1570–1850* (London, 1975), p. 126.

[7] Christopher Haigh, *Reformation and Resistance in Tudor Lancashire* (Cambridge, 1975); Scott Michael Harrison, *The Pilgrimage of Grace in the Lake Counties 1536–7* (London, 1981), chapter 9; F. Walker, 'Historical Geography of Southwest Lancashire Before the Industrial Revolution', Chetham Soc., n. s., 103 (1939), 114; Henry Fishwick, *The History of Garstang in the County of Lancaster*, Chetham Soc., n. s., 105 (1879), i, p. 150.

whole.' Sir Thomas Tyldesley of Myerscough and Richard Gerard of Bryn were Catholic veterans of the Thirty Years' War who brought their military experience to the king's side. Prominent recusants such as Charles Towneley, Sir John Preston and Robert Molyneux and his son gave their lives for the king. Above all, Richard Viscount Molyneux set the example for his co-religionists, using the county as a recruiting ground for the king, taking part in key engagements at Bolton and Liverpool and in 1642 leading his infantry regiment against Manchester. This town, was said to have 'multitudes of papists near unto it, and being reputed a religious [i.e. Protestant] and rich town . . . [was] much envied and often threatened by the Popish and malignant [i.e. Royalist] party'. Likewise, when the earl of Derby marched on Lancaster in 1643 and sacked it, it was reported that 'the papists [were] rising wholly with him'.[8]

It is true that during the civil wars a gap opened up between Catholic gentry activism and Catholic plebeian neutralism. A parliamentarian comment that lower-class Catholics 'had a good ground to have been neuter in this war' was borne out by the fact that, in contrast with the high rates of active royalist support by the Catholic gentry and nobility, a lower figure of 21 per cent of rank and file troopers were recusants, and even that figure may have been inflated by impressment and various patronal and tenurial pressures. Nevertheless, the revival of organized Catholic militancy in Lancashire during the civil wars, sedulously advertised in parliamentarian propaganda so as to link royalism with 'popery', seems likely to have perpetuated a lasting Protestant fear in the region of papists in arms, which was reflected in intense commitment to Whig anti-popery in Cheshire in the Exclusion period.[9] In turn, deep suspicions of aggressive Catholicism, above all among Lancashire Dissenters, created an unfavourable climate for Catholic-Nonconformist collaboration to by-pass the Anglican hegemony when James II opened up such prospects. This is not to say

[8] J.M. Gratton, 'The Earl of Derby's Catholic Army', *Trans. of the Historic Soc. of Lancs. and Cheshire*, 139 (1987), 38–9; J.A. Hilton, *Catholic Lancashire from Reformation to Renewal 1559–1991* (Chichester, 1994), pp. 34–5; P.R. Newman, 'Roman Catholic Royalists: Papist Commanders Under Charles I, 1642–60', *Recusant History*, 15 (1981), 396–405; Michael Mullett, 'From Reformation to Renewal: Lancaster 1450–1690', in Andrew John White (ed.), *A History of Lancaster, 1193–1993* (Halifax, 1993), p. 71.

[9] B.G. Blackwood, 'Plebeian Catholics in the 1640s and 1650s', *Recusant History*, 18 (1986).

that such alliances in local government were totally out of the question: as we shall see, Lancaster offered the reality of a working collaboration of Dissenters alongside Catholics in the government of the county town in the royal revolution taking place during the last months of James II's reign. However, memories of the reality of Catholic aggression during the civil wars were likely to dispel belief in a pacified Catholicism, and to encourage the kind of suspicion fed by the marquess of Halifax in his *Letter to a Dissenter* of 1687 to the effect that Catholics continued to harbour monopolistic ambitions.[10]

The return of peace and civilian government in 1660 made it highly unlikely that Catholics would receive any further encouragement to take part in politics in any military capacity. Passively or actively royalists, they had no incentive to become involved in the flurry of radical Nonconformist bids in the north to destabilize the Restoration state in the years immediately after its establishment. Nor were the recusants to be admitted into the arena of civil government at the regional or local level, and, as for parliamentary or corporate voting, the aim of the county political establishment was its restriction, if not its elimination. As Sir Robert Carr, a post-Restoration chancellor of the duchy, wrote, 'Let one thing be observed . . . what number of papists vote'.[11] In the Lancashire towns, however, and especially in those such as Preston and Wigan where they had their greatest urban demographic strength, Catholics might revert to the politics of riot that they had used as their collective system of self-defence since Elizabeth's reign. Most notably in Wigan, a town with an established tradition of demotic direct action, as in riots of 1640 and 1661 against the restriction of the franchise, Catholics resurrected their well-established rhythms of collective and militant protest against any invasion of their position. In 1681 Wigan recusants and their local allies, in an action orchestrated by two local Catholic doctors and spearheaded by the 'pour wemon in the streets', strenuously and successfully beat off an attempt by the clerk of the peace, Roger Kenyon, to levy arrears of fines for non-attendance at the parish church. With the officers of the peace beaten up, these riotous scenes may well have raised new questions about the

[10] J.R. Western, *Monarchy and Revolution: The English State in the 1680s* (London, 1972), pp. 227–8.
[11] Michael Mullett, '"To Dwell Together in Unity": The Search for Agreement in Preston Politics, 1660–1690', *Trans. of the Historic Soc. of Lancs. and Cheshire*, 125 (1975), 61.

docility of Lancashire Catholics. More to the point, and with longer-lasting political consequences, this victory over a Protestant offensive in Wigan, coming at the beginning of the Tory Reaction, accompanied a swing to Toryism promoted by the High Tory crypto-Catholic Sir Roger Bradshaigh. This move was expressed in the rhetoric of an attack on local Whigs and Nonconformists, which was voted through the corporation, sent to the king and given pride of place in the government's propaganda sheet, *The Gazette*. It described Whigs and Dissenters as 'Republicans and Factious Zealots . . . Fanatick Sectaries and Seditious Conventiclers'. Bradshaigh, with his coal mining interests the most powerful economic force in the Wigan area, having been effectively shut out of Wigan politics during the Whig and Dissenter ascendancy of the Exclusion period, was showing a determination to recover his political sway by vilifying the Presbyterian figures who had enjoyed considerable importance in the borough's religious and corporate life. Bradshaigh's Catholic sympathies were well known, as was the fact that he was able to deploy them all the more effectively under a thin veneer of conformable Anglicanism. Following up on the victory of 1681, when Catholic plebeians had defeated the attempt of the Protestant county authorities to enforce the laws in Wigan, what Bradshaigh was doing in 1683 was linking local Catholicism with a witchhunt against Dissent and the denigration of Whiggery. This was, arguably, a short-term strategy of considerable utility during the Tory Reaction, when, nationwide, Catholics were largely being spared the onus of penal laws that was instead being loaded on to the Dissenters. Bradshaigh's kind of anti-Whig, anti-Presbyterian vehemence was readily taken up by the people of the Wigan streets, in this 'ancient and loyal' borough, with its carefully cultivated reputation for civil-war royalism. Fresh mob action in 1682 accompanied with denunciations of 'all presbiterian Rogues and Whigs in the Towne', targetted leading corporation officers and prominent Dissenters.[12]

Perhaps we need to take account of these events when we review the failure of James II and his agents to build a workable Catholic–Nonconformist alliance in such a place as Wigan in the late 1680s. Crucial to the king's plans was the winning of support from corporation members, and other electorally influential

---

[12] Michael Mullett, "'A Receptacle for Papists and an Assilum": Catholicism and Disorder in Late Seventeenth-Century Wigan', *Catholic History Review*, 73 (1987), 391–407.

men, for his plan of repealing the Test Act and penal laws which shored up the civil position of the Church of England. In borough corporations, committed Anglican Tories who refused to comply with James's plans were being replaced in 1687–8, sometimes by Dissenters, at other times by Catholics, ideally with a mix of both. In Wigan, despite the town's important Presbyterian traditions, only Catholics served on the governing body, in two groups making up fourteen new members to replace Anglicans who refused in 1687–88 to go along with the king's drive to secure agreement on the repeal of the Test Act and penal laws. The hollow triumphalism of the corporation's Catholic ritual, the 'Sword and Mace . . . carry'd before them to a popish Chappell there erected', along with the fact that the new Catholic corporation members were recruited from rural gentry families, served only to underscore the isolation of the newly constituted civic body from the mainstream of the town's life. It is true that in 1687–8 James II had a good chance of success in constructing a viable national coalition of Catholics, Whigs and Dissenters to form a 'synthetic ruling class' made up of all the minorities traditionally excluded from positions of power.[13] However, in Wigan, a town with considerable potential for forming a successful Catholic–Nonconformist treaty, earlier moves initiated by Sir Roger Bradshaigh to discredit Nonconformity and Whiggery by hitching the fortunes of Catholics to the High Tory cause left local recusants without allies among the Dissenting community. In addition, their position was made worse by the spectre of assertive Catholicism and the hysteria of the wild 'Irish panic' of the autumn and winter of 1688, which provoked a marked local popular anti-popish reaction.[14]

James II adopted what may be described as his Nonconformist strategy after it became apparent in 1686 that the Anglicans, despite all their protestation of utter loyalty and non-resistance, would take no part in the demotion of their beloved Church of England. The impracticality of an 'Anglican strategy' is well illustrated in the case of Preston which, unlike its rival Wigan, did not acquire a Catholic-dominated borough government in 1687–8. This was not for the want of trying. Indeed, a special 'regulator' was appointed to assist the new Catholic

---

[13] For the source of this quotation, see Michael Mullett, *James II and English Politics 1678–1688* (London, 1994), p. 64.

[14] Mullett, 'A Receptacle for Papists', 406–7.

lord lieutenant Molyneux in his efforts to bring the town's government around to comply with James II's policies. But ever since the Guild of 1682, when Preston corporation had been flooded with loyalist freemen, the town had been the powerhouse of Lancashire Toryism, and the dominant influence there of the Protestant earl of Derby helped to keep local Catholics firmly under control. Although the Preston Tories were deeply, indeed ostentatiously, loyal to the king personally, their loyalty to the Church of England took pride of place. Not only did they stand out against the repeal of the Test Act and penal laws, albeit more by evasion than by open obduracy, but they also failed to prevent performances of an anti-Catholic comedy, *The Devil and the Pope* in 1688. Overwhelmingly, the Preston Tories managed to survive Molyneux's attempts to dislodge them in 1688, and the viscount had to admit his frustration at being checked by the political acumen of Preston's Tory Anglicans.[15]

Elsewhere in Lancashire, Anglican resistance defeated James's plans. Liverpool, ringed around by Catholic villages, on the face of it had a trading town's blindness to credal niceties. Good neighbourliness dictated helping a Catholic squire from the hinterland with his little difficulty over exporting currency to his daughter with the Grey Nuns in Rouen; common courtesy suggested a civil and civic reception for James II's vicar apostolic. However, when it came to *popery*, the public face of Catholicism, the Liverpool corporation remained unwilling to see the repeal of the laws that upheld the Church.[16]

In 1687–8 the patterns in the Lancashire towns generally show that James II's radical plans were defeated, though not necessarily doomed to defeat. For the county town displayed the reality of a working Dissenter–Catholic alliance, one indeed that managed to include some Anglicans in support of the king's policies. The partnership was coordinated by a Whig aristocrat, Lord Brandon, popular with Lancaster's freeman electorate, a 'favorer of all sorts of dissenters papists and phanatiques', 'gracious with the dissenters' and 'so high an actor for the papists'. Brandon showed how workable the Catholic–Whig–Dissenter coalition might be, if promoted tactfully through the avoidance of any swamping of the borough

[15] Mullett, 'To Dwell Together in Unity', 76–8.

[16] Michael Mullett, 'The Politics of Liverpool, 1660–1688', *Trans. of the Historic Soc. of Lancs. and Cheshire*, 124 (1972), 53–4.

corporation by rural Catholic gentry. Instead James's agents, the Whig Brandon and the Catholic Molyneux, worked through the town's established Nonconformist, and especially its Presbyterian, elements, securing a Presbyterian mayor in the person of the local apothecary Augustine Greenwood. The thread that held the coalition together was a pledge to religious toleration and civil rights. As the Lancaster Quaker William Stout put it, 'none [were] permitted to any place of profit or trust till they would promise up[on] election for parliament to vote for such who would be for the repeal of the penal laws and the Test Acts'.[17]

As for Quakers themselves, it was difficult to fit them into normal political plans. The comment that Preston's regulator was a Quaker and/or a Jesuit, a variant of a long-standing allegation that Quakers were Jesuits in disguise, was on the whole intended to discredit a man rather than illuminate a situation. There were more or less technical difficulties in the way of Quaker absorption into local government and politics. In Clitheroe after the Restoration the Quakers' refusal to swear oaths was sufficient to debar them from the vote. In Lancaster a prominent townsman, the Quaker sugar refiner John Lawson, was admitted to, then disqualified from, the corporation in the 1660s. Following a decision by the lord mayor of London in 1688 to the effect that 'Quakers should now . . . be allowed to serve . . . without taking any oath', five Lancaster Friends assumed the council office of common burgess. However, oaths were not the main problem. Even in Cumberland, it was Catholics who moved into the lieutenancy in 1688 and the mayor of the county town of this most Quaker of counties was not a Friend but a Catholic. For, in the final analysis, both Presbyterians and Catholics, but not (generally) Friends, could be said to come from social strata, in town and countryside, whose members had traditions and expectations of rule that were in part checked and in part fulfilled, albeit very briefly, in Lancashire towns during the reign of James II.[18]

---

[17] Michael Mullett, 'Conflict, Politics and Elections in Lancaster, 1660–1688', *Northern History*, 19 (1983), 81–2.

[18] Nicholas Morgan, 'The Social and Political Relations of the Lancaster Quaker Community, 1688–1740', in Michael Mullett (ed.), *Early Lancaster Friends*, Lancaster, Centre for North West Regional Studies Occasional Paper, 5 (1978), p. 22; Michael Mullett, '"Men of Knowne Loyalty": The Politics of the Lancashire Borough of Clitheroe, 1660–1689', *Northern History*, 21 (1985), 109–10.

INDEX